THE
POWER OF CLIMBING

'It's having the power to link the moves together'
Ben Moon, Ravens Tor, Derbyshire.

THE
POWER OF CLIMBING

Interviews   Photography

David B.A. Jones

Illustrations

Patricia Donnelly

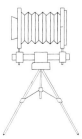

Modern climbing terms.

Bolt to Bolt: Free climbing each section of a route between bolts, and usually resting by each bolt.
Cleaning: Preparation of a climb, wire brushing holds, filing down sharp edges and glueing back on any loose flakes.
Conditions: A term used for the relative humidity in the air which causes handholds to absorb moisture and become slippery.
Crimp: A very small hold and is usually very tough on the skin, invariably splitting it near the fingertips.
Dogging: Practising small parts of a climb, falling off purposely as not to get tired and consequently working out the easiest sequence.
Dyno: A climber using mostly arm power to leap for a hold out of reach, momentarily losing all physical contact with the rock.
Egyptian: A resting position in a groove, all the body facing one way, knees bent, with one heel dropped and the other raised.
Figure of Four: From a good hold, placing the inner thigh over the wrist, locking the arm (fig 4) and reaching up with free arm.
Flash: To climb a route from the ground up to the belay without falling off.
Frigging: To cheat on a climb, in any form or way i.e. resting on the rope, standing on a bolt head, pulling on a runner etc.
Jumar: A device which grips thin ropes such as 8-11mm climbing and caving ropes. By using two jumars a climber can easily ascend a rope.
Match: A useful term and often used in bouldering, bringing both hands together on the same hold, often critical in a sequence.
Numbers: Inside information on how to do a climb, i.e. which fingers on which holds, footholds, dynos etc.
On Sight: To do a climb or problem on the first try.
Project: A bolted up climb which still awaits it's first redpoint – even though it may be free climbed by top rope.
Quickdraw: A piece of tape which joins two Krabs as safely as possible, also known as a tie off.
Redpoint: To lead a climb in one push, clipping all protection having practised the route on a top rope or bolt to bolt beforehand.
Sloper: A flat sloping hold which looks good until you are forced to hang from it, a standard limestone bouldering problem.
Smear: Using toe rubber friction on rugosities where there are no footholds.
Sport Climbing: Climbing which uses in-situ protection only, such as various types of resin and expansion bolts.
Spotting: Standing behind someone bouldering, the hands ready to catch a fall and support the back.
Working a route: Dogging a climb firstly, then practising certain sections to build up strength, then going for a redpoint ascent.
Yo Yo: Not working out a hard move when falling off, lowering down to a natural rest then carrying on again; not a clear cut ascent.

Acknowledgements.

Alison Taylor, Andy Goring, Andy Pollitt, Anne Kirkpatrick, Ben Masterson, Ben Moon, Ben Pritchard, Bonny Masson, Chris Gore, Chris Plant, Claudie Dunn, Corinnie Jones, Dave Kenyon, Dave Pegg, Dave Turner, Dave Wark, Dennis Gray, Dougie Hall, Ed Morgan, Fred Simpson, Gary Gibson, George Heydon, Gill Kent, Greg Rimmer, Gretel Leeb, Grimer, Ian Dunn, Ian Horrocks, Ian Vincent, Jane Antoine, Jason Myers, Jasper Sharpe, Jeff Jones, Jerry Moffatt, Joe Healey, John Dunne, John Hart, Johnny Dawes, John Redhead, John Welford, Joanie Sharpe, Ken Wilson, Kitt Hart, Malcolm Taylor, Malcolm McPherson, Mark Leach, Mark Pretty, Martin Atkinson, Martin Boysen, Matt Birch, Matt Saunders, Mick Lovatt, Neil Gresham, Neil Pearson, Nick Dixon, Nick Harms, Nick Sellars, Patty Pickle, Paul Craven, Paul Ingham, Paul and Pauline Innes, Paul Pritchard, Paul Widdowson, Pete Chadwick, Pete Gommersall, Phil Davidson, Quentin Fisher, Rachel Farmer, Richard Davies, Sean Myles, Seb Greave, Simon Nadin, Stephanie Snowball, Steve Earnshaw, Stuart Lancaster, Terry Tullis, Tim Freeman, Tim Lowe, Tom Proctor, Tony Greenbank, Tony Mitchell, Tony Ryan.

Equipment acknowledgements.

I would like to specially thank two firms in supplying equipment very essential to the compilation of this book. Firstly and perhaps most importantly to BEAL ropes. They have supplied excellent ropes which have given me confidence, and allowed me to concentrate fully on photography when endlessly abseiling over Malham Cove and other such daunting cliffs.. Also to LOWE rucksacs who provided me with a very ergonomic sac the 'Alpamayo' which has fulfilled the task of carrying all my climbing equipment plus a battery of Hasselblads and Nikons up to the crags, without any back strain or discomfort.

The Power of Climbing
Published by Vision Poster Company,
The Stables, Ivy Cottage, West Bank, Winster, Derbyshire.

Copyright text and photographs © David B A Jones 1991
Copyright illustrations © Patricia Donnelly 1991

1st Edition September 1991

ISBN – 1 873 665 00 8

British Library Catalogue – in – publication data.
A catalogue record for this book is available from the British Library

Packaged on EMG International Shakespeare.

Printed and bound by Biddles, Guildford, Surrey.

All trade enquiries to:
CORDEE, 3a De Montfort Street, Leicester. LE1 7HD

Contents

—— *Introduction* ——

Waking up in the morning is so easily understood, the dream finishes just as it becomes exciting, the clock stares violently, presenting a time far later than it should, and the inside of the mouth, well it's usually like an arid garlic field in disarray. Essentially it is the only part of our lives which we never can dictate, we either wake up, or at some time or another don't. It is from this quiescent moment that we begin to analyse and question every other second of our lives, theorise as to what makes us do up the right shoe first, why we cannot remember everything; to the ecological future or disaster of mankind. But 'what of the benefits' we ask ourselves, do we have control over our destiny or just tumble along with the rest of the human race. If we took no notice or care, then reading and writing would be at a very simple level, debate would be non existent, and perhaps the term fulfilment would hitherto be uncomprehended. It is valid I feel, not to question ones existence, but to understand ones actions throughout life and to derive either satisfaction or dissatisfaction from them; in doing so one is made aware of the appreciation, benefits, hardships and even the cruelty, made available to us within society.

I feel though as a climber, the want to question the justification of my climbing as a singular activity, I am tunnel visioned into thinking that it bears only fruits and hardships to myself. Yet it is something which happens in the world's environment, the birds, the animals, the flora and fauna, the winds and rain; It is from this that I feel compelled to seek explanation of why I climb.

By looking at myself I can make many conclusions, and 'yes' feel totally at home with myself, but to understand others is perhaps as important, since the world cannot exist for one man or woman alone, and immediately I reach my quandary. I talk to passers by in the pub and exchange comment: politics, music, literature anything in life. Quite often climbing can be discussed and analysed, yet is invariably ridiculed; the latter being the layman's comic cynicism, to almost self pity in the face of hearty respect for others gumption. Their comments if such are equivocal, should be answered with silence.

We ask ourselves, do people upon waking up, actually sit bolt upright in bed and shout "Climb! Climb! I've gotta go climbing, ahhhh!", leap across the room to grab a rucksac and set forth to the hills. Well if you did, all would be explained by the simple fact that we probably are completely and utterly bonkers. No, not at all, people are compelled for many other reasons and least of all is it an ascetic direction. It is however more often than not, others who play within the sport that dictate the rules, the byelaws, the parameters which define enjoyment from insanity. These onlookers, these parasites of climbing testament, are the ones who lay thinking patterns for today's rock gladiators. In stating so, I raise the question of dissent amongst our climbing peers, those with the skill and technique of climbing, their acceptance of ethics, challenge and enjoyment. In asking these questions I fall between a conversationalist and perhaps a psychiatrist, neither of which is my intent. I am merely here to serve as one who opens up the minds and thoughts of the interviewees. It is not for me to conclude why people climb, I know already, but my view is so tainted by personal thoughts, it has to be for the reader to judge for themselves, their experiences, their upbringing's, their mishaps. Their experiences must serve to colour in the pictures painted in Black and White by the text, the reader must perceive, assess and judge, the 46 interviews; what POWER does climbing have over people, then they can perhaps question why they either climb or they don't.

The Interviews

In starting the book I came up with a list of over 400 names to interview: Allen, Arocena, Atkinson, Austin; Bancroft, Bonington, Boysen, Brasco, Brown, Burke; the great names: then the Punters, the Beginners, the Retired, the Gifted and the Squandered. That was the easy part, but to choose fifty or so names from that list would prove lo be far more difficult.

I looked at the various areas within climbing and from this derived eight or nine chapters. I came up with *Professionals* - people who worked in climbing but didn't actually climb for a living. *Legends* - here I tended to shy away from the obvious historic names that have been so well documented, instead I choose characters of great historical respect that hadn't written their own books – yet. *Graduates* - climbers that didn't fit into the other chapters yet individually represented valid parts to climbing: the lads and the ladies, the young, old and bold. *Addicts* - who represent many of the traits that climbing forms in people.

After these four groups I looked at the best climbers in the country and made a list of everyone who had climbed 8a and above. I came up 100 names; how standards rise. To get down to 25, the cut off point was raised to 8b which left three convenient chapters, The *Hustlers* - 8b, *The Elite* - 8b+ and the *Masters* - 8c. A few positions have changed, Mark Leach has climbed 8c, John Welford had come on very strong and others are climbing 8b, but not many other changes – see the roll of honour in the back for up to date credits. You may well ask 'but what of the bold E8 climbers,' do they merit inclusion. It is difficult to quantify because of our antiquated grading system. All bold E9's today are rehearsed on a top rope, yet are only French 7b+ in standard. At the same time a lot of French climbers have solo'd 7c+, take Jebé soloing CHIMPANZAD-ROME 7C+ at Saussois, you won't walk away if you fall off that. A lot of routes in France have been solo'd that are a far bigger achievement in terms of world boldness in climbing. Britain is only up in the top league by a Frenchman, Antoine le Menestrel soloing REVELATIONS 8a+. I have included the great loose rock enthusiasts in the book such as Paul Pritchard, but on their own grounds, in their own chapters as specialists in their own right.

The two chapters I decided not to pursue; competition climbers, and foreign masters. Both are of world importance, however play a very small part in British climbing and are not reflected in everyday life at the British crags. The list stopped at 46 climbers yet could have gone on so easily, Dave Thomas soloing LORD OF THE FLIES, young Malcolm Smith from Scotland doing MAGNETIC FIELDS 8b at 17, Denny Moorhouse the Welsh Wizard of equipment, Pat Littlejohn, Whillance etc. But over a fascinating 12 months I ended up with 46 names chosen for intense variety, honesty and interest. They in no way reflect a definitive character analysis of all climbers, but do represent involvement with the sport at the top level.

I have often thought essays to be false, thoughts are premeditated and written to a style which represents what people would like to think, rather than what they actually think. I therefore chose tape recorded interviews as the best medium to translate personal thoughts into published form whilst retaining spontaneity. They have been edited to make clearer reading, some more tightly than others but each trying to reflect individual characters. In every case, the interviews were resubmitted to the climbers for clarification of truth and meaning. Some edited more vigorously than others, yet all remained quite in line with the original interview upon my insistence. Contentious issues have arisen, and hopefully they will not offend since all is part and parcel of everyday climbing life, the ups and downs of a personal subject. The questions are immensely varied, which in turn was a response to the climbers in question and from this point it made the somewhat exhausting and painstaking task of tracking them down, very worthwhile. The climbers on their behalf were exceptionally helpful, hospitable and generous in freely giving their time to this historic project.

As chapter headings I have used illustrations by Patricia Donnelly, which capture the stillness, the quiescence and the flavour of the beautiful English countryside. This is today's climbing environment, not the mountains as in the sixties or seventies, but gentle countryside which is in contrast to the crags that demand the brute strength of today's power climbing.

In photographing climbing in it's present day form, I decided on a completely journalistic feel, non-posed shots, black and white throughout. Only on rare occasions did I plan to meet climbers at crags, it was very much a case of turning up to a crag and capturing what was happening for real. A lot shots were on a telephoto lens, tight in, getting to the root of the action, capturing the essence of the mood. Modern climbers in the hot summer months sneak around in the dark, dim foliage, which in many cases needed film speeds of 1000 ASA basic. With the dedication to medium format cameras I managed to get some shots with detail, but mostly the content of the personality had to come first. The intensity of real life reportage photography is addictive as climbing to me, and survived entirely throughout the year of photography, most lucky of all was being present to capture first ascent shots of HUBBLE, and bear witness to the new world standard of climbing at 8c+ here in Derbyshire. The portraits could to some degree be classed as self indulgent, yet I feel the reader will agree that they do bring to life the individuality of each climber in a striking way, that the written word however poetic, lucid or descriptive cannot.

In conclusion the text does represent the physical and mental power that climbing has over peoples lives, and the photographs illustrate the power contained within climbing at it's highest level.

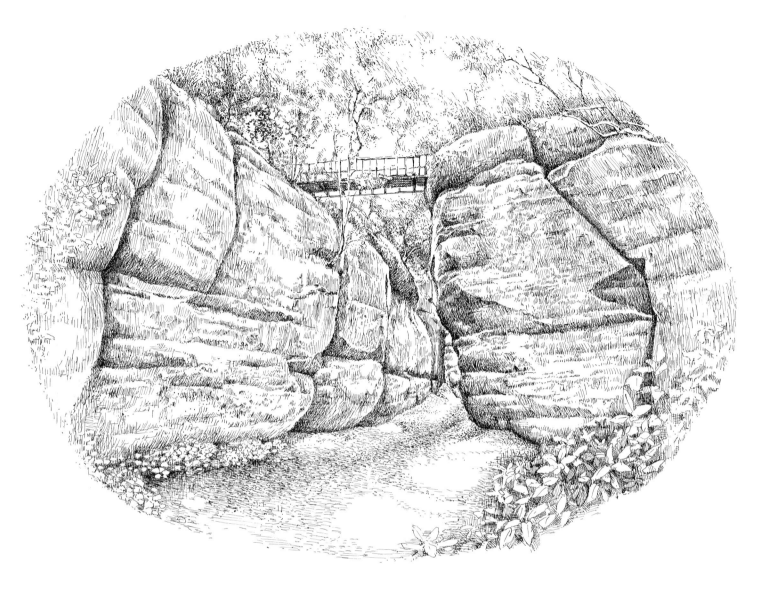

The Grand Canyon of High Rocks, nestled in the woods close to Royal Tunbridge Wells, Kent.
A delightful sandstone outcrop where climbing and pleasure walks can be had
amongst the boulders, narrow gorges and rhododendrons.

The Professionals

There are those that make money from climbing yes, but there are those who make money from climbers and some even succeed in selling climbing to non climbers. Some make a lot and others make a pittance. All are professionals at what they do, if they're not – they cease to do it. Most enjoy climbing, it starts from an enthusiastic spell, early in their career, then get side tracked to making money, it takes over and climbing gets put on the shelf. It occasionally gets resurrected to the odd day on Cloggy and glimpse at a European snow covered blob. But the affinity for the sport never dies, far from it; the protection and support for the sport grows to a feverish level. The money making endeavour then gives the ultimate ability to exercise control over the sport. But then also holidays allow the resurrection of activity, training to increase, standard to rise; and all is forgotten. Then there is a financial crash and the entrepreneurs go bust, return to the bed sits in Sheffield, and start all over again; professionals in a sport, they truly love.

Terry Tullis

Anybody who has climbed at Harrison's Rocks in Sussex over the years will have met Terry. He is very much a father figure and respected all over the world for his affinity to the rocks and indeed climbers themselves. I can remember at 14, cycling 62 miles down to the rocks and being totally over awed by this climbing game and consequently loosing my jacket. A few days later Terry found it, then managed to unravel the almost washed out phone number, and without a thought returned the jacket safely. This is very much Terry's nature, a long lasting friend and guardian to the Sandstone outcrops of the South East. He has climbed well and upholds the basic ethics of the sport, a more down to earth person you could not meet. His wife Julie died tragically on the descent of K2, the second highest mountain in the World. She was also a lovely girl whose presence was always part of Harrison's. Terry now looks after the rocks and supports climbers with the tea caravan, the main venue of topical discussion prior to sampling those great Sussex Ales.

Interview 28.12.90 Groombridge, Sussex.

When did you first start climbing?
About 1956-57, I was 20 when I came out of the Army in 55.

Was that National service?
Very much so, it was not something which I would have done willingly, but it was good fun in retrospect.

What career did you take up?
I'd never been career minded, my mother looked through the papers and came up with a job as a library boy for a photo agency on Fleet Street. It meant a lot of filing of plates but I was lucky, because I found that I was interested in Photography. I was promoted to darkroom printing and by 17 was going out as a camera operator. Because of this when I joined the army I was offered the job of a clerk. "No fuckin way" I said. I demanded and became a driver, a great choice, I got posted to Malasia for 18 months and matured somewhat. After leaving I went back to Fleet Street for 6 months; then into fashion and advertising but I didn't like it at all. I wanted to travel so I kicked traces, bummed around and took a lot of odd jobs until I bought the jeep in '57. I headed straight for High Rocks as I'd lived down there when I was a child and knew it; the place to try any jeep out. We used to come down with three guys and take the piss out climbers with the inevitable result that,'If you can do any fuckin better, you do it'. I did, HUT CRACK at High Rocks, my first climb it's not hard but the guys that were on it couldn't do it, I just shot up it, great fun, I liked it.

Was High Rocks then still a Victorian pleasure ground?
No, I'm not that old Dave, Victorian Indeed! A rough idea of High Rocks; the pub was owned by a guy called Captain Doug Lisen, a great bloke. We used to arrive about 10 o'clock on a Friday evening, go straight into the pub and if Doug wasn't there, then you poured your own beer or rum and cokes. You had just spent an hours ride in the jeep and were bloody cold, you poured your own and put the money in the till, closeing the door behind you, then have a big bonfire on the rocks. In lots of ways there was more anarchy then, than there is now; climbing has always been anarchic but was slightly more so in those days. The public weren't there, you paid peanuts to climb. When it changed hands to a chap called Gibson Cowan, he started to make the thing pay, which antagonised climbers. Before that it was just great fun, Doug got the better deal because climbers helped him no end because he was fair with them. Climbers, as soon as they feel they're being ripped off, don't do anything. It's like that today, the guy now is having a rough time, fences being cut, he's overcharging.

Is that anarchy part of climbing?
I think so, very much so. I've always towed the line, but I've always refused in my dealing with the rocks to accept what the Sports Council would like to do down there. They give me a very free hand, but there are factions within them who want signs saying that it's dangerous to climb, don't climb with bare feet, this way up, this way down. It's in their committee meetings, you say; "look it won't work, climbers don't want signs, they don't want easy ways up, easy ways down;" now they realise that climbers will govern themselves.

Did you become good at climbing?
I was a very spasmodic climber, I've done some quite good routes on Sandstone certainly, but never done much in the Mountains at all. In fact I'm perfectly happy to follow people up easy things. I've soloed what was then called INSPIRATION 5c, I did the first solo of SOUTH WEST CORNER 6a, which the Holliwells them claimed. I climbed very well for a day maybe and then just drifted on happily. I've never, never ever gone down to the rocks and thought well I'll do this today, shit or bust, it's just not in my nature. Sometimes I manage, sometimes I don't. I enjoy being there, I enjoy the atmosphere.

What gave you the idea of having a climbing cafe in Groombridge?
That goes back to Bowles. When Bowles was put up for sale, Julie and I were living in Streatham and not exactly rich. The going price for Bowles was about £400 and we got bidding up to £400. Nea Morin was also bidding so we stupidly (I didn't know Nea at the time), and we were bidding against each other, but were both doing it for the same reason. Then straight out of the blue another guy put in a bid for £1000 and he got it. His plan was to turn Bowles into an outdoor gymnasium, which he set about doing. He was a fairly murky character, very religious on the outside but deep down I think not, he was not a nice man. He had great charisma and asked Julie and I to help out. I could be the warden/chief instructor and Julie could help out. We thought it was a super idea, Bowles was a lovely place; having failed to buy it, we thought it would be good and worked there.

He said we could have £1000 a year and a free house, (the house took a long time to build – it came eventually but took a long time – we lived in a chicken shed). I left under a bit of a cloud, in disagreement with building a chapel down there when we were still using elsan toilets. So I left and bought a house, got a job in Tunbridge Wells, after about two years we got itchy feet and decided to do something, so we put the house on the market and went off to the continent with the kids. We went out for six weeks and when we came back the house was sold and Julie was panicking about where we were going to live so we went out and bought a caravan which we parked just behind Bowles and lived in that for a year. After a year I still didn't know what I wanted to do, I was cutting wood for local farmers and messing around, earning a few bob here and there, living on the sale of the house. Then Saxby's in the village came up for sale, which at that time was a grocer's store with the tiniest of tearooms – two tables and that was it. I'd been using it for a long, long time, I thought that's it, it seemed a sensible idea so we bought and ran it. Then we sold it to a couple, Molly and Olly. They went down the tubes very rapidly because they wanted to live high on the hog, go out for meals every night which you can't do with a grocers shop, there's not that much profit in it. We offered to help since we lent them some money to buy it and they weren't paying us so we were in dire straits. Eventually they went bankrupt and Julie and I decided to go back in. The place was just a shell, the bailiff's had taken everything including a lot of my stuff. So we said that's it, we'll just run it as a climber's cafe at weekends. We got a gas

stove in there and started serving teas again, we only opened at weekends, we put a football machine in the front room and it just became 'the' centre for southern climbing. We sold it to go to Peru in 1978, we went with Norman Croucher - the man with no legs – who wanted to do a 20,000 ft mountain.

What made Peru more important than the success of the shop or mixing with the climbers?

I don't have a great deal of time, I suppose to conform, so we sold it to someone who said he was going to run it as a climbing shop. In the end he turned out to be a trifle odd and had very little idea at all, really now I miss it like my right arm, but now the caravans taken over, that's great fun instead. Going to Peru was something to do – it was a chance. I'd never been to South America, I get on very well with Norman, I like his company enormously and I thought it was something very worthwhile to do, so that was it, we sold and went.

Were you successful?

Yes. His aim was to climb a 20,000 ft mountain, eventually Julie and he climbed Huascaran, which is 21,800ft, so he was delighted. I wanted to go off and see the places which were so close and I felt I must see eg. Machu Pichu and places like that. I was out there and carrying loads and quite happy to carry them, Julie and Norman hit this terrific partnership right away which was nice to see. They were doing very well together, hell, let them do it. So I went off and looked at earthquake sites. In fact I met 7 Peruvian lecturers from the University at Lima, all extremely pretty girls, I went off with them for a week which was great fun.

Do you feel it's important for climbers to just leave their normal climbing and go and climb something else?

I don't know. I came from a family where it was the norm to have one job all your life and then retire, which is what my father did then promptly died. All he wanted to do was to get his pension and retire, he didn't use any of it, so I thought that's a bit silly. Everybody has their thing deep down inside that they want to do. If they feel they want to be terribly serious and pursue a career and have a mortgage and 2.5 kids – that's great, but I don't look down on people who don't have those ideals, it's quite good. I suppose it's the anarchy in people.

Have you noticed that climbers who go to the rocks are addicted. Is it sandstone or is it just climbing?

I think there are those who are totally addicted to sandstone but I think they are in the minority. I think most are addicted to climbing.

Does a greater addiction corollate with the standard?

I'm not sure. I think that climbers who climb at a high standard are basically talented. Not all climbers that are addicted are talented, they have to work very hard for what they get out of it. I suppose that's where I look on with a little bit of humour because I've never been dedicated to anything except being lazy.

Is there an average age that goes climbing to the rocks?

No, I don't think so. We have the 60 year olds and 70 year olds and you have the youths. They start coming down with girls, then with their girl friends, then get married and vanish for about 6 years. The next time they come down it's with their children, it always seems to be about a six year gap between getting married and coming down. Then you find that's sub-divided into the girls who came climbing because they enjoy climbing, and the girls who came climbing to catch the poor bastard. The one's who were caught come down with the kids on their own and the ones who actually did climb together come down together with their kids. There's that gap and I've seen a lot, now I'm on the third generation of people I've taught which is really nice.

Is there a type of profession which climbers come from?

I think profession wise we have everything from total bums to brick layers to plumbers to doctors, dentists, nursing, social workers, we've got one millionaire – Judging from the cars you see on the car park there must be a lot of high flyers, as well as the really beat up old mini drivers. The fact is that we can see all these people together, there is no social bar at the rocks, everybody gets on.

Does that make them go to the rocks do you think?

I don't think so. I don't think they go to the rocks to rub shoulder with anybody who's necessarily rich or famous.

Climbing is physical but is also a mind game, which is more important to you?

To me the physical. I've always been very powerful in the shoulders, so I used to be able to cream up really powerful climbs and thoroughly enjoy them. If anything though I'm much happier on slabs, the joy of movement to me is far more important than the joy of success. I'm quite happy on a Hard V. diff. where every move is in balance and every move is neat and tidy, I can thoroughly enjoy that. But I've been repulsed on things like GOLIATH'S GROOVE at Stanage which is not hard and I can do it but I didn't enjoy it, it was not something I could hack, because I couldn't make one move nice and I'd rather not bother, that's not what climbing is about to me – I can thrutch up anything because I've got the power but it's something I don't enjoy.

Have you ever found climbing mentally straining?

No I've never climbed that pitch which requires it to be mentally straining. I think that's why I like seconding so much. I know I'm strong, I know I can do things, I know there is not much that when I was climbing well, would hold me back. I know I'm a good man to have around in adversity, as it were. So I knew I could pull a few stops out if necessary, maybe it's the teaching thing, you feel you're playing a supporting role and you're bringing someone else on. It's very difficult to explain how my mind sees this. I remember a couple of climbs in particular where my leader was really pushing himself. They were climbs I'd never climbed before, around HVS but I was absolutely in control as a second, and perfectly happy as a second, maybe I don't like being at the sharp end. I can also remember climbing with Julie and failing on dismal things because we couldn't climb together, I couldn't do CREAG DHU WALL, which I'd done three or four times before. But with Julie I just couldn't do it, I thought bugger this if I fall off, she'll fall off, it just didn't work, we didn't climb together. She was quite a powerful climber though.

Do you get a lot of enjoyment from teaching climbing or is it something you do to make money?

For a long time we got immense enjoyment out of it, then when they raised the school leaving age to 16, all we had down there were rebels – the people they wanted out of school. They were two terrible years, they just wanted to cause chaos wherever they were, they didn't want to be in school for the next three years; that was a very very rough patch. Then we had good schools like Skinners which is a high quality school, they are always very good to teach, but then you get other schools which are absolute bastards. Although we can't teach them to climb, we have always had a lot of success turning them into human beings. Julie and I always believed in a thick ear if it was necessary, we've always believed in firmness and manners, all those things they don't seem to bother about in schools these days. So we have an incredible number of youthful friends throughout Tunbridge Wells. Teaching the handicapped kids of course is also enjoyable, it has never ceased to be enjoyable, you get a phenomenal amount out of that and you see them get better every week.

Jasper Sharpe on the final moves of Gary Wickham's route KINDA LINGERS 8a, High Rocks, Kent. He added his own direct, start straight up the arête, previously it was approached from the right with a figure of four move.

Dennis Gray

The name Dennis Gray has become synonymous with the British Mountaineering Council over the last two decades of climbing. He led what was initially a very small amateur group of enthusiastic mountaineers to become a highly respected professional sports body for climbing. During that time he made friends and enemies as any figure head does, but he retained the finest quality of all, in being known to most climbers, as someone you would always bump into from time to time at the crag, or the wall, or the bar. In becoming a high flying exec. He never lost touch with the voice of the regular climbers, and over 20 years has put an unparalleled drive into the sport at every level from leadership and instructing schemes, to political lobbies on free access to Britain's countryside environment. He persuaded the BMC to run bi-annual international conferences on climbing with involvement from all the big climbing names such as Scott, Bonington, Messner, Bonatti, Cesen, Moffatt to name but a few. To combine the love of the mountains with the frustrations of a paper pushing job, was always going to be a heavy undertaking, but Dennis has fought well in debate for the voice of climbing and now enjoys the benefit of retiring into the sport he has always loved and tried to protect.

Interview 16.2.91 Baslow, Derbyshire.

When were you born?
1935

Did you start climbing at an early age?
Yes, I was about 11, living in Leeds with my parents, our family was very much a theatre family, my father was on the stage all his life, and my great grandmother a concert pianist. Nevertheless at 11, I joined the Boy Scouts in the middle of Leeds. The first weekend we were due to go out to the Cow and Calf at Ilkley. Well I missed the Scouts at Leeds but with a bit of initiative I got out to Ilkley on the bus and wandered up into Ilkley quarry. I saw Arthur Dolphin climbing; I'd never heard of climbing, I'd never even thought of rock climbing and this was the first time I was exposed to it. I was immediately gob smacked by it and decided, that's what I wanted to do. So the next week I gave up the Scouts and took up climbing.

Were you enjoying school at that time?
I was very fortunate to have won a scholarship to Leeds Grammar School, but was made to feel very uncomfortable in coming from the inner city in Leeds, eventually I moved to the modern Grammar School and I enjoyed that until about 14-15. Then I became rebellious and my schooling suffered proportionally, I became totally disenchanted with school and the only subjects I was interested in were English Literature and Art. That in turn took me into Fine art printing for a firm in Derby. Before that I went to study printing at college whilst working for a firm in Leeds.

Did you need to enjoy your work?
Not at school because of the format, but at 18 I did because I was so much more interested. It later led me back to university as a mature student to read Psychology. I like taking on a subject and trying to understand it, particularly if it's academic with an artistic influences.

Did you succeed?
Yes, I'd become very interested in Psychology. I'd read a lot of books on it, and I'd also helped on a scheme set up by the Home Office to treat youngsters who were psychotic.

Did you then make a study of the psychology of climbers?
One of the things I was interested in was personality in climbing. In my course as part of my final years programme, I took what was then the top climbers in the country and subjected them to a Personality Inventory: 20 people who were top grade, 20 people who were medium grade and 20 who didn't climb at all, and the idea was to see if there was any differences between the groups.

Was there any?
Yes there was, the top climbers were shown in certain areas of personality to have traits in common, as did the middle group and the non climbers. In the top they were anti rule, evaders of the law as one would expect, they were shown to be very free thinking, also in layman's terms to be rather ruthless and obsessive. They were also the people who did not recognise societies obligations, for instance in areas like the family, and they all had more or less these traits in common.

In your study in climbing did it give you an insight that perhaps you might be able to join that top group of climbers?
That's a difficult question. It was done very arbitrarily, I was picking people that now you would consider the top mountaineers rather than the top climbers such as Tom Patey, Joe Brown, Dougal Haston and so forth. One hoped that one might be part of that elite band but did see them essentially as a peer group.
Where did that lead you to?

I'd really misunderstood the nature of the problems of Psychotic young people and I found it wasn't for me, besides working day in and day out. Then I got odd printing jobs which then landed me up in Kenya, being one of the major cogs in running a printing factory. I then came back since my father was taken ill, and thereby got involved with the BMC by accident. Tony Moulam who was then running a very much makeshift operation invited me to join, since they needed people; climbing was growing faster than anyone could have envisaged and the organisation couldn't even cope with opening the mail. So in 1972 the job of National Officer was created which I took on.

Did that bring a conflict by then actually working in climbing?

Up until then climbing was very much for me an escape from work, absolutely. I had very strong views against professionalism in climbing at that time, and people who were in fact making a living from it I felt were prostituting the sport. I looked at the job and in fact realised that I wasn't working in climbing, I was working in administration, rather like any other service organisation. It was simply running the office, and the climbing I did was quite separate from the BMC.

When you set up the committee structure of the BMC in 1972, did you feel that both with rock climbing and mountaineering that you were dealing with the same bunch of people?

Yes, more or less, but I did become very aware through involvement at Leeds university of the radical changes afoot. The building of the climbing wall there in 1964 which we initially didn't understand and that of it's use as a training medium! It was John Syrett who first shocked everyone by starting this form of training, and after a few months from starting this programme, he was zooming through the grades. A whole new movement was happening and bouldering was developing to a large extent.

Did you believe that the BMC could serve both boulderers and Himalayan mountaineers?

Yes, I was rather tongue in cheek about it, but I felt that it was very easy to do. The problem was mainly it being an organisation run by older people; as most are. Those who have retired, and the new movements aren't going to relate to bureaucracy anyway. You are not going to have Simon Nadin spending N weeks going to BMC committees, he would certainly be bored out of his bloody skull.

Did it worry you in leading an organisation in presenting climbing, where it's forefront members were the first to rebel against society?

I think that's true of a lot of other sports and climbing is certainly not unique in that respect. Rugby, athletics etc., and one knows a few inside stories which gives you confidence that you're not the only one failing to find support from 100 per cent of your members or

participants. But I did feel particularly in the 70's very torn because of that dichotomy, worried about the BMC becoming a rule orientated organisation. Through good sense we managed to let climbers make their own decisions on an everyday climbing level and let rules govern more technical matters such as training and the safety aspects of equipment manufacture rather than it's common day use.

Did you always feel capable of communicating the voice of mad rebellious climbers with a more conservative society and straight faced politicians?

One of the things I always used to say, "Climbers are unique", particular to the sport political system, which whatever people say is very self evident. It's incredible, it's the first card on the bartering table of trade negotiations, exchange contracts be it under the cover of whatever is happening in the world at that time, and every nation tries to use it as a vehicle to get what they want out of it. I used to address National Coaches conferences with "Climbers are unique". And people started to immediately fall around laughing and say, "that's what every sport tells us and if you think climbers are unique try to run the Rugby Union, these guys beat up their officials quite regularly in the bar after a few heavy pints". It's true that every sport is unique and every sport has it's problems, climbers do have a uniqueness since obviously it's beyond the boundaries of what other sports do. It plays for keeps in certain areas, with a death toll in the Himalaya that is quite staggering. I think in general that climbers do exaggerate this because I've seen inside a lot of sports over the years, especially running and observed very similar trends.

How did you feel representing climbing, a poor sport, up against the big rich sports like Tennis, Cricket etc?

Well if you look at climbing across the board and count the numbers of participants from basic hill walking to Himalayan mountaineering, then we have as many people, and worldwide there are certainly more people involved with climbing than a lot of what are considered as major sports! Also it's one of the sports that we do hold a very prominent place in the history, and also in terms of modern day performance. Which ever way you care to asses things, if you want to asses them, and sometimes you are forced to asses them, you have to conclude that we've played a major role in the development of mountaineering and rock climbing. We have people at the very highest standards of the sport in all the modern day disciplines of climbing and it's a great pride.

What climbs have you most enjoyed in your life?

That's a very hard question because I've been climbing over 45 years now. One climb that sticks out very much is a climb I did at Hell's Gate in Kenya, which was a first ascent. Rockclimbing is really unique in East Africa because you have these really unbelievable objective dangers, things like the killer Bees, the Baboons who throw boulders at you, the snakes etc. I was climbing with two American climbers and we cracked this route which was then, one of the great last problems at Hell's Gate, we had a lot of fun and I really enjoyed that. I think another climb I enjoyed immensely was doing the first ascent of the highest of the Manikaran Spires in the Kangra Himalaya, a lovely rock spire nearly 18,000 ft high.

What are the best memories of climbing in England?

I think that the best overall memories of climbing are actually in this country. They are the best because British climbing is unique, you've got every type of rock and a very varied weather system where you have good and bad weather. With an incredible landscape where you can climb on sea cliffs or the grit edges of Derbyshire, sandstone of Northumberland and lovely sweeping granite slabs of Scotland. So we do have this incredible environment to give us such memorable days.

Will you carry on climbing forever?

Yes, as long as I'm able to.

Tony Greenbank

To any committed professional working within an artistic medium there are always financial hazards which deliver hardship more often than a splendiferous lifestyle. The choice is nevertheless always that of the writer, and accountable more to themselves than perhaps the reader could ever conceive. Tony has always respected this but uses it to enable himself to live in the heart of the English Lake District, and climb whenever time dictates. He is not young, but then in character you could never refer to him as old since his energy to climb is immense, his enthusiasm has always been admirable and to many climbers epitomizes the ability to get 100 per cent from climbing without pitting oneself against a particular grade of climb.

Interview 3.2.91 Ambleside, Lake District.

Does writing about climbing compare with doing it?

No, no, no, no! Nothing can compare with actually climbing, writing about climbing is extremely second hand compared with the experience of climbing and I don't often write about climbing for that reason. That is why I've gone into freelance writing and written about anything but climbing. Over the years I haven't written that many climbing articles in journals and things, and with books only those early instruction books like 'Enjoy your Rock Climbing' and 'Climbing For Young People'. It is so hard to write about climbing, as the climbing actually is.

Have you always climbed?

Since I was a teenager, I have tried other things but climbing is always the thing that has brought me back, or I have come back to climbing. It's either brought me back on the rails or I've actually come back to it anyway. It was always climbing that has been the constant thread through my life from when I was about 19; even through 10 years in the wilderness when I didn't climb very much, climbing was still there, but then climbing actually brought me out of that bad period, otherwise God knows where I would have gone.

If you ever have an EPIC on a climb do you feel as though you want to write about it?

I suppose so. As a writer the whole purpose I think is to entertain people, and you must entertain people, the reader has to be entertained and if it's an epic, then that actually could be the opening part of a piece of writing you're doing to grip the reader. I'm not sure about this but I think that is probably what I would do if I had an epic.

Do you enjoy reading other peoples writing about climbing?

Not generally, no, only when it is well written and I don't find many writers who write well enough for me to persevere, so I read very little on climbing really.

Would you say that's more from today's era than older generations? Do people like Abrahams and Owen Gwyne Jones stand out at all?

Probably, perhaps...... I think I used to read all those books, those are the books that really fired me to climb, I used to like them but now would probably find them a bit hard going. The writer has to carry me through the text, I can't persevere if I can't get past the first page without feeling a tendency to yawn, which comes on very quickly now. I just don't persevere and certainly that is basically what happens, or maybe I get through the first few pages and then I just can't be bothered any

more. When it comes over well and it's by a good climbing writer, like that etheral article by John Barry called 'Mountain lovers and gratuitous couplings', that is different; I love reading it then.

Can you think of any great books?

Well 'The Void', Touching the Void. A marvellous book, particularly because the way it was written. A lot of climbing books give you the impression that they have just been written and perhaps altered once or twice, but you feel it's flat and there is no life, no class to it. That was a book that was WRITTEN...this is the way that real writing goes. I think that he wrote forty thousand words and then threw it away because it was stylized, it was all for effect so he scrapped it and started again. He told it like it was, and then it flowed out of him in just eight weeks, THAT is what writing is, but there are very few writers I think who are prepared to do that. If you say you had written and thrown away forty thousand words, to most people it's shock horror! But to me it's perfectly natural, that is part of the process of creation, it's essential and Joe did that, it's why the account of the story is absolutely dead on. Publishers will take anything, especially English publishers, much more than American ones. Prepared to take any old shit at all, as long as it is readable and literate, and can keep the printing presses running, they don't mind. They don't like it particularly if you say you want to change forty thousand words, and yet that is the way things go if you feel it in your heart.

What makes climbing difficult to write about?

If you love something so much, which I do, then it's like writing about a woman you love. It's very hard to do and you wouldn't normally do it, it's something you keep to your heart, it's so very very good, it's so very personal. Climbing, writing about it, so many streams come between you and the actual experience of climbing that when it's actually written, it's all a bit diffuse and very second hand as to how it actually comes over. Now and again a writer will pierce that, and the text won't be opaque anymore, it will be crystal clear and that it marvellous.

Do you think it's by virtue of the ability of the writer or just simply the experience lent itself?

It could be both, but I'm sure it's the ability of the writer, but anybody could have it without knowing they had it, and it's just the experience perhaps brings it out, the tremendous moment of climbing.

Are there any other books in the past that have done the same to you as Touching the Void by Joe Simpson?

Hermann Buhl's book, I've read that several times, Perrin and Dave Cook's work, articles by the great Jimmy Marshall, Jim Curran; Bonington's first book because it was written during his lean years and the writing shines as a result, and rock climbing guidebooks by the score, some of the best climbing writing today is done by guidebook writers, there are some brilliant passages and I read them again and again, even if I am incapable of touching those particular routes, like the Yorkshire Grit guide, solid gold. You may only climb 5a but it gives as vivid an account of routes up to that grade as it does E5's. But the one book I return to all the time is The Hustler. Everyone knows the film but the book itself, written in the late 50's is something else again. Crystal clear. Walter Tevis also wrote 'The Color of Money', 'The Man Who Fell to Earth' and 'Queens Gambit'. His theme is the clash between having talent and bringing a wayward character to heel to capitalise on it, and will he – won't he succeed?

That's why it's such a cliff hanger. I can identify with every moment from when Fast Eddie Felson first walks into Bennington's – that's right, Bennington's billiard hall in Chicago and drops the first of a whole series of momentously heavy bummers. No gain without pain is the theme. I hang in there on every bloody sentence. I know the feeling.

Do you think it's possible for writers who don't climb to write about climbing?

I suppose it is, it's certainly possible for them to write about climbing, I must say I only know this from my experience of writing for SHE magazine. I once wrote about Sailing through the great whirlpool of Cory Vrekan, between Jura and some other Island. It was totally fictitious and I told SHE at the time, that it was written for real. Dennis Norden who wrote a regular criticism at the end of the magazine said that this was by far the most riveting and gripping piece of writing he had ever read in SHE; that it was the most edge of the seat stuff and he could identify with it all the way. I hate sailing, I hate water, and it was totally fictitious so I'm sure it's possible for someone to write about climbing without experiencing it. I think if you're a good writer and you get the facts together of what is going on, you could probably write a very good piece of climbing writing.

All the people that write about climbing are climbers; is that's where it's gone amiss over the years?

Yes..... I honestly don't know. I mean some of the writing is so essentially pedestrian, and I just despair sometimes, but when a good piece of writing comes up, like that jewel by John Barry; Oh man it's great.

Does the Boardman Tasker prize excite you to want to write something?

No, not particularly. I'm just indifferent to awards or bursaries or scholarships for writers. I don't think writers should see beyond the money they initially expect, though very nice if their work THEN collects extra remuneration. Money for the actual piece they're writing is the thing that drives them on, and I think that a writer won't produce their best work unless they're up against a deadline. I've been full time writing since 1961 and I know from experience that if I've had any hard times, then it's through my own fault; because if you're a writer, there's lots and lots of good markets for writers, and millions of pounds are paid annually in fees and royalties. You have to produce the goods, and so what happens is that the writer, the full time writer, you only really produce the goods when you're up against it. Anything like expecting grants from the Arts Council and Society of

Authors etc., is absolutely wrong, you associate good writing with lean times, not with sleek, well fed times, or subsidised times. The best writing comes from when you're having a really fuckin hard time, like Dickens for instance. He had written Pickwick Papers and something else, he was already a name as a writer, and yet his royalties started to fall off and his publishers told him that they were going to cut down on him. He had about 5 kids and he was really desperate, and he got a writers block for about 6 months, or even longer. He couldn't even think and he didn't know what to produce, he was running out of money and he faced absolute failure did Dickens. He went to the south coast, walked along the headlands in search of inspiration, didn't get any and came back to London, and one night he though 'oh well, sod it', and went down to these dismal gaslit streets, into the East End, where there was absolute squalor

and poverty, and THAT triggered him off. He thought, 'Well I'm going to write about all of this, it's what I know,' and he wrote A Christmas Carol, and that was the whole thing that revived him back, brought his flagging career back to life. The Society of Authors go on and on about how authors shouldn't take contracts unless they get such and such terms, and you shouldn't give a lecture unless you get such a sum of money for it. Well it's rubbish because it's swings and roundabouts, if you're a freelance writer then you take the good and bad breaks, but you have to accept all that. Dickens didn't get very good terms for Christmas Carol, but he knew what he was doing when he wrote it, and he thought 'Sod it, I might not be getting very good terms for it, but it's going to bring my name back into the fore', which it did; but by today's Society of Authors standards he shouldn't have written that book because he wasn't doing it for the right kind of advance etc. I see a writer very much as a gunfighter, a high plains drifter who goes out there, he doesn't have any other job, he just writes for a living, even through the lean times, never giving in. You never give in, you persevere right through to the end and I think that's, what makes writing.

Do you think that mentality is very similar to climbing?

I'm sure it is, yes I do. I see parallels in it, like you have to produce the goods when it counts, which is the crux thing. It's that being committed and out there feeling that you cannot get if you have a job on the side like teaching creative writing at some university. To quote the novelist Anthony Burgess 'The freelance writer has the most lonely and maverick job in the world' which of course is true, you have to attain the psychological concentration that only the solitude of being out there can bring. So it's just like climbing. On my window is an ON THE EDGE sticker which says it all; that's where I'm at, what retirement? Christ, what a laugh. I'll still be here into the year 2000 with luck just like Haydn when he wrote The Creation, head bowed over the keyboard and tongue working away furiously and desperately still striving to keep the wolf away from the door. Others in the same boat know all right. I wrote a piece about the smugness prevalent in some climbing writing and behaviour today and Jim Perrin sent me this card..."Right on! If only the Fuckers knew..." Had it pinned to the wall for ages.

Did you ever feel that your writing was getting in the way of your climbing?

Oh yes, well of course, this is the whole conflict. It's interesting, it's the penalty I've paid for not wanting to write about climbing. So I've had to write a whole lot of shit really for magazines like Weekend and Titbits, stuff like that. Now I'm trying to get away from that, it's only recently I can begin to see the light after doing this present book that is so different from anything I've done before. I've found it deadening writing journalistically through the years like flying in a Jaguar jet on a Nato exercise and sailing in a nuclear submarine to Gibraltar etc, people say Isn't this great to go on these exciting trips, but I don't think it's great at all because you still have to come up with the goods, your head is on the block. Oh yes, for a wealthy magazine you still get a kill fee even if you fail; but if you collect too many of those then you're soon out of business. Besides, these assignments are not at all like climbing. Then of course while you're struggling with all this to bring in the cheques, you just can't go out and climb so writing definitely gets in the way of climbing probably more so than for people in the 'secure' jobs or those who have taken early retirement. It's even worse when you hit the jackpot. I've had two best sellers, one sold a quarter of a million in the States, another topped the Sunday Times best-seller paperback list for 5 weeks, but it's when the money floods in , that the writer is most vulnerable and at their most wayward, or at least I am. So it's soon back to the 'Welcome to Hard Times' again.

Has it been the will to climb or to do particular routes?

I would say both, sometimes a climb but generally just to climb, in the winter for instance it is lovely to go to Scotland, Maybe Lochnagar in a few weeks, but that's only when the damn cheque comes in for this bloody book I'm doing, I'm still working on the sodding thing, I should be out today really.

Do you feel that they play against each other, in so far as that you could possibly have been a GREAT writer if you had no interest in climbing?

Yes, I might feel like that when I'm feeling down. And that the climbing demon inside every climber has been responsible for holding me back, a bit like that ace lecture by Warren Harding at Buxton, HOW CLIMBING ACTUALLY RUINED MY LIFE WITHOUT ACTUALLY KILLING ME. But it says in The Hustler self-pity is the world's universally most popular indoor sport. Really I'm stuck with what I have. I was guest speaker at the Rock & Ice dinner and they have a character assassinator who imitates a hen and who introduced me as a failed Chris Bonington. "Hell, that's not right," I said. "I'm a failure in my own right." There's only one thing I can do, to write and climb better as Fast Eddie is told repeatedly by his mentor; and that is to bear down when the clutch comes. But you'll have to read it for yourself.

What makes you live in the Lakes?

I've really chosen the lakes but I still do get very excited when I go to Scotland or Llanberis. Perhaps it's something that just appeals. There are some places aren't there where you feel at one, and I always have with the lakes, the only other place I've felt totally at one is Manhattan where I lived for three years in New York. I loved it and had that feeling of being totally safe and secure, and at one with New York. John Lennon in his famous Radio 1 interview said exactly the same thing days before he was shot. It's a place where I didn't have to make any effort to get into the city.

That is surprising, the Lake District and Manhattan!

Yes right, but a lot of similarities, people do see it but they're in the minority. I don't know what it is, but it's this feeling of being totally at home. There is tremendous bouldering in Van Courtland Park and Central Park, it's illegal but you can go at night, they have these street lights and if you've had a few you're alright. All the boulders are chalked up and are really good. The best area is in a woodland where all the perverts hang around in the shrubs with shiny macs! There are little bridges, viaducts and big boulders.

Does it worry you that you won't be able to fulfil all your dreams in climbing?

Good God no! But there are still lots and lots of things that I would like to do.

And in your writing?

Oh yes definitely, I certainly want to improve in that. I have lots and lots to learn. I was thick at school and hadn't passed any exams and didn't know what to do really. Going to the Outward Bound as an instructor at Eskdale, was an experience like going to university really. I didn't know what to do beyond that, I decided I certainly didn't want to be a social worker or teacher which is what a lot of the instructors ended up in. I took this correspondence course in writing and in the end I was writing and earning more than I was at instructing. The writing success showed the true character of friendly rivalry between some of the other instructors who, unlike myself, had been to Oxford or Cambridge and saw Greenbank as a thick'o. They would see these cheques coming into my pigeon hole and be thinking 'bloody hell if he can do that, we're going to start'. This instructor started who had been to Cambridge and he wrote a true story about how he had been mugged in Paris, he sent it to a magazine called Wide World which published true-life dramas for men and all stories had to be true; but he had it rejected, saying it didn't have the ring of truth about it. I sent mine which was a totally fictitious thing about a guy falling off the Cima Grande and spinning like a spider on a thread, and having to cut the rope with a pen knife. I got fifteen guineas for it and I had never been near the Dolomites at the time. In truth of course I still have lots of writing to do, and plenty to improve upon.

Do you see a future conflict in wanting to climb over wanting to write?

I see it as coming together providing I can work hard enough, providing I can get my head straight, providing I keep working hard. The whole thing is wanting to do it, you have to have the appetite to do it, which you have when you're having lean times as opposed to well fed times. I want to get some success in my writing, that is what I want; and it will give me more freedom to do the climbing I want, definitely! There is something inside me which makes me rejoice when I see good climbers, I love watching young climbers and good climbers. There is something in me that really responds to that even though I know I can't climb at their standard. I love to lead, and can cope with 5a on a good day but generally 4c; but to watch somebody doing something really hard, I just love it! Like climbing competitions, I love watching them and I respond to it; and it's the same thing, my heart leaps when I see good writing - tremendous!

Ken Wilson

There have been many people who have made forays into the mountaineering publishing world. Many have come and most have gone, yet Ken remains, aloft at Fort Wilson, standing high on the battlements, always ready to engage forcibly with anyone who should attack the most sacred of sports, Climbing. He became involved in publishing with the foundation of MOUNTAIN magazine back in the '60's. From there he edited vigorously to produce, THE most highly respected climbing literature magazine in the world. He saw the market for good descriptive climbing writing and compiled two great books, HARD ROCK and CLASSIC ROCK; which even today are musts on the bookshelves of any climber. After nearly 60 issues he sold the magazine in 1977 and set up his own publishing firm DIADEM; which enabled him to direct all his energy into publishing good climbing literature. The list is long and

formidable; anthology's, biographies, translations etc. The list is long and is full of the great names such as Tilman, Shipton, Gervasutti, Cassin and Bonatti. Ken has delivered time and time again, insights into a medium that is not easily expressed with words and photos alone.

Interview 3.2.91 Langley, Cheshire.

How would you actually define climbing?
It's going out and having an adventure - going out in the open, sorting out the problems of tackling a wild environment. It's really an extension of playing when you are a kid. I used to climb trees when I was young which was a a big thing in the post war period when there wasn't any organised recreation, there certainly wern't leisure centres or anything like that and of course the only transport was bus or train, very few people had cars. You either

went to the baths, played football in the street, or you played in the fields and climbed trees. If you compare a tree with a crag, there isn't that much difference, it's relatively straightforward providing you know what you are doing. But there is alway that menace, that if you make an error and slip, you could really hurt yourself. For me climbing was very much an extension of that whole childhood, life of woods and rivers and trees, instinctive, right from the word go. When I first touched rock it felt absolutely right, something about actually feeling the rock that felt right.
Do you feel that people who write books on climbing have the same attitude as yourself?
Obviously everyone comes to it from their own perspective. One of the things that has been very valuable to me is that I've got this very tactile feeling for the whole thing. That's not to say that other people don't have it, but a number of people who are involved in this

Jerry Moffatt – licenced to drill at Ravens Tor.

Mark Pretty 'The demon of Bosch,' belaying amid todays hardware at the foot of the crag.

and other deeper aspects of the sport isn't as great as it should be. Now we are disappearing down this gymnastic dead end. It may be society which is changing and climbing is just reflecting that. It's very interesting to see the way sports climbers are trying to marginalise adventure climbing, Mark Pretty wrote an article in an American magazine a year or so ago which gave the impression that Gogarth was virtually a suicidal cliff. He even implied, that only a madman would do a route like DREAM OF WHITE HORSES. Now that's terrible. If you get to a situation where you can't go on a cliff because it's not bolted up, you're going to miss a hell of a lot of fun and challenge in the sport. Climbing is much more than that, it's an art form; it's a dangerous art form yes, but it is an art form in the sense that at it's most committed level it searches down to the soul. Perhaps 'cultural expression' is a better description - the nature of climbing is fascinating and it needs a far greater level of discussion and debate than we are capable of here. I think Nick's point can be answered; and climbing can be justified as a fundamentally elevating thing, not a derivation of Russian Roulette, but if we are not careful it can easily degenerate into that and we must be very careful of that part. Obviously there is no way that I could have put those things in the magazine with any degree of conviction if it hadn't been part of the way I climbed and my whole ethos to climbing, I totally identified with that and still do.

field don't seem to have it. Somehow you can tell when they do, it reflects in the way they present things. Hiebeler used to do it with ALPINISMUS magazine back in the old days, he had it. He often used photographs that were taken quite close to the rocks, you could see the texture of the rock and this is one of the reasons why I'm so virulently anti-bolt. Because the bolt in effect ruins the rock. Pegs ruin the rock to a degree but at least they have to follow cracks and placing them from below involves some struggle, some inter relationship with the rock and it's weakness. But putting in bolts with a bolt gun hanging off an abseil rope is a soulless rape. It has cold cynicsm. It's like somebody putting nails into a tree and carving their names into it. I can't stand the sight of all these iron things sticking out of what should be left alone; because the rock itself is actually very pleasing to look at.

Do climbing books give a good medium for the adventure spirit of climbing to be reflected in?
I think so, that's what I tried with Hard Rock and Classic Rock, and I think we – and I say we because on all those books a lot of people made major contributions – achieved it with both of them. I have always tried to do books that reflect that. If people don't have an adventure, then there is no way they are going to write an interesting article about it. With Hard Rock and Classic Rock, I was getting people to write the essays who found climb's hard, people who had been balls-out when they did the route, or at least where something

unexpected and eventful had happened. Otherwise you just get a flat, half-baked article that just doesn't add up to anything.

Is it within the confines of your job to either support or to dissuade people from adventurous climbing to the point that it's dangerous?
It's an interesting point. I have been seriously criticised on just that point by Nick Colton who did a lot of big rock routes, and alpine climbs back in the 70's with Alex Macintyre, Tim Leech and Roger Baxter-Jones. These people were part of a group that were very much the 'Mountain' generation who read the magazine and who may have been influenced by it when I was editing it. Nick today looks back on the whole thing in a rather jaundiced way. and in effect implicit, in that he was accusing me of drug pushing., 'You edited that magazine' and 'You inspired everyone to go out and a lot of them didn't come back.' This is true. I did inspire everyone to go out, and I did edit the magazine in such a way, that people did want to go off and do big routes. I've thought about it a hell of a lot. It's a very difficult question, but I don't believe what I did was corruptive, and anything other than healthy, but it is a difficult question. All I can say is that I edited the magazine in the best way I know, and of course editors are constantly pressured by their peers. So really it was a broad expression of the sport at that time.

One of the things that saddens me about climbing these days, is that the level of debate and the level of inquiry into matters like this

How far afield have you climbed?
I've obviously had a lot of alpine seasons and I've climbed in America and I went on an Everest trip once as a journalist, I got to 23,000 ft. which was quite nice. It's a spectacular place Everest, when you get up in the Western Cwm it's gob astoundingly beautiful, you really feel that you are somewhere when you are there.

Did it make you want to go back there?
Not back to Everest, but a light-weight trip. I think the big heavy-weight expedition in some ways is good fun because there are a lot of people, and if it's well set up you have a good time. But really you just sit around with your feet up all the time, you do a bit of work now and again but there are all these sherpas, lugging things up and down the mountains for you. I think it must be very good if you are on a small trip and you can keep moving and

maximize the use of your time. We did the wonderful Omnibus of Shipton's. The first book in that – Nanda Devi – is what it's all about, it's a tremendous all round mountaineering book. It describes his adventures with Tilman in a wonderful trip to the Garhwal, they got up the Rishi Gorge and did some climbing, with a small team of really good sherpas. Shipton describes all this very vividly in the book which for me sums up what climbing is all about, it's not just climbing it's exploration and a hell of a lot of adventure. The degree of commitment was awesome. They crossed passes not known, what was on the other side, on two occasions descending 5,000 foot icefalls – real white knuckle stuff! After one of these descents they came down into this uninhabited valley and they had to fight their way through bamboo jungles, down steep ravines, crossing swollen rivers and at the end, when they ran out of food, they had to live off the land.

Does that entice you to go and do that sort of thing?

I In our hearts it's what we all look for and we are all inspired when we hear of such adventures. Every now and again one gets involved in some smaller version of that type of thing, and I can remember a few trips like that, but alas my life had led in a rather different direction. I am desk bound in a sort of purgatory way, producing books about it. I also find it difficult just to drop things and go out for a quick 'adventure' as I've always found it very difficult to get and stay fit. Even when I was at school playing sevens rugby and at my fittest, I would get desperate cramp, and this creates big problems - particularly with snow and ice climbing. Whenever I've had an alpine season I have to spend weeks of serious training and even then, usually on the big route at some stage, I've started cramping, my fingers have cramped, my knees and my legs have cramped; and that is pretty frightening. It means that you've got to keep quite a lot in hand.

Why did you choose a career in publishing?

I didn't, it just happened, well; it sort of developed. When I was in the scouts I would take snaps on our many trips and organise them into a factual record, assidiously captioning them and presenting them in an album in a pleasing way. That probably owed something to my previous hobbies of stamp collecting and train spotting. One thing led to another and I produced a small magazine for in the Scouts. Then after leaving school I studied architecture at night school and in that I got very used to doing what is now my everyday life; working weekends, burning the midnight oil. When I did that book with Chris Bonington, he is an 'early bird' – that's why he is a good alpinist – and he'd be phoning me up at 6.30 or 7 o'clock in the morning, asking me 'what do you think about this' and I would be half asleep. Then I'd be phoning him up at 10.30 in the evening and he'd be tucked up in bed. I am a night owl and get my best work done between 10 and 2am.

Then how did Architecture get you into magazine editing?

I went down to London to work for an architectual photographer who had a studio in Islington. You had to go out every day to photograph buildings and this made you very aware of the weather and more importantly light so that helped a lot in photographing cliffs. Also I ended up sharing flats with some other climbers: Pete Crew, Chris Jones, Nick Escourt, Malcolm Howells and others, all of whom were very active. Crew was a big influence, from a humble background, he creamed through the system and got into Oxford, didn't like it and was in London, working with computers. He was a real action man, fascinated by books and magazines and was also writing guidebooks. He had a complete set of Alpinismus which at that time was the best magazine. I was a photographer was a photographer so it was not long before we started working on joint projects.

Didn't you want to climb with Crew?
He was in a different league to me, he operated at the top level and there was a much bigger gulf between the top performer and the average performer then than there is now - though that part can be We did the odd pleasant route together, but usually the main reason was that I had a unique opportunity to photograph him at a time when he was at the peak of his powers. We also teamed up Jack Soper to produce THE BLACK CLIFF and I gave up climbing for a whole summer to take photographs that were necessary until it was finished. You either go out to get proper photos, or you're going out climbing. I was going out of my mind having to spend all those weekends taking snaps when I wanted to be climbing. After Cloggy the whole Gogarth thing broke so again I had to concentrate on photography again as I realised that major climbing events were happening, and if I didn't get them recorded, it was just going to be gone. Once I'd done all that, I just put the camera away and started enjoying my climbing.

Did the effort you made to get the pictures, reward the effort?
Of course it does, you don't need to ask me that question, you know the answer, what a bloody stupid question. It was definitely rewarding, but very hard work and I missed out on a lot of good climbing days. I was very sad with Black Cliff, in that it wasn't very well printed, it energized me at a very early stage to get better results. In fact I can remember going to Kaye & Ward's office, ranting and raving at them, but they didn't know what I was talking about. That was my first introduction to the some what relaxed world of publishing: In general the publishing world aren't too hot on reproducing pictures. Mind you I have been trying to get it right for 30 years and still haven't solved the puzzle.

That particular application of wanting to see something through really well, has that applied when you've been trying a route?
Yes, obviously. I'm the same as any other climber, particularly when you get into a good run. Usually my partners have been better or more skilled but it quite often happens that I'm in less good shape than my partners and have to take the minor role. But every now and again I climb a little better than them, and it feels really good. It's very difficult to know how the alchemy works, because it may be that if you are climbing better than somebody, you get better whilst he gets worse. Your morale goes up, while his correspondingly goes

down, you have a separating effect on each other. If you're the underdog it's not so good because if you're not careful you get pushed to the bottom, and there it's impossible to develop your own aspirations at your own speed, because you always want to do a route that is best for the team. The reality is, that the team always seeks to maximize it's potential, so if you have two people in a team they will always try to do the hardest route that they can do as a combination, then the whole team has an adventure. Consequently, if you are the less able person in the team, you'll be tending to go on routes that are a bit too hard for you. There are occasions when you get into the deep end, a difficult route and you lead a hard pitch, that you are not expecting to lead, other occasions when you're climbing better than anyone and you have a wonderful day as top dog. But it's pretty shambolic, particularly if your climbing is spasmodic because of deadlines, going to print etc. Take now for example, I have been locked up in this office now for months on end finishing a cave diving book, I went out on the Black Ladders the other day with the wild ambition to finally do Western Gully in winter. I have been to do it about 4 times over the years. Got there at first light and after a couple of pitches, I was an absolute gibbering wreck.

Does it worry you that a lot of climbers today are developing on their own, the concept of a team doesn't exist?
Yes, I think it is very bad. I think that's one of the worst things about sport climbing - they spend days in what appears to be self obsessed meditation where the partner exists merely to hold the rope. One of the big pay-offs of climbing is the shared adventure, getting in, up to your neck with somebody, and having to fight your way out of it; not this summer thing of poncing around on sun-baked crags in the South of France, and somebody holding the ropes. It was the beginning of the eighties, the concept of a rope holder came about. I think one of the most telling incidents that I had, was at Buoux about three years ago. I'd never been to Buoux before and I went with a friend, we did a couple of route on the left hand end. We took all our runners and looked at all these idiots flying around on bolts, doing routes that were far too hard for them, all the stuff down the left hand end doesn't need bolts anyway. God only knows why they are in, because there are cracks all over the place, you could climb it like a normal British crag. To the left of the Pilier de Fourmis in the centre of the crag is a big wall, there was this guy on this it and it looked really exciting, so we stayed and watched. He got to the end of the pitch which he was finding it hard; fell off once but he got to the end all right, and we thought wonderful,

his mate's going to second it and carry on up the route. But he lowered off, that was it! end of story, tedious! Climbing is as much about watching other people do it as doing it yourself. You get as much thrill and inspiration from watching another team having a genuine adventure on a big route; you go off and think great! That's what it's all about, we'll go and do that. When you see some wally going on a crag like that, bailing out when there are three wonderful pitches above it left to do; that's pathetic. I think those guys haven't got a clue, they just don't know what they are doing. They have changed climbing and turned it into a load of gymnastic nonsense, what they should have been doing, is carrying on up the crag and finishing the route and that might have involved a struggle; they might have been forced to use aid, but it wouldn't have mattered, it would have been an adventure.

Weren't they just enjoying themselves?
There's a form of words going around at the moment that I was criticising at the BUXTON CONFERENCE last week, "We put bolts in the route because it enables more people to enjoy it", now I think that is UTTER and COMPLETE HERESY, because they've totally misunderstood what climbing is about. Enjoyment doesn't come from making it all easy; enjoyment comes from keeping it hard, keeping it challenging, so that when you do achieve it, you get the enjoyment out of the sense of achievement, otherwise why bother to lead why not just top rope everything, big deal. But I promise you that you won't enjoy it at least in any profound or lasting way. You'll have a quick fix, a little bit of physical exercise, but you won't remember it tomorrow or the day after that! it will be forgotten. Enjoyment comes from the profound experience of facing up to a challenge and overcoming it. I'm not for a second saying that big jutting bits of limestone can be climbed in any other way, than protecting them with bolts, that's self evident, and that part of climbing satisfies the advance on the physical and technical front. But rather than plaster all the crags with bolts, routes should be top roped if at all possible, just like at Harrison's and Bowles Rocks. Eventually even the hardest routes will be solo'd or natural protection will be devised and we can look to that as a tremendous achievement. It seems to me that if we go on as present, every one of these sport climbing cliffs will get totally plastered with bolts, one every six foot and even closer, then those crags will be effectively ruined and what's worse, the whole adventure seeking instinct and attitude of climbers will be ruined too. It takes years to build up but it will be lost in a generation if we are not careful.

Gill Kent

Climbing is no exception to other sports, it too needs media magazines to communicate the ideas at the forefront of the sport to the armchair aspirants. Of the very early climbing magazines, most were very heavily involved in mountaineering and alpine endeavours. The first real magazine which applied only to climbers was CRAGS, first published in newspaper form, it was a shock to the conservative climbing world. Geoff Birtles took the idea or a real climbing magazine, flavoured with humour; a great big phallic needle of rock glossed the cover, tits on page three and a pull out centre spread of Ron Fawcett. The magazine was inspirational and over the 30 or so issues, it clearly shaped British climbing into a very competitive fore. It's boldness was also apparent and perhaps reflected the climbing style of the day: Tom Proctor was nicknamed 'The Hydraulic Man,' Pete Livesey as 'Michelangelo,' and Ken Wilson as 'Moses.'

Eventually it developed into a more typical financial venture of mainstream journalism. It closed and reopened as High magazine, catering more for walking and mountaineering, than climbing. The gauntlet was laid down, Ian Dunn and Nick Dixon took up the challenge with Rock Action. Although this was a very factual production it failed to amuse and identify with the whole spectrum of climbers. This was taken over by Ed Douglas who turned it upside down, and came up with On The Edge, a true climbing magazine; rock news, photo's and humour. Ed produced some magnificent issues but in the end, threw in the towel of exhausting hard work after 13 issues. Gill Kent took up this challenge and now heads Britain's only magazine which is purely for climbers.

Interview 9.4.91 Greenfield, Oldham.

What did you do after leaving school?
I went to Bangor University and did a pure Maths degree. I went there because of the climbing, back then in 1978 Bangor was the place to go, not Sheffield, it wasn't in vogue.

Had you done climbing before hand?
Yes I came from Buxton originally and there used to be a very active caving scene with the Eldon pot holing club. They were absolutely notorious for wild living basically, and they used to congregate in a hostel at Spring Gardens, Buxton. About 20 people used to live there and it was an awful place, but of course when you were 16-17 this seemed very glamourous, all these chaps with beards etc., and in the caving club, were a lot of very good climbers.

At what standard were you climbing when you went to Bangor?
It was very much the same old story, I had done a season in the Alps when I was 16, then I went to the Verdon at 17, and did a lot of big climbs. I was following about 6a and leading VS, like you do.

Did you have any career in mind by going to Bangor?
I was going to do maths and I always knew even from primary school I was going to be a maths teacher. I got a reasonable honours degree but there was a big gap after leaving university to getting a teaching job. When I left university I went to America for three months with Ron Fawcett, then when we came back and did just enough to survive.

Was it a good climbing partnership?
I think so, it was a very good partnership, not particularly fulfilling for me to lead, but he got up major routes in that time. Nobody else would have put up with the long hours you have to put in as a belayer more than anything

else. You have to stand there in all weather's and say "I'm fine, I'm fine, you carry on;" when you're not really, you're not at all.

Why were you attracted to teaching?
Holidays!

How did you then get involved with editing the magazine ON THE EDGE?
Over the years climbing with Ron I had the perfect opportunity to write the odd article for magazines, which in many ways stemmed from letter writing. We were living in the middle of the Peak District in a old house near Monyash, the back and beyond. I got into writing really long letters to everybody as we rarely saw anyone. This led to writing an article which was published and I never looked back. I then wrote a book on the alternative guide to climbing, ie. pubs and cafes of Britain. That and other articles led me to write for ON THE EDGE, the crux came when Ed Douglas, who was running the magazine, said that he was going to sell out to one of the big magazines, who I imagine would have closed it down. I

asked to take it on and he was thrilled to see that it would have a future, and I got a lot of help from everybody. It wasn't really skill or talent but just opportunity.

Is it something that you've enjoyed doing?
Oh yes, I enjoy it but it's bloody hard work. Incredibly hard work, I couldn't believe how stressful it would be.

Is it hard because climbing is a struggling market or is it because climbers are very difficult people?
No the climbers are the nicest part of it, it's really great the people that write to the magazine. In all the time I've been editor, I've only had one what you might say, disparaging letter over two years from which I got annoyed, because it was a blatant attack instead of constructive criticism which I totally accept. Climbers are great. They are what make the magazine.

What's it like coping with less climbing than you once did?
I think I did too much climbing at one time, not in terms of achievements but in constant going out every day to the same places, doing the same routes and same bouldering. Now when I go out, I enjoy myself and have a wonderful time. I get pissed off that I can't do the routes that I did in the past as I'm a bit larger these days, I'm not so strong as I once was. Now with a family it becomes very much of a compromise.

If you had developed in climbing on your own, do you think you would have got any better?
Yes, and this sounds churlish in retrospect because I went to some fantastic places with Ron. In a lot of ways I would have done far less, but then he was such a dominant personality, even though you wouldn't think that probably when you first meet him. He's a shy retiring personality but very, very strong willed, You don't achieve what he did in terms of technical difficulty unless you were straight down the line about it. But I don't know, I only started to get up decent routes when the relationship was deteriorating and when I was unwilling to say "no I'm not going to hold you're rope, no I don't want to go to that crag, there's nothing there for me, I'd rather go here and do this." I suppose then I started to apply my own climbing more and it led to doing INDECENT EXPOSURE 7b+. The best on-sight I ever did was BEHEMOTH 7a. Climbing INDECENT EXPOSURE for me was very difficult, it was a red point ascent and that wasn't acceptable in 1986; not considered a proper ascent, because it was practiced and top roped, of the ilk that if you spent long enough on a route then you're going to get up it. I myself thought that anyway because I used to follow

Ron on a lot of these routes anyway. When I did it I thought great, but so what, I just worked it into submission. I was dead chuffed because it was the first E6 to be led by an English woman and that was nice and there was gentle rivalry between all the top girls of that time. Being in Ron's shadow was hard of course because whatever he was doing was miles better, fair enough.

Did you feel surprised at the time that women weren't generally climbing that hard?
There weren't that many women climbing in Britain. We had been climbing in Buoux that Easter and seen the French girls doing 7b and 7b+ in the redpoint style, it was then that I knew I could do the same.

Are more women climbing in Britain now?
In the mailing list for the magazine we see a lot of women's names which now amount to about 15%, and when you go to walls and crags you see a lot more women.

Do you think it will increase?
Oh yes, certainly. If bolts get onto the lower grade climbs there will be a lot more women climbers. That's why a lot more women climber in France, instead of having to place nuts, get frightened on HVS and E1's, they can just clip a bolt.

Do you see a magazine such as yours in having a major dominant role in that part of climbing?
Well if we have a dominant role, then it's 'God' help the climbing world.' I don't know how much influence we have as a magazine because I'm so involved in it, that I can't see from an outsiders point of view, I can't remember if I was influenced by what the magazines said. I can remember photos being instrumental in wanting to go and climb in certain areas, but I knew in myself what was right and wrong anyway, I didn't need a magazine to tell me. It is difficult isn't it, it's alright to say this, that and the other, but I don't think people appreciate getting things rammed down their throats, I certainly wouldn't like to be told what to think, or told what to believe. Yes, you can influence and you can do it subtly, but I would always try to give a balance on all matters.

People have commented that now days climbing literature has taken a nose-dive in oblivion, do you agree with that?
No. The past is revered and the present is always decried, particularly in Britain, but I don't think that is right at all. There just isn't a fantastic wealth of brilliant writing. We turn away more articles than we take, there is a lot of rubbish, but when you talk about English literature, perhaps climbers are not as well educated as they used to be, they come from

different social classes now. I think you could probably get away with one well written, heavy-weight article in an issue and with that you are probably doing quite well. We have had some good articles and I believe their under-rated. I remember going to the Mountaineering Literature festival last year and somebody said that there was no good writing any more, 'there's no decent writing in High or Climber and Rambler:' but what about On The Edge. A lot of people don't give the magazine it's due and they don't even know it exists, because it's small circulation and it's not available in W.H. Smiths. It's still got the image of being just for young, sports climbing weirdos, which I think is a bit unfair.

Do you feel conscious that On The Edge is a pure rock climbing magazine and that you are trying to break it away from moun-taineering?
Well, in the last couple of issues we have been trying to break it into mountaineering, be-cause a lot of rock climbers do go moun-taineering and do go alpine climbing. I think the vast majority of rock climbers probably just go rock climbing and that is the end of it, but we need to broaden our base so that we can get more readers; that's the CRUX of the matter. We have mountaineering articles, big wall articles, alpine articles, Himalayan articles and international articles. We have to broaden the base, but still do what we know about. I don't really know much about ice Climbing but I know a man who does, so we use other peoples expertise. We wouldn't ever go into parapenting or skiing, that's diluting it too much.

Can you in your magazine do anything to stop the growth of drugs, or do you feel completely helpless?
I'm pretty innocent about what people take or don't take, it comes back to the role of the magazine – are we there to preach to people? should we? I certainly wouldn't promote it.

The fields surrounding Monyash in the middle of the White Peak, a quiet yet most beautiful countryside where hay is still made into bales.

Ian Dunn, Better known to the climbing world as Squawk. Born 2.4.61 at Hartlepool, started climbing at the age of 13 and has not looked back since. Ian's enthusiasm is immense and early in the eighties when working at Middlesbrough, began the climbing magazine ROCK ACTION. This in typical style of bumbly climbing magazines went under but did lay the foundations for ON THE EDGE magazine. He then landed the job as a Technical Manager, in charge of climbing walls with the British Mountaineering Council. From this he left to join the firm Bendcrete making the most futuristic of the climbing walls in Britain. They always resemble crags in shape and form and seen the obvious way to go. He is now a director of the company having worked his way up and looks quite optimistically to the future of climbing walls.

Interview 14.1.91 Stalybridge, Lancs.

Is being involved with building walls not enough, do you still have to climb?
For sure, yes. I really enjoy training, I really enjoy climbing, for example I won't work weekends unless, a job has been held up for some reason out of our control, and therefore you would let someone down because of it. In the summer I would probably have a mass walk out, the work force is more into climbing than money. The lads who work here really get into building the walls, they get very enthusiastic but still have to climb.

What buzz do you get from climbing?
When you just keep on going, pushing it, and when you get to the belay, everything is going, your legs are trembling, your arms are pumped, you get there and just clip in. It's just brilliant. The real buzz that I get nowadays from climbing, is the same kind of buzz that you get if you solo something hard. The thing is with bold routes is that you've only got to do them once in a while. You're not going to go out every weekend and say 'right then, I'm going to put my life on the line today', then put it on the line tomorrow and the next day after, because sooner or later you're going to fuck up, and if you fuck up, you're going to fuck up big time, you know; you're going to end up as a Jam Sandwich.

Do you like the struggle on a route?
Oh Yes, you go to France at Easter and try a 7a or 7a+, you're climbing crap since you haven't done any routes that year. You get there and really bumble about, you have a massive fight and think bloody hell, I'm really unfit. That's just as bigger a buzz, as you would have had in the summer if you were climbing well. You can get that even with on-sighting, where you're totally pumped like. That's hard to do in Britain because there aren't enough routes to go on. You've either done them too early, when you dogged, worked, and ticked them. Or they're too hard for you to on-sight anyway.

Do you find that redpointing climbs is psychologically pressurizing?
Oh yes, you can come back totally drained sometimes from a weekend. If you are on a route, and you're close to redpointing it, but you're really tussling with it, you've got a block on a move, you keep getting up there, and falling off that same move; it's really hard work. It's really hard to drag yourself back to it and think, right you bastard, I'll get the sodding thing this time, go up there, and get stuck in.

Have any particular routes done that to you?
BIOLOGICAL NEED 7c, at Kilnsey did. It's not that hard actually, it's been flashed by a lot of people, but I just found it really hard. I kept going on it, and having bad days. Where as, on RAIN DOGS, every day I failed on it, I was getting half a move higher, or one move higher. I kept thinking if I don't get any higher I'll give up. Next day I got a bit higher, it was a matter of time before I wore it down. It was great the day I got my fingers through the biner at the top.

Having climbed ZOOLOOK 8a, and RAIN DOGS 8a, does something like the INDIAN FACE E9, appeal to you?
Yes. It's always appealed to me. Throughout my climbing I've been to loads of different areas and when I started climbing I went to Cloggy quite a few times. Obviously that line has stood out to everybody, it's a big blank wall crying out to be climbed, but nowadays I wouldn't even go and work it and then lead it. I wouldn't have a hope of leading it on-sight anyway, I'm just not interested in dying. I don't solo hard routes now, I have done some in the past, but there's too much to lose, I enjoy life.

Why has sport climbing taken since 1980 to evolve in this country?
Basically because people in Britain were scared to put bolts in for a start. Also that all the top people climbing in Britain then, were into doing boldish routes as well as protected

routes. So you had things like STRAWBERRIES 7c, which was your well protected route and hard, and stuff like THE BELLS E7, and THE CAD E5. You had a lot of people doing those sort of climbs, but on the hard nut protected routes people were climbing French style because they were so hard, dogging and yo yo'ing. When Basher and Gore came back from France they said "Stuff all this let's get into proper redpointing." Then it spread to places like the Lakes where people started redpointing nut protected routes at Reecastle. Then Malham took off because people like Ghersen, Jean Baptiste and Antoine le Menestrel came over. Antoine soloed REVELATIONS 8a+ and everyone said, let's get out and bolt up routes so we could compete with the standards on the continent. It was obvious that without those routes here, we wouldn't even be in the same game. Malham was like French crags in shape and style, that was it, end of story. It got bolted up, no fuckin around, belay chains, dogging bolts, it's great. What was surprising though was Isabelle Patissier, she did ACID TEST E5-6,6c at Pen Trwyn, but couldn't even top rope DOWNHILL RACER E4 6a, the classic gritstone route at Froggatt. She spent a whole afternoon trying and got no where, it's a totally different up bringing of climbing, which is quite an interesting comparison Something that certainly wasn't picked up in the magazines. The French magazines said of course that Isabelle roasted everyone in Britain, and was, ever so wonderful, as the French magazines are inclined to do.

Do you think the invention of the Friend stopped bolts in Britain?

Yes, quite significantly – RP's and Friends. I went to Yosemite, California in 1981 and RP's had only just come out. RP's, rocks and Friends were really significant in stopping bolts happening here. If they hadn't been invented, then sports climbing would have taken off massively in the early eighties. It stopped sport climbing for 10 years, but it just meant that all the crack climbs or all the routes that you could possibly protect were done. It's like all these weird and wonderful things that equipment manufacturers keep trying to insist that you buy every year, like gems and God knows what, rock and rollers. The things cost you 30 quid each and if you are going to buy a full rack of them it's £300, then try to carry all this stuff up to the crag, you'd need a rucksac the size of a Himalayan haul bag, no way man. Climbers can't be arsed to buy loads and loads of tackle for one particular climb. Some people buy that sort of gear, yes! Gear manufacturers might want to hope that everybody will buy them, but at the end of the day, people are just going to go and bolt routes rather than try and fiddle around with all sorts of weirdo things.

Does it worry you, the split between sports climbers and Alpine climbers?

There's always been a split between Mountaineers and Climbers. I remember a Ron Fawcett quote, something like "I've got no desire to be a snow plodder like Bonington and Scott, give me Rock man, Rock," and I thought that was a bloody sound comment. That was Ron Fawcett in the late '70,s and obviously he was into adventure as well as protected climbing.

What climbers use your Bendcrete Walls?

Well, Simon Nadin's the total Master of Bendcrete. He trains a lot at Keele, Preston, and Glossop. He's well into Bendcrete, he really likes the surface. Joe Healey really enjoys it, both are outstandingly good technicians. You also get a lot of other people like Tony Mitchell, Nick Conway; Leach goes along and powers his way up a few problems without using his feet, but Nadin is probably the Master. Simon won at Berkley 1990 in the USA, on the Jean Marc Blanche wall which had good friction, and that's the thing we have been very careful about producing on our walls.

Do you see a lot of women climbing on Walls?

You do see a lot more women climbing on walls, I was at Newcastle last weekend and there were stacks of women on the wall, absolutely stacks more than you'd ever see on

Ian Dunn testing some of the single bolt on holds that his firm makes. These are made of purpose designed resin cement mixes and developed for steep plywood boards in excess of 40° overhanging.

The social side of climbing a few yards down the road from Kilnsey Crag in the Yorkshire Dales. Chris Plant, the driver opposite the heavy drinkers going for it, Mark solidarity Pretty and Sean Kit Kat Myles.

the crags in Northumberland or wherever. You just look at any of the climbing walls in Britain, if you took the percentage of people using walls, roughly 65% men and 35% women, you go to the crag and it would be 90-10. It's obvious that there is something significant about climbing walls which is attractive to women. Is it because they are nice, warm and cosy. You can go down there, put a decent pair of tights on, get changed, have a shower afterwards, spizz your hair up, go to the bar and order your orange juice in comfort. I'm sure that attracts lots of women to the climbing wall. I mean you see just as many blokes going down and spizzing their hair, I'm not trying to be sexist at all.

Could you ever give up climbing?
No. It's such a part of my life now, right from the word go. If I had a really bad accident and couldn't climb anymore, then I would still be interested, I'd take photos or just have something to do with it. It's a way of life. I think it's the same with a lot of people, it's funny how

many people who give up climbing or disappear, then you see them back at the wall or the crag every year. You see people and the classic quote is 'I haven't been climbing for a while, but I'm BACK AGAIN.' Joe Healey is the classic example, he's always coming back. I think it's very hard to give up climbing. You occasionally get someone like Pete Crew, who just suddenly drops out of it, but they are very few and far between. There are lots of the Boysen's, Rab Carrington's, people like your Joe Brown's and that. It's just such a way of life. They may not go out so much, but they'll still go out and have a good time, still go up pub, and take piss out't people, that's one great thing about climbing, anyone who sets themselves up on a pedestal like, is there to be really knocked, right off it!

Is the social side of climbing important?
Yes, I think the pubs are perhaps the most important part. There aren't many climbers who haven't got pissed once in a while, I don't think climbers are different to anybody else.

Obviously top climbers who are training hard, don't go out and get pissed every night, you can't do that nowadays. It's no good turning up on a 8b with your guts churning, your head spinning, then as soon as you put your arms above your head, all the power drains to your feet, you haven't got a hope. In the 60's it wasn't the case since you were climbing E1 maximum, lets face it, you can climb E3 blind drunk anyway. Whereas, today on an 8b you haven't a hope of getting up them. It is significant though that a lot of British climbers still like to go to the pub, even if they're not drinking, just for the social scene. That's another great thing with climbing walls, it's a great place to meet people and have a good chat. Even if it's dead busy you still go down there and take the piss out of people, and half of British climbing is about having a good time and taking the piss. It's something which a lot of people don't seem to realise, it's part and parcel of the sport.

Tim Freeman

Born just outside Shrewsbury, Shropshire. Tim started climbing on the Southern Sandstone and enjoyed Bulls Hollow the most. He developed fast, then ended up at Bradford University studying Maths. Then he became absorbed into the Sheffield scene and climbed with Jerry Moffatt at the beginning of the eighties. Tim's natural strength has always been phenomenal, at 16 he could do a one arm pull up on either arm. A real lightweight and a very good boulderer. He had an incredible amount of talent and strength, on his second try of REVELATIONS in 1984 he cruised past the crux. Without doubt, had he carried on climbing, routes like AGINCOURT 8c, and HUBBLE 8c+ would have been within his capability. He now works full time as Financial Director for The Tube, as it is known to most climbers. A firm which specializes in vertical access to buildings and bridges. It also does industrial drilling on the sides of cliffs and can just about perform any task in a vertical surrounding.

Interview 6.1.91 Hunters Bar, Sheffield.

How did you get into work after being involved in the Hunter House, Sheffield dole scene.

Well, I was really into bouldering in the peak, that lasted about 3 years before I got bored with it. Instead of going out climbing every day I'd be sitting in the house not doing much, occasionally going down to the gym with Jerry. I used to go down there do a couple of one arm pull ups, smoke ciggys or play with Quentin doing double dynos, it was more fun. I didn't so much give up climbing, I just sort of drifted out, particularly when I started working for Can UK in '85. I was working on the ropes, abseiling down tower blocks all day. I worked all over the country, so I never had a steady base, and when I did have spare time, climbing was the last thing I wanted to do really.

How long did that last?

I was with CAN UK. for 3 and a half years then became disillusioned with the set-up, unhappy

with various management decisions etc. I heard Technitube were starting up, so I joined them. It was a small affair in those days, literally only a couple of people working. I was doing most of the jobs for them and as it grew, I changed my positions.

When did you become financial director?

It was just under a year ago (1990), when I acquired that official title. I'm quicker with figures than anybody else in the office so I ended up in charge of the finances.

Are you directly involved with employing climbers?

Yes. I end up with a lot of my friends working for me. I don't think it's particularly good position to be in as half of my mates are always working down in London. It is good however to see everyone working and getting a good deal from it, which is I guess, something directly under my control.

How much can a good climber earn with you a week?

I'd put it at about £600-£700 on a good week.

How does this situation compare to 10 years ago?

I think that it's a good thing. I wish that 10 years ago I had had the opportunity to earn a bit of part time money. Then the only way, was to go on the dole and improvise an income from the DHSS. I think it's a very good thing for a lot of the climbers around. However a lot of climbers are getting hooked on working instead of climbing, because the pay for the jobs they do is pretty good.

Do climbers ever miss work because it's a nice day and they'd prefer to go climbing?

The majority are good workers and generally turn up. I think if people say they are going on a job, they will go. For us long term, we are looking for people who are more committed to working than to climbing. It can be a bit of a drawback if you are planning work and some climber wants to go off for 3 months to the States, it can shock your plans to a certain extent.

Are climbers essential for the work that you do?

They are certainly an asset for a lot of the work, like aiding around in the roof girders of a shopping centre, cleaning windows. Then the climbers fitness does come in very handy. Some of our workers aren't climbers but are maybe much more experienced at working, it's a combination work force.

Do the climbers that work for you appear obsessed about climbing?

Not as obsessed as they were probably a year ago when they weren't working for me.

Is that because of the money?

Largely so, I think a lot of the people working for us now have had a taste for earning money and maybe are becoming more financially motivated.

Is there any room for girl climbers within your work.

Yes, certainly. I've had girls working for me before and will continue to do so. The girls we've employed have been excellent.

A lot of the climbers are your friends, do you find yourself being drawn back into climbing because you employ them?

Well, I haven't done up until a few days ago. I've been training on the finger board which is the first time for, God knows how many years. But I wouldn't say, that was a reason for me doing so at all.

Do you feel that British climbing is developing in a good way at the moment, away from naturally protected routes to bolt protection?

I think that was an inevitable step in British climbing, so I've got nothing against that because, it's the only way to push the grades forwards. We've had various battery drills and resin bolts in the office, people have asked me for them and I'm quite prepared to let them borrow what they want. The only thing that disturbs me really about bolt routes is that it is attracting too many people out onto the crags for perhaps the wrong reasons. I remember a year or so, going out to a crag in Wales, where there were just hundreds of people hanging around on about 3 bolt routes and just getting nowhere. They were on routes miles above their standards. Okay they are trying hard, but there seems something wrong to me. I think they would get much more enjoyment out of going and trying some E4 and putting runners in. I know I would. I don't particularly know what is going on in the British scene at the moment in terms of top routes or anything.

Can climbing really link itself with climbing in a job?

Yes, I think it can, there's certainly is a place for it. A lot of the climbers we've had working for us this summer do it, take Mark Leach for example. I think they can find a good balance of working, earning some money, and having planned months off to go climbing on the various trips. The sort of work they do as well keeps them reasonably in trim for climbing.

Is it nice for the employer to be able to offer this?

It is. We will use it as almost a selling point occasionally.

Do you see that as the future?

The access business is changing all the time. I think roped access, my line of business, is going to be a boom industry - it's going to get a lot bigger.

Do problems of safety worry you?

Yes it is one of my personal fears that there will be an accident. We've been going for 3 years now, totally accident free. We haven't had a accident but the level of training amongst everyone in the industry has got to be increased, even in Technitube because one accident could create a very bad atmosphere for the industry.

Do the other workers resent the fact that the climbers can come and go on a freelance basis?

No, they don't I feel. Work for subcontractors is always up and down, swings and roundabouts as we call it. The climbers get no special perks. Generally speaking we employ cavers and climbers, The cavers are probably in a lot of ways, better than the climbers to be honest. The climbers are a lot better swinging around in steelwork, but the cavers have generally got a much better attitude towards safety. If you think about it, climbers they only know how to tie a couple of knots on the end of a rope, the rigging for various pitches is very basic. Caving rigging is much more complicated, they have a much sounder knowledge about jamming up and down ropes and everything.

Do you find climbers the same mentality as cavers?

No I think they are a different breed totally. Cavers have definitely got a good few more screws loose.

Dinas Cromlech in the Llanberis Pass of Snowdonia National Park, the great fortress of rock, stands like an open book citing verse 'thou shalt go forth and climb.'

The legends

What makes a climbing legend, is it skill, talent, or just being in the right place at the right time? It is perhaps the combination of all three. There are many great climbers, those who have pioneered great new climbs, always climbing at the forefront of the sport. Yet legends, there are far fewer. They do not always shock the world, they don't have to climb the hardest routes, but they do have to reveal a special character, way above that of the ordinary climber. They are made by their compatriots, treasured as figure heads within climbing conversation. There are of course many climbers who are both great climbers and legends alike, yet it sometimes only takes the luck of being born at the right time to be a great climber. To be a legend it takes far more; character, drive, friendship and thought. The five I've chosen span from the 60's to the 90's; from characters to performers, all very different from the rest of us.

Martin Boysen

Some climbers are exceptionally famous, others are exceptionally good, Martin perhaps is best described as somewhere between the two. Certainly around the sandstone outcrops of Tunbridge Wells he is legendary for his pioneering efforts in the '60's. Many climbs boast his name, BOYSEN'S ARETE 6a, at Harrison's Rocks, BOYSEN'S CRACK at High Rocks, yet never thought of as pompous gestures, but a tribute to someone a lot more talented than most on his home ground. Indeed in the '60's Martin started to climb all over Britain and leaving a wake of important routes, few were desperate yet many were great classics such as GOGARTH, and the majestic PINNACLE ARETE E1 an Cloggy. From here a legend unfolds to the Alps: South face of the Fou, Dru and the Grandes Jorasses, and to the Himalayas. Expeditions with Chris Bonington on Annapurna, Changabang, Everest SW Face, Trango Tower and the American filmed ascent of Ama Dablam.

Interview 22.1.91 Hale, Cheshire.

What got you first into climbing?
The family was always interested in walking and outdoor holidays, and it crystallized really when I went on a walking holiday to Scotland when I was 15. I was walking all over the Cairngorms by myself and had bugger all money, I spent a fortnight living on ten bob, had a desperate scrap, hitching back home and was living off the dregs and scrapings of a youth hostel cupboard – scavenging basically. I remember in the youth hostel there was a magazine with a picture of someone climbing PORTCULLIS, a climb at Eridge Green, and I thought, that's really close to me. It had never occurred to me that actual rock climbing, was going on in the Weald of East Sussex. I went out to High Rocks and met a couple of climbers and watched them, eventually they must have realised this little waif was wanting to have a go, so they tied me on and I scampered up this route. It was quite an easy route but when I did that first route, I thought 'God this is wonderful'. I knew immediately I'd found the sport which was going to give me more fulfilment and excitement than anything else.

You started with a rope but then found delight from soloing?
Yes, I've always been an enthusiastic soloer, basically the rocks are not very high, the landings are mostly good, and all this nonsense about bad rock is largely an excuse for top roping. One of the main reasons for the rock's suspect reputation is that you get these pig ignorant people, yanking on holds with the

benefit of a top rope, which they would never dare treat so badly if they were soloing. I feel quite strongly about this, the overuse of top roping on sandstone.

When you were climbing on sandstone, did you climb with purist ethics?
When ever possible yes, I had tight ropes at first, particularly when I couldn't manage to do something, I wasn't any great pioneer as far as slack ropes were concerned, but we never considered we'd done a route until we had done it on a slack rope. We used to make fun of people who pretended that they had actually done something on a G sharp rope. There were quite a few characters around who would never climb on anything but the twanging top rope.

Did that automatically lead to climbing in the mountains?
The convention of climbing in those times was, you always looked to bigger things all the time, and mapped out as a progression. First of all you went to Wales and did the big routes, then you went to The Alps, and then maybe you would go to the Himalayas. Books like Nanga Parbat Pilgramage, were the climbing bibles of the young people at that time.
Did The Alps impress you when you first saw them?
Yes immensely, they were very, very big, and you had so little knowledge of them. Certainly the most dangerous climbing I've ever done was my early seasons in The Alps, the number of times I think I could have died, it horrifies me now.

Did that not ever make you give up?
No. I've never wanted to give up, and danger is the least of my worries. Danger is definitely one of the things which gives climbing, it's extra spice. It's one of these very tricky sort of things which you want just enough; it's like a curry, you want it hot, but not too hot and getting it just right is a delicate art. Get things badly wrong and the penalties are awful. The danger of it was certainly one of the things I really enjoyed about climbing. Pitting yourself against the danger and overcoming it was very exciting.

Talking of hot curries, is that what took you to the Himalayas?
The Himalayas were the ultimate mountains, Nepal and India had all sorts of romantic associations, the remoteness and the sheer exoticness of the place, it seemed like an amazing privilege to go to the Himalayas. On my first expedition I really did feel tremendously privileged. Travelling to the Himalayas at that time was not something which you could do as easily as you do now. It was too expensive and there was great difficulty with permission, so you tended to have to go as part of an organised trip. I was very fortunate that I went with Chris Bonington and his team, it was an immense privilege and tremendously exciting.

Do you think it needs to be an important part in every climbers life?
I have certainly enjoyed a tremendous variety of climbing experiences and some of the best and worst experiences have been whilst climbing in the great ranges. As I have got older I have started on reverse progression, these days I get as much pleasure and excitement as I need from tiny scraps of rock. Going to the Himalayas is definitely an extremely hazardous form of climbing which for one reason or another I've stopped doing now. I think if you can get the chance to go on a Himalayan expedition, there's no question about it, you should go.

Would you say you quit while you were ahead?
Yes, I suppose so, but it's more than that. I've had quite a few expeditions and I would certainly love to go out again and potter up a few easy mountains. But for the big ones, it's something you have to do whilst you are young, very, very keen and committed, because you have to expend an awful lot of energy, time, money. It's a very selfish activity Himalayan climbing, because if you are living, married with kids, you are putting your near ones through a lot of pressures and pain, basically I'm not prepared to do that anymore.

You left school and went to Manchester University. No thoughts of being a climbing instructor?
No. I didn't think about it at all. Climbing instructors were funny people in woolly socks and tartan shirts when I was young, they all had beards. I went to university because it gave me plenty of time and avoided having to work for a few years. I wasn't thinking about a career.

Is travelling an important part for you in climbing?
Yes, the travelling is always undoubtedly the best bit of the expeditions, I think most people would agree. Many of the best memories are of the walk in with it's changing views, peoples and the ever present sense of anticipation. Once you get to the mountain, the the horrors begin, humping bloody great loads up and down; the amount of pleasure to humping loads is pretty low, the proportion of pleasure is fairly low. The highs are tremendously high, the few moments of exhilaration on the trip make up for a lot of the agonies and the messing about.

Did it surprise you that a lot of the sports climbers aren't interested in being michelin men in oxygen masks?
No, no one wants to do that. There's endless scope for enjoyable rock and ice climbs in great mountain ranges. If you want to have a fantastic rock climbing adventure in a foreign place with all the fun of travelling it's all there to be done – I'm sure it will be.

Is being good at climbing important to you?
Yes. I remember when I first started climbing, I realised straight away that it was a talent I had, and that gave me tremendous satisfaction and self confidence to know that I was good at something. I enjoyed being good, I enjoy it now being moderately good and I hope to carry on doing so even when I am quite hopeless!

Is climbing always a serious thing?
No it's not serious all the time, in fact I think that is one aspect of climbing which I think has deteriorated markedly over the last few years. It's taken far too seriously by many climbers, especially the young climbers you see, who really are very, very serious about it, there's not much laughter and fun or piss taking the way there used to be. Maybe I'm just getting old, but when Rab and I go out to a crag in Derbyshire we always seem to have a bit of a laugh, it's noticeable that a lot of people don't seem to be enjoying themselves that much.

Are you embarrassed not taking it seriously?
No, it'a a pretty silly thing really, it's a ludicrous activity a lot of the time, you've only got to stand back from it and just imagine what climbers look like really, to see the silly side of it. Laughter and good companionship are as

important and vital a part of climbing as getting 'gripped' and overcoming difficulty.

Are doing first ascents necessary for your enjoyment?

No but I have always enjoyed doing first ascents. It's a different sort of enjoyment you get, it's a very creative enjoyment but I've never been prepared to put that much time into them. I prefer to do things quickly and move onto something else. First ascents tend to bog you down a bit and you get struck into something for some time cleaning it etc, etc,. So I've tended to pick off the odd first ascent here and there if it's come fairly easily, I've done quite a few first ascents in Scotland for instance. Some obscure crags in Scotland with first ascents on sandstone, have given me a lot of fun, but I've never really been methodical about going for first ascents.

Were figures like Bonatti figures of greatness?

Yes, when I was young there were the various figures which I hero worshipped, Bonatti was obviously one of them, Herman Bhul was another one, Joe Brown and Don Whillans of course.

Did you ever feel that they were in a different league, and if you attempted those climbs you'd be putting yourself at unnecessary risk?

In the Alps certainly, because at first I felt like a novice. Most of the time I was climbing in the Alps I kept thinking 'do I know exactly what I'm doing here?' During these early seasons we were doing what were then regarded as quite hard routes, and you didn't have as much experience of alpine climbing as the continentals.

Was it a lack of self confidence?

To some extent yes. We had poor route descriptions – often mangled translations. Then of course we had often read about the routes in the colourful words of Bhul and Rebuffat. If they had struggled, endured epics with storms, stonefall and losing their way, how could we fare better? When we actually got to grips with the climb we were often pleasantly surprised, the climbing was often much easier than we had dared to hope for, the horror was all in the imagination.

Would you say Bonatti was a better writer than climber?

No, Bonatti was obviously an extremely tough climber, there is no doubt about it, all those early great climbers, they undoubtably were fantastically good climbers. I think it's very easy to belittle the achievements of people before. I hear it all the time because I've been around a long time and people just don't appreciate how climbing has changed, and how the psychology of climbing has change. For instance in the Alps nowadays you are rescued from any bit of any climb almost, and that has a tremendous psychological difference from the old days, when you knew that if you got stuck on a big face, there was nobody to get you down except yourself, and that was it.

Are there any big challenges for climbing that you feel you've shy'd away from?

I suppose in a way I've been too sensible, caution has held me back when success was perhaps a daring possibility. There are times when I think – if only I had held out a little longer, risked a bit more. But then I am alive, and many of my friends and contemporaries are dead. If the price of greatness is death or a brief blaze of glory I am happy to have avoided it and carry on quietly enjoying myself.

The guide translation said you could go up and down in a day, and that the temperatures would be extreme, with 'glacé' - ice creams at the top.

Tom Proctor

As a climber, if Stoney Middelton is not in your memory then you have missed out a very important part of your climbing career. Some love it, yet many hate it; slippery, polished and alarmingly steep limestone. In the 1960's it was one of the aid climbers domains, yet in the '70's it became the centre of British climbing activity. More remarkable was that new routes were being pioneered, single handedly by the now legendary Thomas Proctor, a joiner from Chesterfield. The routes Tom pioneered were hard and brutish, giving need for a strong pair of arms, and a steady head. The routes still stand out as test pieces in any modern climbers career: WINDHOVER E2, WEE DORIS E3, OUR FATHER E4, and CIRCE E5, are the real all time classics. They are often attempted by most young climbers, too early, too weak, too poor in technique; they fail, but not until the struggle has become intense and their forearms almost burst with agony. The routes do not reflect Toms gentle and quiet manner, but do however represent his quest in climbing, a challenge both physical and mental.

Interview 18.1.91 Holymoorside, Chesterfield.

When were you born Tom?
1st of September 1947, here in Chesterfield, just up the road in fact.

What made you first go climbing?
To start with then between 10 and 12, I collected birds eggs (don't tell anybody but.....), I used to climb the big trees and was the climber for around here. If someone couldn't get up to an egg they would come and fetch me, they'd come from miles on their bikes. From there I went out to Stoney Middleton and went caving two or three times at weekends, I met climbers there and went up a little crack which the climbers were attempting. I had muddy wellies on and just shot up it, it was fun.

Did outdoor adventures appeal?
I liked the outdoors, but I never went walking, climbing etc., before leaving school. Then at 15 I started climbing because I had nothing to do on Saturday and Sunday.

When you were 15 you then started going to Birchens on your bike, was there any difference then between limestone and gritstone?
Yes. Limestone was loose, white, tottering, slimey, grassy, something that you didn't climb on a lot. I'd seen it a few years before out caving at Stoney, and I didn't really believe what I'd read about it. I thought there could be some good climbs there, I knew it was dirty and greasy, especially in EB's on a wet day so for quite a while I stuck to the gritstone and Birchens. I climbed solo for the first year because I had no one to climb with, I didn't know anybody. I treated it like a job, I'd go out at 8 O'clock in the morning and take my sandwiches, climb to about 12, eat my lunch and then climb to about 4 O'clock and then go home. I did about 4,000 foot of solo in a day and that was every week. I went about 38-39 weeks on the trot around Birchens, finding new bits to do and treating it as a bit like a workout. I found Gardoms a little bit frightening, if I fell off there nobody was going to find me because it was a bit deserted. I'd go up and down, up and down, traversing and generally enjoying it. I was getting better and also growing then. When I first started I really had difficulty reaching some of the holds, then just a few years later I could reach them so easily, I must have grown a good six inches from when I started at 15. It also helped my standard to go up. Being 6 ft and just over 12 stone seemed to suit me very well.

Did you have a guidebook to the area?
No. I Knew it was called Birchens and that was it. Eventually I learnt all the names and I did some of my own climbs that were new, I never recorded them and other people claimed them.

If someone had given you a guidebook do you think you would have used it?
Yes, but I'd not got anything but a rope. The first bit of gear I'd got was someone had left a

sling with two krabs on it, so I thought I'd keep that, I could use it. I abseiled off Nelson's monument at Birchens after standing one footed on top of it!

When did you start progressing to harder things?

As soon as I got somebody to climb with. Barry Dixon, he'd been on limestone and he'd been along to Froggatt which was miles away to me; so I just went along with him. His dad used to take us out in the morning, sometimes to Stanage, Cheedale or Water Cum Jolly.

What was Curbar like the first time you saw it?

Frightening! Bleak! It was steep! There weren't any of today's desperate routes but: PEAPOD, LEFT and RIGHT ELIMINATE, INSANITY still looked intimidating. What are they now E1's? HVS? INSANITY is given E3 now, even with friend protection? I think it's given E3 because you're meant to put 7 friends in, so you have to be that strong and INSANE, to hang around long enough to get them all in! You have to be rich as well!

When you first looked at Curbar, did you think there were routes up there or...?

I knew they were there, but I knew I didn't dare do them. I think I looked back later, came back and did little snippets, messed about on things and abseiled down a lot of lines to see if I could do them, that was early on as well '65/66, it's a long time ago!

Were you surprised that they hadn't been done by anyone?

In a way I was a bit disgusted that they had not been done, because they didn't look hard enough to be impossible. You'd think if someone got their finger out, they would do them. I knew they frightened me, I suppose they frighten everybody, but I just assumed the big climbing types could do anything; but they weren't doing these things. You never saw anyone doing RIGHT ELIMINATE, I've seen it done about 2 or 3 times, and I thought it must be very, very hard; and if that's hard the wall must be even harder because there was no protection. I think that was probably the reason why I didn't do it, because there was no protection – I didn't trust a top rope, I never have trusted a top rope. I don't like to second at all, I find it horrendous if I look down and there is no rope....gulp!

At that time did you spend all your time climbing at weekends?

In the summer yes, and evenings because it was just over the hill, if it was a nice night I'd nip over and do an hour and come back.

What did you do in the winter?

Artificial climbing for a while, then that went out of fashion. I realised that it was wrong, but we seemed to base those expeditions around Stoney Cafe, then went up to Stoney Cliffs and realised that there were artificial climbs there, that could go free and that was three years after I'd started climbing. The first route I freed was JASPER E3, I didn't do the first ascent but I did the first hard version of route. It had three pegs in and I used two, which to me seemed reasonable, better than the peg route all the way with 15 or 20 pegs, and at the time it was a step forward. I met Jack Street, and Geoff Birtles. Nobody would climb with Geoff, I was the only person who would climb with him, we were like chalk and cheese, but his abrasive manner didn't bother me and we're still friends. He pointed me to where there were routes and encouraged me to try everything.

Do you regret not having a regular partner?

No. I didn't want one because you got into a routine that I didn't like. I sometimes got into a routine with people for perhaps 6 months. I also had this break so I'd never go, like year after year after year, endlessly climbing.

What would you do in that break?

I'd still be out on the rock but I'd just be soloing around VS's cleaning routes. I'd spend a whole summer cleaning routes.

Do you feel that was important to sustain your enthusiasm?

Yes, I got very fed up with climbing. If Stoney was bigger I'd have climbed a lot more but it wasn't. I spent weeks down Cheedale, cleaning steep walls on High Tor, cleaning CASTELLAN, TWILIGHT, things like that. I'd reverse peg to get in, and clean them with a view to having a purge next season. I missed out on a lot of routes that way because people saw me clean them.

Could you ever envisage that today, High Tor is now just dismissed by the top boys as being a slabby easy cliff for beginners, did you ever see standards getting that high?

I knew they would, but I didn't know when. What I could see was what people could do on a ten foot boulder, and I thought right, just extend this you could free climb Malham which you can now. I couldn't see myself doing it, but I knew it would come.

Do you regret that you missed out on free climbing Malham?

Yes. If I knew then what I know now, and came along when Joe Brown was about, it would have been great, there would have been thousands of routes to do, nothing so desper-

ate that you felt absolutely pushed. I enjoyed the climbing that didn't wreck my fingers, but gradually it got harder and harder. Before, it was comparatively juggy, swinging around on your arms in good situations, it was enjoyable.

Did you ever have any conflict wanting to give up your job to climb?

Not really. I had to keep working to pay my way. I couldn't envisage myself becoming a professional dole climber. I wanted more out of life than just the climbing, it doesn't pay the bills does it?

Did alpine climbing have ever have any interest?

I was interested, but only in what other people were doing. I saw lads coming back year after year from Chamonix. Just down for about 3 weeks or a month and they'd not done anything, and I thought that it's just not worth going. Year after year it was just the same, but the thought of being out there was just great. We went to the Dolomites, got terrible weather, then came back and went to Cornwall.

When you heard MASTERS EDGE 7c+, had been done, did that impress you?

No, I'd sussed it out, it was one of those that I shelved.

What made you leave it?

I wasn't good enough. I couldn't reach quite far enough, and I didn't know who could belay me quick enough if I fell off high above the runner. I would want someone who could whip my rope in quick, someone big and heavy, even have two people so that if I came off, they would just have to run.

Do you think you will ever climb again?

I did a few E4's this summer in the Horseshoe Quarry, above Stoney. I just go out if there is someone to go with, but I'm interested in following what happens.

Would you be disgusted if people started bolting up your old routes?

Yes. It would take the element of danger away which you need in adventure. If you knew you had to go 15-20 foot before self placed runners, you know you have to work to the point, before you're safe. It's not like going up to a bolt, you have to get there and be able to hold on long enough to fit the nut. I'm for easy protection, I can't see the point in spending half and hour wiggling a little nut into a corner, it becomes a bit petty then. You might as well be putting the effort into getting up the route in a case like that. I don't like these fluorescent tapes that hang down, but something that you can't see doesn't bother me at

The river Wye flowing past Chee Tor in the heart of limestone climbing country in the Peak District.

all. I've never had the choice of whether I'd clip into a string of bolts as they were never there. I've put bolts in myself, occasional ones, but not many.

Do you think the routes that you created, natural gear was the right thing, and remains the right thing?

Yes. Looking back they're not hard routes now. A modern climber should be able to climb them easily. It's like looking back at some of Brown and Whillans routes, they were desperate in their day, but they're pleasant HVS's now. You wouldn't expect to protect them any more than they did. They have better protection now, but you can't help but protect them better can you.

Have you any particular fond memories of climbing elsewhere?

A few routes in Norway and Yosemite, I enjoyed that. I did THE NOSE, The North West face of HALF DOME, I did 45 routes in the valley, I thought that was just lovely.

After doing El Cap, could you then find interest in Stoney?

It's just scaled down. It's different, it is totally different. I really enjoy granite climbing but didn't see much of it, I think it's quick climbing, you get on it and can cover 1000 feet, I like that. It doesn't all have to be desperate, as long as there are hard bits here and there, just to remind you. I'm not keen on rounded gritstone, if I didn't like any rock it would be rounded grit and sandstone, I hate it. I went down to Harrison's; that's the limit for me, it was just terrible, you can never clean it off, you can brush it till the cows come home but there will still be ball bearings on it. Another thing,

to start with I didn't really like the thought of chalk, not what it did to the difficulty but the mess it left, I just hated it. I used it but I didn't splash it all over the place, I wish someone would invent either green or brown or grey so that it wouldn't leave this horrible white mess. I stopped climbing not long after chalk came in. If we had chalk a few years earlier who knows what I might have done, harder routes and then progressed on to even harder things.

Do you think it's a pity that today climbers really aren't given a chance to use their own brains, literally all the gear is so perfect.....

It's like climbing by numbers isn't it, yes it is a shame. Well they haven't got the scope for new routes that we had. I thought we were pretty hard done to, the generation before us squandered it although they didn't realise, they climbed for different reasons I suppose. Now all the rock has been climbed what can they do? I feel almost sorry, they just haven't got the rock. The routes have got to get harder so they have to do something. Perhaps in the future it will all be bare foot solo on-sight, no guide and take pot luck as to what you are going up, blind fold! Or even a handicapped system like they do with horses and jockeys who are weighted down. There has to be the challenge, you have to be on the border or possibility. If it's predictable you know you can do it, it kills it. It's like having a fight with someone and you know you can flatten them, it's not a challenge is it? You have to be pushed or else you don't now progress do you.

Do you have anything against people who just like going out climbing bolt to bolt?
No, great. It's a bit like being a jogger, they're on the same routes week in week out, it's like a form of exercise and you try and cut down your time.

Did you just progress steadily in climbing harder and harder?
I became almost fanatical about getting rid of aid on routes, I just didn't like to see anything on a crag. That's why I tried to clear the whole of Stoney Middleton of pegs.

What form of protection was there at that time?
Home made wedges on wire, that's a sore point with me, because when I was actually climbing in the early days, I made a Moac or exactly the same, only wire sling, they hadn't even got them out on rope. Then and about two years later they started making moac's, I thought there's nobody else using these and I didn't bother. I drilled out nuts.

Did it work, did you ever fall off?
Now and again, well perhaps once a year. I remember flying but never hitting the floor.

You were satisfied that all your home made equipment worked?
I was satisfied that I wasn't going to hit the floor, if I had a good nut more than half way up the route, in theory I could go to the top, and if every thing else stripped there would be a good stopper. I've only seen about two people fall to the floor, and I don't think that was because runners came out, probably hadn't got any in! I was frightened of falling, but I didn't see much of it.

Do you know where you got this fanaticism for cleaning the aid routes?
It just seemed wrong banging pegs in. Pegging was too easy I think, that was the top and bottom of it; and there were all these holes to put fingers in, why put a peg in it, I thought

with a bit more effort......It was a progression, it wasn't like doing hard routes straight off, just sort of HVS which had pegs in them, I just whittled those away. Eventually they just got harder and harder, but they got harder because I realised that routes would go, things that looked impossible you realised were possible. You probably couldn't do them, but then two years later you'd have another look and think, if I don't try it I'll not get up it, so you have a go and eventually these things get done!

Were there any particular routes that were way ahead of their time?
WEE DORIS was harder than most, OUR FATHER was a scary one but not hard, it was impressive. WEE DORIS I found hard because there was no resting place. LUCY SIMMONS stuck in my mind, I top-roped that before I did it quite by chance.

The route names at the time were very inspiring, have you wanted to name routes or have you not felt they were important?
They needed a name but if it went free the name still remained the same. Other people seemed to enjoy naming them. You'd sit in the cafe, and say shall we call it this, that or the other and we'd agree what it was going to be called. LUCY SIMMONS, Geoff named it, and OUR FATHER; WEE DORIS – Bruce Andrew named that. Most of the routes had been pegged and they had a name.

Did you think routes like CIRCE E5 would go free?
I thought it would in the future, but I didn't think I'd do it, I didn't know. It was a line and anything that's a line you have to go at. When I first went to Stoney I pegged CIRCE and KINK, then I pegged KELLOGG and SCARAB, I did them all and realised that they weren't impossible. I could see how you'd do it, but what I couldn't see is where you could rest. I could see each move but I couldn't see anyone doing the whole route. If you had a little platform to step off at 30ft., have a breather and then get back! As I climbed more and more it became obvious what was possible, and I suppose finger strength and stamina got better, through spending hours off the floor traversing up, down and around.

You did GREEN DEATH E5, was that an epic?
That was a turning point. I realised then that I could climb apparently blank rock, because when you get to it, it's not blank. From below you just look up and don't see the holds, but you've got to literally, get a rope, and go down and have a look.

Was that frightening?
Yes. I tried to top rope it but couldn't, so I thought right I'll lead it. I could see it was possible but I couldn't top rope it because I

didn't trust a top rope. I can't see the point in pushing yourself on a top rope because it doesn't count does it, it's nothing. But it is worth pushing yourself for a first ascent.

You say you didn't top rope routes, did you ever top rope a route that was too hard to lead?
No, only little snippets, nothing major. I'd rather abseil down, learn the moves, and then have a blitz from the bottom, I prefer that approach. I don't know if it's allowed now, pre-inspection!

Now anything goes! No one really cares how anyone deals with a route.
As long as you don't alter the route it doesn't matter. As long as you don't go up with a hammer and chisel and carve it up, I think anything goes. I don't know about bolts, I think they are too close together, there isn't a scare factor now like there use to be. I think a lot of routes are done now because they have got bolt protection, I wouldn't have even considered them. I also wouldn't have done them because I wouldn't have put the bolts in. I suppose if I was still climbing I'd have a change of mind or see that it was holding us back. It depends on why you want to climb; if you try to do hard good climbs, or if you want a really desperate workout.

When did you stop climbing?
In November 1979, I strained my tendons that's why. It was on MENOPAUSE as well, of all things, it hadn't been done free. I'd got up into the top groove and my forearms just tensed up, I'd done something in my left and a lot in my right. It was cold, November, I was a bit fed up with climbing. I've never climbed more than 18 months and then I've had a break from it. I thought I'd do something to keep fit over the winter, so I went cave digging. I'd seen a little hole in the quarry and wondered where it went, I started digging and never stopped.

Did you enjoy the danger element of climbing?
To a certain extent, but the thought of hitting the floor was appalling. As long as there were runners somewhere along the line, you can afford to fall 30 foot, so if you've got a good runner above 30 foot, you're pretty safe up to 50 foot. Some real stocky runners up the route, or a big hole below to fall into, it's not so bad.
That was very much a good part?
It was the buzz. I also got an ambition to do routes that no one else could do, and that spurred me on, that was the reason to climb harder and harder. The ultimate would be to do a route that wouldn't be repeated for 10 years?

Phil Davidson

Looking back through history books it is very easy to say 'he was good, look at that brilliant new route he put up' and so on. But of course there are others, and there were many with far greater ability and courage than the first ascentionists when you examine the cloudy detail of their ascents. They number too many to list but are perhaps best represented by Phil Davidson, soloer extrodinare! In 1974 Pete Livesey climbed RIGHT WALL E5 6a, on Dinas Cromlech in Wales, a major climbing landmark, Then three years later Phil Davidson did 4th ascent of RIGHT WALL, he was only 17 and it was completely on-sight. A couple of years later he was fast on the heels of Ron Fawcett by doing the 3rd ascent of LORD OF THE FLIES E6 6b on the same cliff. But then in 1982 he did the first solo of RIGHT WALL, at a time when E6 was still bloody hard, and E5 was definitely not a walk. This was by far the most impressive solo in Britain and illustrated the incredible level of skill that that Phil had. The next person to solo it was Jerry Moffatt, a year later.

Interview 22.1.91 St Helens, Merseyside.

Has bold climbing always interested you?
Absolutely. If you sit back at home every weekend or watch the tele, perhaps play a football match, go to the pub drinking with your mates; that is the normal run of the mill pastime, and it's relatively safe. Now if you don't agree with the general rules, or societies norms, then something else is needed. Well, that's the way I felt, I didn't particularly like what was going on. I certainly didn't like work, and I definitely didn't like the holidays they were giving me...!! To step out against that, climbing offered me something normal society didn't. It offered me danger, it offered me an incredible challenge, it was something that nobody else ever did, or very few did, and it was just the whole attraction of getting out from where you live and getting to somewhere which is a nice place.

Why not move completely from St. Helens then?
Occasionally I've been on the dole and I've had plenty of time to myself, those particular times I've still had to, understandably earn some money, and usually that coincided with earning money in some sort of town or city. The jobs and the opportunities in the outdoors are not quite as proliferous. Having said that, one of the ideas of going back to college and to doing a degree in outdoor education, was hopefully to open that avenue up. As soon as it was opened, the government in their infinite wisdom, shut it down. The national curricu-

lum, and everything that goes with it ensures that outdoor education along with many other practical subjects doesn't come very high up, in the levels of what people feel are important. Alternatively Llanberis in the winter doesn't really appeal to me, there is very little to do, it never seems to stop raining. There is little live jazz and getting in with that sort of scene is more difficult. Although it may exist in Wales it isn't anywhere as common as in the city.

By 1974 you had climbed all the Extremes in the Llanberis Pass, did you think of doing any new routes?
One of the reasons I didn't, was that I was quite happy to underestimate my own ability. I did the routes of people who were seen as the

top climbers in the country; Pete Crew, Boysen, Brown and Whillans and all of the rest. It came as a surprise that I could do them, because these were my gods, and in most cases I found the routes relatively easy, well within my capabilities. I never got pumped or fell off. While that was going on there was still new routes being done and the standards were going up. Ron had come on the scene with Chris Gibb, and those two were seen as the pillars of the climbing world, pushing the standard forward. In retrospect I really should have done more new routes but I just wanted to be driven to a piece of rock, where the challenge is; then do it with the minimum effort. New routes usually take a lot more effort than just going and doing one which is there to be repeated. In many instances I did early ascents, and I think few people would doubt that the second ascents were probably better than the first, because they were always on-sight, and usually without falls. It was very seldom I fell off, something I used to pride myself on, I still detest falling off, even now with bolted routes, but at least it is safer. The actual moves are getting very much harder but at the same time there is the safety aspect. I can see the attraction. But personally it wasn't why I started climbing. I started climbing because it was dangerous, because it was adventurous and you were putting yourself in positions where your average Joe Bloggs wouldn't dare to go. It made me feel a stronger, more together person through doing that.

Did you have problems controlling yourself psychologically in dangerous positions?
No never. That's not to say that I'm not frightened but I can't actually remember being frightened whilst climbing. I did the second ascent of DEATH WISH E7 6b, and even facing 90-100 foot ground falls from soloing, I can never really say I'm frightened. I always had the confidence in my ability and never really got worried. Early in the season you might feel a bit gibbery about gear and what have you, but that soon wore off, and certainly if I was climbing well the fear aspect could easily be put to the back of my mind, getting on with the job in hand whether it was 2 foot off the ground or 100 foot off the ground.

What are some of the best on-sights that you have done?
I was quite proud of doing the 4th ascent of RIGHT WALL E5, when I was 17. Soloing it was good but I was more confident. I was climbing with Jimmy Jewel at the time and he just expected me to do it, I wandered up there on my own one evening and soloed it, it didn't seem any big deal. Soloing COCK BLOCK E5 6b, I felt was another descent effort, flashing THE ANGLER which is now 8a but then was about 7c, and nearly flashing TEQUILA MOCK-INGBIRD 7c, in front of the Peak's leading climbers. They had spent days on it! I had to pull their ropes down to get on the route. Perhaps more important though was LINDEN E6,6b at Curbar, it had never been led on-sight and that was in 82. At the time that was quite a hard grit route and again I just wandered along there one evening and soloed it. Other things were the first complete ascent of MIDSUMMER NIGHT'S DREAM E6 on Cloggy. WISE BLOOD OF THE VIRGINS E6, amused me a lot because Ron had failed on it, I did it then Ron tried it again and took quite a pisser off it. I was pleased with that. Later in '84 I virtually left the climbing alone because I'd got such a poor mark in my canoeing, (I don't like that sort of thing going on...) I can still remember it today.

I'd been on the water (Grade 2 water which is pretty flat), then 30 seconds later I was swimming and the lecturer was laughing, a D minus in my first year. After that I virtually stopped climbing and it was all canoeing; three years later I took the same lecturer down a particularly hairy piece of water in Wales at The Fairy Glen, grade 5, serious stuff. He actually wrote a college boat off and I had to rescue him, so my final canoe mark was higher than my climbing. Actually I got A minus for my climbing because my rope work wasn't any good.

Is doing well at a sport essential for you?
Yes, I don't like doing things badly. Lots of people can't really cope with me, they can't understand my obsession and my fanaticism, but I hate doing things badly. When I started canoeing I was the worst in the year at college, it just felt wrong and I couldn't put up with it. The climbing was no sweat for me, to be one of the best in the year, again this mattered to me, but a new challenge. Canoeing offered me something that climbing had really lost, a challenge. Athough there was still a challenge, it wasn't new any more, that is really why I got attracted to canoeing.

When Jerry did REVELATIONS though there was something to go and do?
REVELATIONS – I admired it but it seemed such a short piece of rock which didn't appeal to me, I still feel that way. When I see the likes of HUBBLE and the pictures, I could never decry the ascent, it's phenomenal, the moves and the amount of effort that Ben put in to do it, he's brilliant; but for me it still lacks something. Anyone however good, will spend a month doing an 8c+ and for me to spend that much time on it, detracts from the climbing experience itself. I personally cannot focus my attention on 30 foot of climbing, I prefer looking at something, like INDESCENT EXPOSURE 7b+, I did the first on-sight flash of that by the way, it's 150ft of really good climbing. REVELATIONS never really appealed to me in that way, it was totally bolted, and I wasn't really fond of bolts. Now I'm in two camps, I'm doing quite hard routes because of the bolts, moves which are harder than I would do normally, but I still feel the number of climbers in this country who can climb hard routes without bolts, is the same as it ever was, and that is very few. There are lots of climbers who are brilliant but can't do hard routes without bolts. Perhaps they don't want to have the danger aspect. I know there is redpoint pressure, but if some dude falls off a redpoint he isn't going to die but if someone falls off The Bells there is a very high likelihood that they will die. The people who are going to lay it on the line are few and far between, those

are the people I admire in sport, the dudes who take the risks.

Was there any reason that you stopped soloing hard routes?
Yes, because it is only a matter of time before you die. I'm convinced of that. No matter how good you are it only takes a hold to snap, or one foot to slip, and there aren't any second chances. While I still solo, the routes I do are not particularly desperate, things on Suicide Wall, like CAPITAL PUNISHMENT, E4. But some of the guys who are soloing these days, I feel are pushing the boat out. It's like a drug, I climbed with Jimmy Jewel for a long time, and before he was killed, I was spending quite a bit of time with him in Llanberis. We both came from similar backgrounds and climbed. I did try to warn him about soloing but he wouldn't have it. It is like a drug, and the feeling you get with soloing is fairly addictive; but the only way you can get it is by soloing. I can remember I'd seen him the weekend before he died, I did try to warn him about the risks, that perhaps he should cut it down a bit. But there were a lot of people (I don't want to get off the subject of why I'm climbing but I do think it is an integral part with the soloing) who produced these solos for the media. There were a lot of people who wanted to film him, a lot of people who wanted to photo-graph him, and it was easy to get on the band wagon, just carry on with the euphoria of the fame, your name in magazines and everything else. It is easy to carry on trying to solo things that you shouldn't, because the people want you to do it, I'm convinced that is why Jim carried on.

Did you ever feel you were under that spell?
Oh yes, definitely. It's a strange feeling, Johnny Dawes in his Stone Monkey programme spoke of doing moves without thinking, about being weightless and being on a different plane, and that's happened to me many times. It's hap-pened to me climbing with a rope at a high standard where it is dangerous, but more importantly, it happens whenever you are climbing solo. The feelings that Johnny was talking about, I have experienced as well, you are not aware of thinking about the moves, they just happen, and your body is weightless, you're not aware of what it feels like until you experience it and that doesn't happen very often. I certainly don't see it ever happening again, I'll never be that fit, but it is an experience which is untrue, when you get it.

Was your fitness different to the top people of today?
Yes, but in a different way though. The climbing of today is mentally exacting. If today's guys make a mistake, it is unlikely that

they are going to die. If you are on a particularly serious route and you make a mistake the consequences are far more out-reaching. Again it is a different sort of mental tuning, but one that needs a particular dedication and quest. I still feel today that the people who do the serious routes, and they are soloing, are few and far between, and that they are the ones with the true talent.

Have you enjoyed coming back into climbing?
Oh yes. I purposely kept away from Malham because I knew there was going to be a lot of people there that I knew and if you like, I wanted to try and portray myself as still being a reasonable climber. After a five year lay-off, I was anything but. Having said that it didn't take that long for me to get back into it, which is a good thing and I don't think I've lost that much as far as psychological control. After going to Malham there were lots of people there that I hadn't seen for years and loads of them were coming up and saying, 'you're climbing again brilliant' they were dead chuffed and I was pleased about that. Soon after that I had things in my mind, objectives at Malham that I wanted to tick and soon. When I packed in, things like OBSESSION 7b+ hadn't been done. I knew Joe Healey, a very good friend from around the corner in St. Helens, had done OBSESSION very soon after the 1st ascent, but he hadn't flashed it, and I was aware that this route wasn't flashed very much, even by today's standards. That was something I set my sights on, because it was a wall climb, it was technical, and it was in a fantastic position and therefore had a lot going for it; but more importantly Joe hadn't flashed it! I set my sights on that and went to work doing as many of the lower routes under Lower Tier trying to get fitter. Then soon after on a really nasty day, cold and windy, I managed to flash OBSESSION on-sight, I was dead chuffed about it. The irony of it, was that Bob Smith, the guy who did it before me had left the quick draws in, hadn't told me the gate didn't open at the top belay chain, you had to take an extra krab. The distance from the belay to the last bolt must be 20 foot, and after flashing it I didn't have any quick draws. I had to untie the rope, thread it through the crab with my arm through the chain, and then tie back in, it was horrendous. Otherwise I would have had to jump off and take this monster.

You may have to stop climbing to enable your fingers to be nimble enough to play the Sax?
You are treading on very delicate territory there Dave, I can see myself becoming totally obsessed with it and having to sacrifice time that perhaps I would use for other things. But

Phil on a historic solo of RIGHT WALL on Dinas Cromlech, Llanberis, Snowdonia.

15 years of climbing seems a long time. It's got something which I don't think other sports have got, it gets you out of cities, it gets you out to areas which are nice and it does keep you fit, you cannot be a slob and climb at high standards, it's just not feasible.

Do you enjoy that challenge of the Sax?
Oh yes absolutely. There are quite a lot of people who have said I'm totally obsessed or single minded about something when I get into it, and I can see that the saxophone playing is going the same way. The only thing

that's holding me back at the minute is that I'm not good enough, but that can only go on for so long before you do reach a standard where you are able to play and perform, so that is my aim ultimately, but at the same time it depends on the season. During the summer when I was climbing I was still trying to practice, but it was no where as near as much as in the winter, and that is the way I can see it since I have no intention of stopping climbing, and every intention of playing a sax!

41

John Redhead

To any climber the mention of THE BELLS, THE BELLS conjures up a vision of climbing on the wilder side of complete insanity. The climb is one of John's 50 or so new routes that typify bold climbing where more often than not the stakes of falling are too high to risk. His contributions to hard climbing in the late '70's and early '80's were immense, classic routes such as COCKBLOCK E5, PRECIOUS E6 and MANIC STRAIN 8a; and incredible lines such as MARGINS OF THE MIND E7 and RITE OF SPRING E8 6c. Living in Snowdonia John explored the mountain crags, limestone lowlands and most impressively of all Gogarth. Provocative route names such as DISILLUSIONED SCREW MACHINE E6, RAPED BY AFFECTION E6, and TORMENTED EJACULATION E7 shocked many parts of the conservative climbing world. His achievement's though have always been at the forefront of climbing in terms of both technical standards and boldness.

Interview 9.4.91 Liverpool.

Do you consider yourself an artist or a climber?

I'm an artist. I don't consider myself a climber. Climbing is basically a part of my creative life and it ties in with who I am and what I want to do creatively. It ties in with my work. I'm not alienated from my work when I climb and climbing isn't something apart from it. It's something that's got to tie in with my work to be meaningful and creative. It's not something separate. It's strange really because they seem quite diverse – painting and climbing. When you think about it, the nature of my work as a painter takes me away from the earth, but is very much part of the world – it is not a product of my own private sensibility. Whereas climbing brings you right back down to earth again, but away from the world when you're actually climbing. You're doing something meaningful and serious. There is a great element of doubt in my type of climbing anyway, which questions what is my motivation for surviving in the world; so it does bring you back down. You're alive in the world and you are actually saying 'am I going to survive or not?' What does my work mean to me? You are questioning all the time; so it is that kind of relationship: opposites but equals.

Do you feel then completely at home with painting and drawing and doing art?

"Doing art" sounds like a pastime. I'm a bit suspicious of the word 'artist,' because most artists displayed in galleries are part of a flippant scenario in which my work has no place. I'm a painter and I have always been a painter, from being dead small and going up through school I always thought.....I had a brief spell doing architecture but even then I realised that I wasn't an architect, it was the wrong path. Painting just evolved and developed from there.

Has the painting always been creative, do you feel in the sense that you have never really wanted to be a reproductive painter?

I'm all for 'reproduction but!' But seriously if painting is to be meaningful it has to be. What other kind is there? It all ties in with my spiritual world as well, my spiritual life. Your spiritual life is actually concerned with how creatively you view the world and that comes into climbing as well. I don't think there is any point of being a climber unless you can use it creatively. That is one of my standpoints against sports climbing, I've nothing against sports climbing but there's not much creativity in it. When a sports climber is judged, creativity is not important. It's like timing and how far you get. It's a very hard aṗßch to climbing, whereas I'm trying to seek a very soft approach. I think my climbing is quite soft and internal and very personal; it doesn't perform to big numbers or popular crags or media attention.

Looking at your history in climbing, of impressive achievements, it would appear perhaps that you have always been seeking the media?

Not at all, no. I've always wanted to be on my own climbing. There are very few photographs of me climbing. When I do serious routes I tend to be on my own; it's a very personal thing; it just happens that I've done a few good routes and the nature of people out there is that they get off on the fact and you do actually attract attention to yourself by doing these routes; but I've never looked for that attention; I don't get off on it, I don't like being on the crags with stacks of people, I prefer to be on my own with friends who I can 'be alone with.' If the crag is full of people then I'll just go somewhere else, go in the hills or just go back to my studio and paint.

In climbing do you appreciate the sense of fear and of danger?

Fear is important. I know fear. It's like 'deep' play; you're putting yourself in a position to question who you are: I think that is dead important to me. It's a controlling of that fear I think which is important, but you also have to know that it's like a field of savagery out there and it's not just the rock face that is the field of savagery: I have a harder time with my painting than I do with my climbing, even on the most serious routes., I'm more in fear of painting than I am of climbing. When you walk across the street you should be in fear, when you go to a night club you should be well fearful, driving a car, it's all fields of savagery; and climbing is just another aspect of that only you're putting yourself more directly in it, more directly in line. Basically it is all about questioning and not because you want to do a particular climb; I think that is secondary. Like what you have to go through to get there in the first place – the searching necessary for gain. When I've done a climb it doesn't really mean anything, it's the act of climbing that's important, the searching, and the need for adversity.

In recent years has that been fulfilled?

Not at all no. You say 'do I consider myself a climber', well I don't because I've hardly done any climbing. I've only done 50 new routes since I first started climbing. They are all classics, they are all very meaningful, they are all superb lines, there's a good feeling to them but there are only 50 new routes. Last year I did two routes, the year before that I think I did one, the year before that I think I did five and they are all E6, E7. When I get on a route there is an element of doubt whether I'm going to climb it or not because I'm not very fit, I can't be bothered to train which I'm sure is bad. What I'm saying is that I haven't achieved very much at all in climbing, I've achieved stacks more with my painting – it's less talked about and that is in the nature of people as well because climbing is wacky and dangerous and bizarre and way out, it attracts more attention; I feel that I haven't even peaked yet, there are routes that I want to do, there's lines that haven't been climbed yet that I would love to do and I'm sure that there is stacks left in me yet to get in there and do a bit more. I'm certainly not satisfied with my climbing performance and I'm certainly not satisfied with the style even though accepted ethics of the day say that I have climbed in good style, personally I know that I haven't – because of the soft approach, because of the the movement; the way it all joins together, the way I feel over my paintings and everything, it doesn't hold together well. There is lots of potential yet, it's quite exciting and I'm looking forward to doing some more climbing.

Do you get that sense of attempting something in the unknown every time you start a painting?

Absolutely yes, you are stepping into the unknown that's what is so exciting about it, but you can't just do a painting. I think it's a very important part of my painting, the way the painting is painted, the searching that goes

before and during the painting – IS the painting. It's the same with climbing, it's not only the climb that matters, it's the stuff that goes before that gets you there in the first place.

Can you not create fully in your mind the final image that you are painting?
It's impossible. No. It doesn't work that way. You can have sketches, you can have a rough idea of what the painting is, you can have all the shapes and the colours and the hues and everything, all the ingredients that can go into a painting you can have in your head. Once you start painting you are controlling that, you're controlling your emotions, making meaning of senses, it's necessary to look down; that is why I say painting is 'up there,' you are looking down, you have no emotions otherwise what you paint is just jibberish and sketchy. The painting predicts and dictates itself. No matter what imagery you have in your mind, at the end of the day the painting will be totally different because it will keep changing as you are painting, it will present

itself, it will move you on in a different way, a different direction, the shapes will change; it will become 'right,' it's actually asserting itself. It's quite a fearful thing to actually have to control something like that and very healing in a way.

Do you want to control something like that?
Yes, because there is no point in painting paintings that are just for you, that are just emotional and how you view the world; a painting that isn't meaningful to other people, isn't meaningful to the world, then what you're giving the world is junk. You get a lot of that in the world now; you go around every exhibition and there is stuff like that in the galleries; it's like 'peoples' laundry in a way. In a lot of ways that's what you're getting with climbing as well, you're getting the laundry, you're not getting the essence of what the sport is all about, you're getting all the ego and the emotions and the media attention and all that crap which I tend to stay away from. But it's useful in a way because I like to make an art out of my world wherever I am, that is why I

came here to Liverpool, to make an art in surviving, to dodge and weave. I think that is really important and you have to use the media now and again for your purposes. You do it because it exists in the world and it's very powerful; that's why I did the TV climb, the Anglican Cathedral. I did that because it's a way through to get into the homes of people who could relate to that kind of bizarre thing. You have to use those tactics now and again, tactics I consider to be like porridge which I dislike a lot; but you have to survive in the world and you have to pay your way, if you are broke you have to do something about it and if that is what the world wants then I can do it - but playing to my own parameters as long as I've got control over it.

Do you have any remorse that people readily accept your climbs as great yet your painting are not heralded as masterpieces?
Who heralds the way it goes? It's just typical of the world, typical of human nature. My climbs are like a claim aren't they, routes like THE BELLS, THE BELLS, MARGINS OF THE MIND,

MASTERS WALL, RITE OF SPRING – they are a claim whereas my paintings......If I have an exhibition in a gallery I think my paintings would be 'destroyed' but would be making tangible claims within transient walls; but that's not why I paint; I'm not in the world to entertain, there are stacks of painters who do that. The galleries are full of entertaining establishment art. I believe that paintings are in the world to confront with the issues of the day with the images of the day to make people aware of what is going on, to make them get off the fence and do something about it; to make them aware of their problems, to make them aware of who they are, to make them aware of the breathing earth. In so doing you can't exhibit in galleries, you can't exhibit in establishment places that would give you fame and attention and stacks of money. You have to exhibit in shopping precincts and in the street or in the cathedral or supermarkets, the Albert Dock here – Liverpool. I tend to confront – I don't entertain, there is a difference there; whereas with climbing there is massive media attention, if you do a good route people are going to know about that and no matter what you say about it, people are going to say things and it's going to get in the press, you don't really have much say about what goes on and I don't really care all that much.

Has at any point in time your climbing taken precedence over painting?
There have been times when, because of the nature of the paintings that I've been doing, I have had to leave the paintings. I've had to because probably I've been painting ad-lib which is a pretty criminal thing to do, just to be involved with the process, just like training in a way without a climb in mind. I've been painting without a painting in mind and to me I'm not a painter unless I've got a painting to do; I can't just go through the process of painting – to me that's commercial, it doesn't mean anything. When I have become alienated from my work then I go and do something about it, that has occurred quite a few times and it's quite a normal process for a painter to go through. In such situations I've blasted through by doing various routes; doing various climbs which brings me back to the bone of who I am and questions what the painting is about and the tones and the colour and just restores me and sustains me for the further battles of my work. Again the battles of my work as a painter are stacks more fearful than the battles on a climb. In the battles on a climb the options are very easy, either you let go by a finger and fall, or you get to the top; the options with a painting are manifestly so fucking complex. In that way climbing can be quite 'therapeutic' for me whereas painting could never be therapeutic for my climbing. I

don't go into painting to get away from climbing and to relax. Art can 'never' be therapy.

Has climbing ever held you from painting for prolonged periods?
No it hasn't. That is why in climbing I've never been fit because for example when I was doing The Bells in 1980, I did three or four good routes and then got into my painting, I lost fitness..... I was getting fit, if I had carried on I would have been fit and I would have been a climber whereas my painting manifested itself again, it reared it's 'ugly-head' within me and I just had to go back to the studio and paint; so I forgot about climbing for months. You get very unfit standing around painting even though you need a lot of stamina. You need more stamina for painting than you do for climbing because you have to keep at it day and night for several days whereas with climbing you don't. If you get fucked climbing, if you've got no stamina or you lose strength you stop climbing – you have to, you either fall off or come down; with painting you can't do that, you've got to keep at it, you've got to control it all the time, you've got to manipulate it, you've got to dodge and weave, you've got to hold it together, you're using judgements and decisions day and night and it's with you all the time.

Can you not force it away?
No you can't that's what I'm saying because it dictates itself and you've got to keep at it, you've got to keep at it to work it. There comes a time in a painting when you can relax, that's certainly true. After a few days you know that the shapes have fought their way through in some kind of possessed way and you know it's right and you can let go of it slightly. In some ways that is when in times past an apprentice would have come in to finish the painting off – the groundwork, the tones and the colours, that can happen. In that situation I would probably go bouldering just to give me some fresh air, do some gentle moving on rock and just feel my body flow in a gentle kind of way.

In that effect bouldering is very different from doing routes?
Very much so, yes. It's a very different thing isn't it. I enjoy the technicality of bouldering but I don't think there's a boulder problem that is any more technical that some routes that I've done in serious situations which I get far more out of – holding it together. Bouldering is like sketching and I hate sketching. I've got the notion of a work in my head and I want it out, I want it out now, I haven't got time to wait, that painting has got to be there in the world and that big white' canvas has got to be full of paint quickly. It's like a climb. I enjoy

bouldering now and again, it's comfortable and it's like a nice situation and environmental thing but it doesn't tie in with climbing at all. If I've got a climb in mind, I want to do that climb even if I'm not fit, I'll get on that climb and I'll have a hard time and I'll scare myself shitless but only if I am getting somewhere. That's the blank canvas, I'm filling it in even though I fall on it and I have to come back to it, I'm filling it in, I'm getting somewhere, I've started, whereas bouldering and sketching don't really suit me personally.

Is there a middle part or a third corner of the triangle, something else as strong as either painting or climbing for you?
I guess that 'hidden God' you are talking about, that invisible ingredient, is like my spirituality which is the pivot for the climbing, and the painting, the way I react to other people and the way I view the world, it's all got to tie in; that's probably the third thing where everything becomes meaningful and becomes part of you. I don't think there is any activity I could do which is unnaturally part of me, to do just for the sake of; that is why I've never been able to have a job as such, that's why I'm fucking broke – how much are you paying me for this!

Do you hold a big respect for society at large?
I'm part of society. I am part of society, we all are, it's not a question of respect, it's a question of knowing that the society that we are living in now is flourishing in music of decline which is one of the reasons I moved here to the centre of Liverpool, to witness that first hand and not be tucked in cosy and warm somewhere in North Wales, cosy fires and wood burning stoves and food; this is raw, this is primeval, the primeval hunt goes on in this town every night. I can't go out, I just can't leave the warehouse, it's scary. It's more scary than climbing – being here on a night. The groups of youths, beer swilling males following the chicks with their high heels click, clacking down the street. The doorways coming alive, the rubbing together of flesh, vomit down the warehouse walls, the noise; it's like a primeval beat, drum beat; just animals, and that's just what we all are basically at the end of the day. I get that feeling that like they just want to screw everything within reach and it's well frightening.... I rejoice! why not?

Is it just the feeling of part of that or does it generate things within you?
We're all part of that and I think it's in the nature of my work to make sense of it. To actually propound that this is society and it is disgusted by it's own body in a way. People in suburbia, tucked away nice and warm, con-

demn what's going on in the world – like buggery or child molestation or massacres and wars and all that kind of thing; it's not these acts that are unclean – but the legitimate children of society, the people who indulge in all that fidgeting aggression - sedentary life! There are civilizations in the world, usually the nomadic tribes, that are I suppose, living in harmony, there are a few left in the world and that offers hope. When I get really depressed about this all I have to do is think about the worm. The worm in the ground writhing in slime and stench because when all fails, when technology fails, society falls, the worm will still be there. To me that is like great hope, that gives me strength to continue. There is also hope in all creativity, without creativity, without culture, there is no future and there are a stack of people in the world who care, many many people that care in the world and you shouldn't forget that just because I'm painting a black picture of society, it doesn't mean to say that it doesn't have the opposite because there are people that care and there is hope and a future....

In that respect does getting to the top of a very serious climb come as a relief or is it more of a power drive?

If it was a power drive I wouldn't do it. Power doesn't come into it; what is more powerful than the rock? It is power, to understand this fact, to understand what is behind the power of a feather stroking the rock, a drop of water mouldering the stone. I was in Parliament House Cave the other day. I went down there with Helen to go camping. We abseiled down and pitched up camp, had some food and a nice big 'cuddle' by the bonfire. I thought it was suspicious at the time, because the drift wood is usually all over the beach whereas this time, it was all in the back of the caves and I thought it couldn't be the spring tide. We were blinded – it was so calm. At 12 o'clock at night the beacon at South Stack was shining across the gorge every ten seconds. There was a deafening roar and I looked out to see a tempest torn ocean. It was just a white, frothy mass. The tide was coming in fast and I told Helen to wake up because we had to get out. She didn't want to go, it was like a death wish, she was comfortable in her pit: but I said that we really did have to go because if we left it much longer we were not going to be able to traverse out. The abseil rope had gone, 150 foot up the cliff it had blown out. It was a real tempest.

We got to a ledge below BLUE PETER and by that time the cave was full, a white frothy mass of water, and it was getting to this ledge as well. A big wave came over. Eventually I had to climb out: I soloed up, got the rope and then jumared out, abseiled down then tied Helen on and she climbed out in the pitch black, a fine effort. We got out at 3 o'clock in the morning, it was an epic. I've never been so frightened in my life. The rock was nothing in comparison, the water was just something else and the energy and the power behind that enveloping amorphous mass – you had to respect or die! So I don't climb for power but to understand it. I think it's a very dangerous thing. If you climb to get to the top of a cliff or a mountain, you should very seriously question why you climb, and I think that's one of the saddest reasons why people indulge in these 'high risk' sports. They should really question why they are doing it, because if they don't do it for themselves, if they do it just to get to top of the cliff or are packaged to perform – then I think it bodes very ill for the world and for themselves. I'm talking about imbalance – it's a carcinogenic thing, and not just in climbing, in anything. I think the path through is what is important, and the outcome is completely irrelevant. When I've done a hard serious route and I get to the top I feel a little dead, there's no elation, it's a deadness.

It's not like finishing a painting, even though the painting is also dead, because the act of painting is important, but at the end of the day you've got a series of paintings with which to confront society, to get out there with and perhaps in a small way, bring about some kind of change; you don't get that with climbing. The energy is there, the creativity is there, but it's negative, it doesn't go anywhere, it can only be for yourself and no one else, so there is no 'power' as such, other than the 'real' power behind it. I'm sure when the climber understands the nature of his language and the harnessing of what is already there, he'll have no need to touch rock? The martial arts, thousands of centuries old, developed in such a way that people can avoid contact. There is no longer a need for 'hard' contact - more like a harnessing of opponents energy - a look or a stare or a gesture and they can rig up barriers, they can just throw people away without using 'hard' force. Climbing is very young, it's a very forceful thing, it's a very hard thing, and I'm sure when the climber understands what he's dealing with he will have no need to touch rock.

Is that a great way forward?

I don't know, it's certainly a way forward just like sports climbing is, I think it's just another approach and it suits me personally. I don't condemn other people for their style of climbing, who am I to condemn them? All I can do is to give you my personal philosophy, and just accept other peoples philosophy. Perhaps the day will come when 'their garden' obstructs my view. I may have something to say, or I may walk away.... If somebody, a sports climber is bolting up a cliff which I've got a particular respect for, then I may do something....! I've learnt a lot from placing bolts and things like that, and I've made a lot of mistakes and hopefully I might have learnt.

Do you make the same mistakes in painting?

I make stacks of mistakes, that's what I'm saying. Oceans of uncertainess I think are just so important, to make any exercise meaningful, there's got to be stacks of doubt to question what you're doing all the time, to stop complacency, to stop you; to be in awe of everything, as soon as you wake up you have got to be in awe otherwise you just get sucked in to all sorts of messy gardens. We are in the hands of 'dogs' – but the grey wagtail still sings in town...

In terms of legends the name Jerry Moffatt stands at the fore of modern rock climbing. Those such as :Winthrop Young, Kirkus, Edwards, Brown and Whillans, Proctor, Livesey, Fawcett, remain classic names and represent the age of traditional climbing. Today's climbing is different because until 1983 the term POWER didn't really exist, 'very hard indeed' was the term used for the hardest climbs. Jerry then went to the Southern Frankenjura in Germany and climbed THE FACE, it was the first POWER climb and received the new grade of 8a and set a new era of eighth grade climbing. In 1984 he climbed REVELATIONS 8a+ and repeated Jean Baptiste Tribout's route BIDULE 8a+, at Saussois in France; the two hardest routes in the world, also at the time he on-sighted CHIMPANZADROME 7c+ at Saussois which was two grades above anything that had been flashed before. In 1985 he suffered from an injured elbow and it became likely that he might never climb again. With hope and luck an operation saw him improve and by 1987 was back heading for the hard routes which had risen to 8b+ by the French. By 1988 he had done the third ascents of SPECTRE 8b+, RAGE DE VIVRE 8b+, MINIMUM 8b+ in France; TO BOLT OR NOT TO BE 8b+, SCARFACE 8b+, WHITE WEDDING 8b+ all in the USA. He was the first person to complete any of the trilogy's. He also climbed Germany's first 8b+ STONELOVE. In 1990 whilst mainly concentrating on competitions he lost out to Ben Moon on the worlds first 8c, but climbed Britain's first with LIQUID AMBER 8c at Pen Trwyn near Llandudno. His competition success has been equally staggering by winning the majority he has entered.

Interview 5.4.91 Woodseats, Sheffield

Do you feel that you've done everything there is to do in rock climbing?
That's the big question first! To a certain extent yes, I feel as though I've done everything I set out to do, I've achieved my ambitions; now it's just a question of repeating them. I feel that I've done the hardest bouldering, the hardest routes, both on-sights and redpoints, and I've won very major competitions against the other top climbers from anywhere in the world. I do feel as though I've done a lot and I'm getting to the stage where you're not finding it as exciting as it was, when you're younger and you desperately wanted to do the hardest routes. I repeated GENESIS 7c+, the hardest route in the USA when I was 19 and it was all new; France in the eighties etc., new excitement. I still have a lot of things I want to do in climbing but now they're slightly different.

Jerry bouldering at the bottom of his own route VERBAL ABUSE on Ravens Tor. Sean Myles spotting him as he makes a 7b slap for another poor hold.

When you were 17 did you set yourself goals?
Yes, I set them in my mind but I didn't write them down, I didn't need to because at that age, things you want to do are really important, you really WANT to do things.

Did schooling interfere with climbing at all?
No, I finished my last 'O' level exam about half an hour early. I remember walking past the room, everyone was still sitting there and I had all my climbing gear with me in a rucksac on my back and was waving, see ya. I thought, 'I'm never going to do examinations again', and I didn't.

Did you become fanatical to get good at climbing?
Once I made up my mind, once I got addicted, I just went completely for it. I remember it was one summer, I wanted to go climbing so I made a traverse at my parents house in Leicester. There was an old brick barn and I would go on it every single day, climb for at least an hour. After that I was really psyched to do this E1, a big roof in Wales called MOJO, I

did that which made me even keener. I then went on routes far too hard for me on a top rope because I wasn't good enough to lead them. Being on a route like QUICKSTEP E4 was outrageous, a 'Pete Livesey' route, it was incredible, there was never any one on it or even chalk on it.

Did you get better quickly or was it a long process?
I got better really quickly, it took one year to get up to top roping 6a's without falling off, I was 16-17. It doesn't sound hard now, but at the time 6a was a very hard route. It must have been 1979 because I remember going up to Dinas Cromlech for the first time, Ron Fawcett was doing LORD OF THE FLIES E6 6b, and I remember thinking, it's Ron Fawcett oooh! That's the day I led my very first HVS IVY SEPULCHRE, I was climbing just above the peg and I slipped off, slithering down and managing to grab hold of a jug, mostly in fear as I was so scared of falling, I didn't want to weight the rope.

Jerry on the 45° lock off wall in his cellar. The left side is for repetitve stamina warm ups, and the right for high intensity body building lock offs. Mattresses make spotters redundant here.

Did you have any vision that you could be as good as Ron?

Not then, no way. But when I was 17 and doing 6a's, getting on the hardest routes of the time, Yes! I led STRAWBERRIES E6 6b with a couple of rests, if I'd had the attitude and working knowledge that I have now I'm sure I would have been able to redpoint it. So at that time I thought when I'm older, I could be the best. I wanted to be the best, that was my goal; the best in Britain, not the world or anything but just the best in Britain.

How did you regard Ron?

Ron was the best at the time, John Redhead was climbing very well also, but Ron was better. The year after in 1981 I think I was climbing as well as Ron, if not better on some things; but I was still very unknown and a young whippersnapper and didn't get the publicity. A bit later I did LITTLE PLUM 7c+, Ron had tried it a lot, Kim Carrigan had tried it a lot, Chris Hamper, Tom Proctor, all the big names, everybody managed it in three days, which in those days was a hell of a long time, also that was then the hardest route in the country. I also did ROOSTER BOOSTER which was a lot harder than STRAWBERRIES and didn't get hardly any publicity.

When did you first go abroad?

I was 18 and had a horrendous trip, I hitched over to France with a friend called Mel Griffiths, we only stayed for a week because it was in August, too hot. It ended up as a big hitch hiking trip.

Have you always gone into things unprepared?

No, after that I prepared hard for all the trips. The first big trip was to America in 1983, I was really psyched to do SUPERCRACK 7c, in the Gunks, GENESIS 7c+, in Colorado, PSYCHO 7c; they were the hardest routes in the world. I trained really hard for 2 months, top roping on SARDINE 7b+. That's where I really first made my mark on world climbing by doing SUPER-CRACK on-sight, which at the time was like doing an 8b+ on sight, people were amazed.

Didn't the Frenchman Edlinger flash SUPER-CRACK on-sight also?

He went there two years after, and as top

climbers know, a year is a very, very big difference, also once something has been done then the psychological barrier is not there. It's one of the hardest things if you're going to a place and know that something has never been done, and it's way beyond what's ever been done before. You're pushing both physical and mental limits as well.

Does that make it easier or harder for you in particular?

It makes it easier to get the motivation but it's still very hard to push the mental limits.

What training were you doing at the time?

I was working out doing problems on Tom's Roof at Stoney Middleton, and that was why I had a big advantage, since I was the only person who was really ruthlessly doing it. I don't think many climbers were applying themselves like that, perhaps Bachar and Kauk in USA but no one else really. I was keener and wanted it more than anyone else, and that's when I got it. Then the next big trip was to France. I did all the hardest 8a's, anything with a reputation and some of those in just a single day. I also did the first ascent of PAPI ON SIGHT 7c+, flashed a 7c+, and many 7c's.

In 1984 you climbed REVELATIONS 8a+, again the worlds first. Did you feel that you were the best climber around, or was it you techniques?

It wasn't technique even though I seem to work things out pretty quickly, it was my strength, my will and determination that got me to where I was, and at that time there was no question that I was the best. Today it's hard to say because it's debateable, but then there was no question. In France the best on-sight flash was 7b and I went along and flashed POL POT 7c+ in the Verdon.

You then went on to climb REVELATIONS 8a+, did that cause your injury?

Not in itself because there wasn't one specific day when I injured my elbows, it was over the years. The skin had grown round the nerve and it was compressing it, diagnosed as tendonitits. I had lots of treatment and thought I would never climb again. Then I saw a doctor in Munich who did some tests on the nerves, he did the operation and after about 20 months it got better, it was a very big surprise to get back into climbing.

Jerry's other cellar 'The Roof', enables sequence climbing to be perfected, non stop footless hand movement from the back of the cellar. Stopping on the problems is imposible since varying direction changes in momentum are needed to stay on!

Did you not feel the injury coming on?

No, in retrospect it could have been avoided if I'd known more about training, if I'd had some rest days when I was younger. I used to climb every single day and if I didn't climb I would do pull ups, I was sleeping in barns and caves where it's all damp, not warming up properly, a poor diet; it builds up and you pay for it some day.

How did you cope, not being able to climb?

I stayed out of it completely and hung out with people who weren't climbers. Deep down I really wanted to climb, I couldn't face the fact of not being able to climb so I just tried to ignore it. I did a lot of skiing and riding motorbikes.

You had to take two years off through injury when Antoine Le Menestrel solo'd REVELATIONS, did that surprise you?

As I had climbed it as in redpoint style without falling off I knew it was possible. I wasn't that impressed because I'd climbed with Antoine that winter before in Joshua tree, and had been climbing better than him. But in retrospect looking back it was a very, very impressive ascent. I climb 8c on a good day now and I wouldn't like to solo it.

You did POWERBAND 8b, at Ravens Tor after returning to climbing in a very short time indeed?

Yes, after climbing again for 2 months I was climbing as well as Ben Moon, I never thought that would happen. I remember Ben Moon

and Ben Masterson were working on the POWERBAND and they hadn't done it. The first time on it I couldn't do the moves, 4 days later I did the moves, then 4 days later I did the traverse, I actually did it before them. In the space of two weeks I'd got from not being able to hang on the holds to doing the thing.

Did you come back to climbing with the same enthusiasm as before?
I wanted to come back and do THE MINIMUM 8b+, THE RAGE 8b+, the stuff in France which was the hardest in the world, so I still had the same outlook. I did them all within 6 months of returning to climbing, they were the names, I had to go and do them.

Have you enjoyed the travelling all over the world to do the climbing?
I have, I've really enjoyed it a lot, when it was all new and I was climbing well.

Did you not want to move to any of the places?
No, I always wanted to come home. I wouldn't like to live in France because even though I like the climbing I prefer the attitude of the British people, I like the atmosphere and the attitude towards the competition more. England is a good mix as well, but saying that if you stay in England you just stagnate and you get bored, you need goals and therefore you need to travel.

Was it a disappointment not to win the world cup in competitions?
No. It would have been fun to take to the crag, sit there shining it, but in truth the world cup isn't really important to me; certainly in terms of a year long world cup circuit. I only went to 3 competitions out of the 7 and beat the climbers who finished in the top three, which cannot mean that they're a better climbers

than me; they're very good but on an individual basis I beat all the climbers in the world cup.

You've been at the top from virtually 1980 to 1990, but now with François Legrand taking a grip on the competitions, and Ben Moon's HUBBLE 8c+, do you feel that your era is over?
In some ways, but not actually climbing at the present moment. I beat François more times in 1990 than he beat me, and possibly I could have done HUBBLE if I hadn't put so much time into competitions. I did an 8c last year and won competitions; that is something nobody else did. But I do feel that I don't want it as much as I did when I was younger. It's not really that important anymore that I'm the best, whereas a year or two ago it was very different. Two years ago I would have done HUBBLE by now, I'd have done it the next day, or even before. I'm not so keen, and I have other interests. I could still do things but I don't have the drive to go out and do them.

Does it surprise you that there isn't one person still out on there own above anyone else?
I'd be very surprised if there was somebody like that, it's so competitive, people exchange on training methods. When I was young I was inventing the training methods and since nobody was copying me they weren't going to catch up very fast. Today if someone wins a competition, or puts up a hard route, then the rest of the pack are in the next day like vultures, and very quick to learn off those who have thought up a new technique. They're all professional climbers and very much on a similar level. Look at the world rating's Patrick Edlinger and Alex Duboc only just scrape into the top 40, yet they've both climbed 8c, it's incredible.

Is that the same with women climbers, is there also a big field very close to each other?
No, there isn't the same level of high standard climbing with women, The girls at the top are very few and way above the rest, there's Lynn Hill, Isabelle Patissier, Robyn, Nanette and a few others then after that there is quite a big gap. There's even a huge gap between Lynn, Isabelle and the rest.

Are Lynn and Isabelle approaching the men's standards?
Not really, they're still about 5 years behind on redpointing and 10 years in bouldering. Actually 5 years is quite a long time in climbing. Like I did the things in Joshua Tree and Patrick went there the year after, if you look at how climbing progresses one year, two years, it's a big time. Five years is massive.

Will mens standards progress?
Yes they definitely will, there's no question, we still have a long way to go.

What will you climb in the future?
I like bouldering a lot. I'm really a boulderer, then I go out and put my bouldering talents into routes. I've never been that keen on routes, a two month spell is about enough. I'd rather go to areas like Fontainebleau or the Peak such as Stanage, Burbage; Stoney's a scruffy place but I like to go back because I have memories there. Fort Collins, Hueco Tanks in America, places like that, Yosemite, all great bouldering areas.

Can you see the top climber in 10 years time being like yourself, in the late 20's?
I think they will be early 20's, say 20-25; but they will be very good when they are 17-18, very very good, in the top 10; but there's a big difference to being in the top 10 and being the best. To get that little bit more is a hell of a lot, especially when you've had to really stretch yourself to even get that far.

Froggatt pinnacle stands aloft this Derbyshire gritstone edge, thankfully left intact by the quarrymen who toiled away at sculpturing millstones over hundreds of years.

The Graduates

To be proficient in an art – a graduate. Not the best, but one who has gained the necessary qualifications. In the case of the men it is 8a and of the ladies 7b+. It is a standard that nobody just steps in at, they may try and for sure they will fail. Others may ridicule such a clarification, but they haven't put in the hours of work, the learning, the development and the research. Painstaking effort is required to reach these standards, yet age seems never a qualification or limiter. The pure essence of a Graduate is that of climbing movement - strength control to the finite degree. It is not thuggery, it is not mindless, brute strength, it is quite simply – an art.

John Welford

John Welford is one of the fittest looking young climbers in Britain today. Over the past few summers he has climbed over 15 8a's in the Peak District, Yorkshire and Wales. Born at Scunthorpe in 1963 he discovered climbing at school and was gradually sucked into the Sheffield scene. In the past few years his ascents of routes such as REVELATIONS 8a+, CAVIAR 8a+, CHOUCAS 8a+ and most recently ZEKE THE FREAK 8b. All have all been completed in just a couple of days. He works full time and looks set to improve a lot over the next few years.

Interview, 20.1.91 Porter Cottage, Sheffield.

What makes the Porter Cottage Pub so special?

I think it's reputation mostly, I'd heard all about it as the centre of Sheffield climbing scene, stories of wild goings on. When I first moved to Sheffield I walked in here and straight away there were the big faces, people you could recognise from the magazines.

Why did you study Geology at university?

It was just a natural progression. I was interested in outdoor activities from doing the Duke of Edinburgh awards, and at school geography became a bit boring with all the population studies and all that. I liked the physical aspect of it thought so I did geology A level at college instead. I did quite well in it because I enjoyed it, then progressed on to do a degree in it. I hadn't decided on it as a career but it was the easy option; do something you're good at and it makes life easier for yourself.

Did you see doing a degree in geology leading anywhere?

No, I was probably too naive to think about it at the time, I wasn't interested enough to want to do a further degree or anything like that. Now I'm a shift manager in a Steel Works which is totally unrelated, except that you needed a science based degree to get the job.

Are you disappointed that you don't use your geological knowledge?

Yes and no. I enjoyed the course but even a degree isn't specific enough. When you get down to the nitty gritty, Geology is quite a broad subject, it's a pseudo science, some people call it anyway; but the bits I enjoyed are very hard to get a job in unless you go into research because I was into evolution and Palaeontology, things like that.

MASCULINE POWER TRIP 8b, at the Cornice, Cheedale. A very short and powerful climb which requires intricate moves on tiny awkward holds; John just before the 'Egyptian' back foot move.

When you first came to Sheffield were you aware that the top climbers were living around?

I'd heard usual rumours that Hunter's Bar was the place to be and seen pictures of Jerry Moffatt hanging from bits of wood in the Poly gym and thought 'wow!' I'd like to go there, I'd like to be good. I walked into the Porter because I'd met someone at work on a course who I think knew Jerry, and he told me the Porter Cottage is the place to go which I didn't know until I came here. I gradually met other climbers through being at the Porter Cottage. I've always been more friendly with the B Team climbers, not the A Team until this year, but I'd never really spoken to Ben Moon until last week at Glossop. I said hello and that was about it.

Is there now a split in Sheffield between the A Team and the B Team?

Not really no. Its more apparent with me I think with being at work because during the week I'm not out with them and during the week you're more likely to meet the full timer, because they can go out any time. I'm really a weekender so it's really a split, it's just case that you don't bump into each other as often.

Do you find that pulls your climbing back because you could learn a lot from them?

Yes, definitely. When I first started climbing I was with a guy that would go out and do the same route every weekend. We'd go to Lawrencefield and do GREAT HARRY every weekend, I enjoyed it but I'm sure if it had been a different environment I'd have been pushing along and trying to do harder things all the time and falling off rather than just going out and having a laugh. I got a lot from it, a lot of experience but purely in terms of climbing hard it probably was restrictive.

Do you think if you applied yourself you could start ticking 8b+?

I'd like to think so but whether I could or not I don't know, I'll let you know in August, the routes list this year is very short, I might spend all year on one route!!

Is it from Sheffield that such a strong sport climbing centre is growing?

It seems like the pot of gold, climbers flock to Sheffield and everyone else flocks to London. I think it's purely because there are a lot of good climbers here that people elsewhere come here to try and cash in on them; not pick their brains, but try and improve themselves by being in the same area.

Being a climber do you like the open air and the countryside?

Yes definitely. I bought a mountain bike last year thinking I'd use it through winter just to get out, get wet and dirty but I've hardly ridden it. Neil built this cellar so I've been into that once – twice a week or more.

What is the appeal of the Sheffield cellars?
It's really good climbing and good moves, it's the epitome of Derbyshire climbing really. In the cellar half the moves you do in there have got to be almost as long as an extended crux on a Peak District route anyway, like the actual flow of moves, depending on the cellar, most of the moves aren't static anyway they are jumping about and moving very very quickly, I enjoy that.

Is it something that people cannot comprehend?
Yes, the guys at work take the mickey out of me something desperate they call me 'Fruit Bat', because I'm a vegetarian and because I hang upside down in cellars, I don't mind, it gives them something to talk about otherwise it would be boring at work.

Is it true that all the Sheffield climbers like the cellar because they can directly compete against one another?
No, there might be some truth in it, I've not been in many cellars. Neils cellar has lots of big holds on it because the other two lads living there climb at E1, E2. It's a contradiction between us, they go in for ten minutes and go around in circles; yet we'll go in and try and work on problems. It's a real contradiction in terms trying to build a cellar that works for both levels.

Do you think a coach could train a climber?
It's interesting to think about but there is still some mental tenacity, a skill to it definitely that you just couldn't teach anybody. But yes, a trainer would improve in general the climbers ability – certainly for someone like me who is basically lazy and should be kicked ass and made to do it. When I was at college in Newcastle, the university employed a guy in the weights training room to coach people, but he knew nothing about climbing and used to make us do things that were totally irrelevant. He would shout at us which is what a lot of people need, but he was shouting at you to do the wrong things and there was almost a clash of personalities.

Do you find the psychological challenge of climbing interesting?
It's a different psychological challenge on sport routes than scary routes, although it is still purely like mind games – you look at a route and think 'shit, there is no way I'm going to get up that' because you know it's hard or you know there is a long succession of hard moves, and if you hit one of the holds wrong then you can't correct it, so you're going to fall off anyway. The actual stakes are a lot lower, you may fall off, swing around you may bang your knee or something, but you're not going to die or break a leg, I do enjoy that.

Do you find hard climbs scary?
Some of them are. Not so much scary, intimidating rather than scary. It's the same old thing, going into the unknown, no matter how far apart the bolts are – it's so hard to hang on, or hard to do the moves, it is intimidating because of that but when you're going for a redpoint you don't even think about that it just seems to disappear.

Do you enjoy bold routes which are unprotected?
I did ARCHANGEL – that took a lot of doing for me, I don't like that, my feet slipped and I was half way up, I pinched onto the arete so hard that it probably left a thread there now for everyone else – I absolutely shit myself - that really sticks out in my mind. Once when I was trying to climb an E1, I convinced myself that if I fell off I was going to hit this tree and die, so I physically made myself calm down and climb on. I thought 'well you may as well fall off trying to do it that fall off here stuck like a lemon!' Looking back at it I would have swung about in mid air anyway.

Did you enjoy the experience of ARCHANGEL, did it put you off?
Yes it's a big rush, even now to go back and do it again I would probably find it scary because I'd think about that while I'm doing it.

Is that enjoyable or just more of a challenge?
It's enjoyable in a perverse sort of way, pervertedly enjoyable. It's like driving a motor bike and you're going a little bit faster than you think you are, you're half way around a corner and realise it's too late and you suddenly get that surge – that's enjoyable even though you realise how dangerous it really is. When you come back and sit down with a cup of tea, you think shit, I shouldn't do that! At the time it's different, it's an acquired taste almost. I could go out now and get really scared on HVS. I've been out bouldering with Robin and he's soloed some routes like E4 5c's, he's strong minded enough to think well if it's 5c I can do it so I'll just get on and carry on, whereas I'm thinking that I don't really know, I'm a bit wiffy in a way like that.

Is being at the sharp end a very personal, isolated feeling?
While you're actually climbing, yes because you're so intense in what you're doing. When I'm psyching up before I start on a redpoint, then the very slightest little disturbance is enough to put me off, but once I've actually started, unless you're on a rest or a lull and might be chalking up, then you can be put off. You're concentrating so much on what you're doing, you're totally oblivious to what is happening around you.

Is that like sitting an exam paper?
I think it has a lot of parallels with things like that – the initial panic when you first see the questions and think 'shit, I can't do any of this', and you think sod it and just start, get engrossed and don't notice anybody around. It is a very personal thing when you are actually climbing even though it is a very social thing before and after the route – back slapping and yes you're good as well – it's enjoyable and good fun. One of the best days I've ever had was when both of us did our routes on the same day. It is very good having you're own success but when you can share it with someone else and they're on a high as well it's brilliant!!! – you're both jabbering away and can relate to each other.

Do you feel after you've had a good day that you want to go and get rat-arsed?
maybe on a Saturday morning I'll think 'if I do this I'm going to get drunk it will be brilliant' and then you do it and think shit, if I don't get drunk I might be able to do this harder route or that route say. As soon as you've done it, the high might last for a couple of hours or a couple of days, but then the jubilation wears off and you need to do something else, you're always looking for the next one, the harder one, the ultimate test of your ability.

Is it addictive?
Yes I'm totally addicted to that high when everything comes right, you spend ages dogging a route – three times out of eight you get the move right yet fall off the next one, then when you actually do redpoint it, everything goes right. Certainly for me if I get one of the holds wrong I'll fall off.

Do you think you'll ever get bored with that addiction?
Maybe, it is very hard to say, at the moment I would say definitely no, but I might change. I have been addicted to other sports but never for as long as climbing.

How does getting married and having children appeal, two up two down?
I think that's a different country at the moment. The reason for getting a house would be to get one with a really big good cellar, it's very childlike in a way, but that's the scene around here.

Claudia Dunn

It is quite ironic that the first ever climbing competition held in Britain in 1989, was won by Claudie, a French girl from just outside of Paris. Claudie moved here when doing a degree in English and ended up staying here. She has never sought fame or press for her efforts, and has now been at the top level of women's climbing in Britain for almost 10 years. Her voice remains unmistakably French, yet her manner is quite English. On the rock she still climbs 7b quite regularly and has shown the way forward for other women by climbing OBSESSION 7b+. All British climbers have been indebted to her for translating the Jean Pierre Bouvier French guide in 1982, and thereby opening up France for easy exploration.

Interview 22.1.91 Glossop, Derbyshire.

When did you start climbing?
I was 19 years old, I would have liked to start earlier but my parents were not very keen for me to join any clubs or go on courses, yet they were mountaineers. They had plenty of books about mountaineering in the house so I read all those when I was a kid and I really wanted to go climbing.
Is that condition still the same in France?
It's a question of responsibility, if you are under 18 you can't do any sort of activity unless your parents allow you to do so. Now with the development of rock climbing it is not seen as a risk sport as much as mountaineering was in my parents days. In those days even when I started at 19 it was more like snow plodding.
Where did you go when you started climbing?
First to the Alps, but more importantly it's where I heard of Fontainebleau. I then bought myself a pair of climbing boots, a pair of EB's and really enjoyed it. It is only when I came to Britain that I discovered rock climbing as a sport in itself.
Did you finish your degree in England?
Yes, I finished it at the end of that year, fortunately for me I had met Ian, and didn't want to go back to France. As Ian doesn't speak French he wouldn't be able to get a job, and I'm not going to work and let him go off climbing everyday because he can't get a job!
Did you realise all the good climbing there was in France?
No, I had no idea because at the time before I came here I studied at Grenoble university and all they were doing was basically peg pulling. We had to climb free between pieces of protection, but free climbing was really in it's infancy and certainly at university everybody was aiding.

Have you ever been tempted to live back in France?
Maybe yes, but I'm happy going back to France on holiday.

When you started climbing in England, did you feel you were the only woman climbing, or have there always been other women?
I remember that there wasn't really any, but in some ways it never surprised me because I think at that time in France, there weren't many either.

Has it surprised you that more women have taken up climbing in France than in England?
No. I think it's a question of safety, because there weren't many women climbing in France until the big development of bolted climbing. I think the safety factor is directly linked to it.

Do you think it's a shame in France that's happened?
No.
Did you ever enjoy natural protected routes?
Yes, I did at first, I found it really exciting after having been doing all this peg pulling around Grenoble, I felt really that added a new dimension to it, it took me a while to understand the bolts.

Did you think all the British must be mad?
No, I thought they were very pure, very ethical.
Have you ever found yourself seriously lacking strength in climbing?
Yes all the time.

Does being light and nimble make up for that?
No. On vertical ground I obviously find it quite easy, but now all the hard routes are grossly overhanging and require power. It's more a question of power than strength, I probably have the basic strength but it's the power I lack.

What do you get most out of climbing at the moment? Which climbs do you like?
Bolt protected ones at Malham.

Can you see yourself ever climbing 8a?
I really don't know. I find it difficult to speak about grades because for example on Main Overhang which is 7c+ I felt quite close to getting it. I didn't think it was that hard, then I go on some 7b's which are very overhanging and I can't move on them so maybe I'll do an 8a but it will have to be one on really tiny crimps, a certain type of climb. The same with the women in the continent they don't do many 8a climbs except those with small holds which aren't too steep.

Would you like to see more women climbers?

Yes, I think women in general would benefit. It was quite interesting last year, we had an activity day at the school I work at. I took some of the girls out and I was amazed, they all wanted to try it because they know I'm involved in it and didn't think for once that it was a boys sport. They all wanted to have a go at it so I think it is very psychological this barrier, and as a sport it's quite suited to women.

Has soloing ever appealed to you?

No, well I've done a few things, easy stuff but nothing serious. If someone else gets a kick out of it – it's alright, they can do it. But I think it's bound to go wrong some day, I can remember quite a few climbers who fell off easy climbs whilst soloing, it can happen to anybody, even the very best.

What for you is the most important aspect of climbing?

Enjoyment, that's why I won't do things I don't enjoy doing just for the sake of building a reputation or whatever.

What sort of moves interest you the most?

It's just one of those things you can't really say, you manage to hook your foot somewhere and make the move really easy and it's really satisfying. There is this element, a bit like playing chess, sussing out the sequence.

What other interests apart from climbing do you have?

I haven't had time for any. In between a full time job which requires quite a lot of commitment, and climbing, that's it. Every evening I've got a plan of what I'm doing, such as work or training, and I can't do anything else out of that, you have to sleep sometime.

Being a teacher, would you like to teach climbing at all?

Well, I think it's a bit of a dodgy area. I think it's too much of a risk sport, a once in a blue moon activity. To get the kids out for one day is alright, but I wouldn't like to do it on a regular basis, I think too many things can happen. Kids or even adults are pretty silly sometimes, when you're a teacher you have to be so very, very careful, thinking about everyone but yourself, and to that extent I wouldn't enjoy the climbing so much.

Do you think climbing is a thing that you should start of your own accord rather than be taught?

That's two different things, starting of your own accord is to decide 'Oh I fancy this sport I really want to do it', but then you might want to be taught at the beginning to know what to do. That's what I did because I had absolutely no idea of how to go about it. I think you should go on one or two courses to begin with, but not more than that, otherwise you're going to spend the rest of your like being guided by somebody, and that's no good.

Have you ever thought of giving up your job as a teacher to climb more?

Yes, all the time, but it would be very difficult really, I had so many years as a student where I had to live on nothing, without all these material things that we have now, I just couldn't give up the money now.

Was there any time that you thought you could be a professional climber?

No.

Not even after winning at Leeds? You won your first climbing competition did that not make you think you could become a world champion.

No. I was lucid enough to see that I was nothing special in world standards, I would have needed to really work very hard at it and even then there are the younger girls coming up behind people like Catherine Destivelle who is very powerful indeed. Also it's difficult not wanting to give up the money that a job brings.

Can you carry on climbing if you have a family?

I don't think so, I really don't. It depends on what standard you can accept, but I'm not interested in climbing at a lower standard, that's the problem. I would feel really really frustrated if I had to go back and climb HVS and find it hard, I think I'd rather stay at home and do something else. It's the big difference between Ian and me. Ian says he'd like to go on climbing because he'd still enjoy it at whatever level he did it, and I think I wouldn't be able to accept it, maybe I'm wrong, maybe I will, but at the moment because I've always improved, I just feel I should be improving all the time.

Do you think you will ever get back into mountain climbing?

No. I think I find rock climbing much more enjoyable. I think I did the wrong thing by going into mountain climbing, I just took what was available at the time and that was mountaineering, I don't think I was meant for it either, I'm far too weak and light for carrying big rucksacks and things like that, I always found it very hard.

Do you think many people go into mountaineering and don't like it and then discover rock climbing?

I think nowadays they wouldn't, but in those days it's quite possible, because it was the be all and end all. Crag climbing was considered a practice for the Alps, and at Fontainebleau you to do the circuits with a big rucksack on your back, typically with big leather boots, running around the boulders and climbing up and down as fast as possible. People used to time themselves doing things like that. It just seems simply ludicrous nowadays but there are still people doing it.

Did you find many friends from mountaineering in France or in France are mountaineers and rock climbers separate?

Well nowadays they are very separate, but when I was at university, as I said we used to practice cragging as a preparation for mountaineering, so it was the same people who did both. I think they recognise each other.

Do you like crags that are busy or crags that are quiet?

Usually the crags that I climb are good crags, and therefore they are busy. But it's not because they are busy that I like them. I like Malham Cove but always feel very self conscious, when I'm trying to redpoint something and I know that I have 20 pairs of eyes watching me.

Does that affect you?

Sometimes it makes me feel nervous but on the other hand it's much harder to wimp out of doing a move when you know that so many people are watching you and will take the piss out of you if you don't do it, so it has advantages too, but in competitions that is certainly one element which bothers me a bit, at Lyon there was that big stadium absolutely full of people and I felt really inadequate about it. I came 26th which was a terrible result, I'd been freezing in the isolation room, it was terrible, really badly organised.

When you go to France do you get tempted by the lovely restaurants, booze and eat all day instead of go climbing?

I hardly booze at all and being a vegetarian I can't find any French restaurant that caters for me so I don't get very tempted.

Does the slate in Wales appeal to you?

No. I don't like the look of it, it looks horrible, I don't like a dark crag it's really off putting.

Have you ever injured yourself climbing?

Yes, many times. I broke my wrist on Altrincham wall. I took my teeth out on SOMETHING STUPID at Malham. I fell off with the rope in my teeth and they just went flying out, (the route was called SOMETHING STUPID 7a+) Last year I injured a tendon in my finger that's why I couldn't take part in Squawk's competition and I couldn't climb at all for about 6 weeks, after that it took me absolutely ages to get back to normal. I've had injured elbows, knees and feet, all sorts of ailments.

What's been the most enjoyable point of your climbing life?

When I did OBSESSION 7b+, I was really happy to do that route.

For any particular reasons?

Competition I suppose!

OBSESSION 7b+ at Malham Cove, in the middle of the crux, a stamina test of finger endurance.

There are very few young climbers coming up through the grades in British climbing at the moment, however Jasper is proving to be the most influential and committed to climbing. Born and brought up in Lewes, East Sussex has made it very difficult to get out climbing, but with the help from his very enthusiastic mother he has climbed in Derbyshire and had three trips to Buoux. With a good summer on the sandstone of Kent and Sussex he repeated KINDA LINGERS 8a, and COOL BANANAS 8a+, still whilst he was 15, and very soon after put up his first hard route at High Rocks SECOND GENERATION 8a, one of the most impressive lines on Sandstone. He then went on to re-climb the route BOONOONOONOONOOS 8a after holds broke off. Now at 16 he has given up school to take a full time career in climbing.

Interview 29.12.90 Crown Inn, Groombridge, Kent.

When did you first start climbing?

When I was 10, I went walking in the Lake District and I always kept running off and scrambling up little bits of rock. Mum then decided that I ought to learn properly before I hurt myself, so I went on a 3 day course with a guide in the Lakes and it took off from there.

Did you try other sports?

I tried loads of different sports, I was quite good at most but didn't really enjoy them. I did quite a lot of horse riding, became good at it but found it boring. I was good at running and the school tried to get me to go into cross country competitions but I didn't want to do that. I won the school titles but I didn't take it seriously so I didn't really try.

Did the school offer any climbing facilities?

Not at all, they didn't understand what I was talking about, they thought I wanted to go and walk up the mountains. In the 4th year when I was already climbing quite hard E4 or so, they organised these trips off to Wales where they did abseiling and jumping into rivers and stuff. Well I then twisted my back when I was climbing and therefore couldn't play football for a while. The sports teacher suggested that I come on the Welsh trip. They would be top roping Diffs and things and it became increasingly difficult to explain that I was climbing about 25 grades harder than they could even conceive or even imagine. So after that I kept away from school sport in general and got really stuck into the climbing on the sandstone.

Did you just get the urge to climb?

I always enjoyed walking quite a lot but as soon as I started climbing it was so much more fun, then walking was just boring.

Did leading at that age interest you?

Not for the first year. We did a couple of V Diffs in the Lake District. They were so different from sandstone, trying to find the route. I found it very daunting but then when we went to the Peaks and climbed on the gritstone, that's when I took off. I went from V Diff. to VS in a day, I was about 12 and then in the same summer I lead my first E1 which was THREE PEBBLE SLAB at Froggatt.

Did you appreciate that it was dangerous?

No, not really at all. I'd fail on VS's because they were steep but I could climb quite hard slab routes and did them easily, I never got pumped on the slabs and never even thought about falling off.

Has danger a larger effect on you now?

Oh yes, I don't think I'd do the routes that I did then now. I lead CHALKSTORM when I was 13 and I thought it was E1, and my second extreme, it only got the grade E1 because you were meant to put a side runner. I didn't realise that so I solo'd it and for that it gets E4.

Then when you were 14 you discovered bolt protected climbs. Do you wish you had found them later on?

No, not at all, I wish I'd had started even earlier. As soon as I started on bolted climbs I began enjoying the climbing a lot more, well certainly leading anyway. Being able to climb something steep and not worry about falling off was a big step forward.

Were there any climbers that you respected?

The scene had no effect on me and I was completely isolated by living in the South East.

What made you try to free climb the aid route at High Rocks?

It was Neil Greshams influence generally I think. I was climbing quite well but not really trying hard routes because I knew they were too hard for me. Neil said I could and encouraged me to try some of the harder routes. I'd done the classic 6a's like FANDANGO, DIGITALIS and HATE. Neil put a rope on the hard routes and I did TEMPTATION 6b the next week, and SANDMAN 6b first go, routes which I'd never of thought of trying. Then when Neil and I were in France together at Buoux he told me about the possibility of the old aid route at High Rocks. We got back and I tried it, it was sandy and horrible. So then Gary Wickham painted it up with this special stuff, a sort of invisible resin sealant which he discovered, working in the antique restoration trade. Dave Turner was trying it and managed to get to the last move 8 times, I went down and as Gary had a rope on it I tried it and fell off. It was a lot easier though with the resin hardened holds, you could actually grip something. I knew that if I left it Dave would do it, so with one last final power surge I did it.

Now you've repeated it, do you find it as hard?

No, it's quite easy now, a bit like COOL BANANAS. It too me five days to do that climb but then the next time I did it, well it was very easy. I think it's because of the tension before doing a route, once I've done it I'm relaxed and climb so much better.

Can you see yourself staying in full time climbing?

Its very difficult to say, my body might grow in different ways but at the moment it's almost perfect for climbing; 6ft tall, 9½ stone and 28 ins. waist. I'm motivated and hope that I continue to improve. Competitions inspire me and having climbed 7c+ in France I've got confidence to do well, I must be able to. But in terms of hard routes 8b+ and 8c they're still some way off. I'll start training when I stop getting better at climbing.

Overleaf: The most powerful line on Kent sandstone, SECOND GENERATION 8a, High Rock's.

John Hart

John Hart, a classic old timer of British climbing, but nevertheless hanging in there at 8a+. John was born 3.1.53 at Holmfirth near Huddersfield in Yorkshire. Whilst studying medicine at Liverpool he climbed and pioneered in the Merseyside sandstone quarries. He was a major developer of new routes and HART'S ARETE 6b, in the 70's was well ahead of its time. At 37 he climbs very enthusiastically and has put up new 8a+'s in Cheedale. His interests are very varied, from playing the Violin at an early age, to now being a full time G.P. running a contemporary Art Gallery, a collector of Victorian line engraved stamps and climbing guide book writer.

Interview with John Hart, 10.1.91, Nottingham.

When did you first develop an interest in climbing?

When I was about 17-18. I'd done a lot of fell walking at school which I thought was great, then I remember going to the Huddersfield public library and getting Boningtons 'I Chose

To Climb.' I read that, and was absolutely hooked, it was fantastic, definitely what I wanted to do.

Did you go straight to university from school?

Yes, I studied medicine at Liverpool.

Did thoughts of climbing as a career appeal to you?

No, I don't think I ever thought of that. Then it was different to the careers that Jerry Moffatt or even Ron Fawcett have enjoyed. The people who made climbing a career either went into instructing, or they had a shop, or they were full time Himalayan climbers rubbing two pennies together. Bonington was about, but even he wasn't regarded as a career climber, I don't think. I never really thought of climbing as a career, and I only actually started climbing just before university anyway.

Were you fixed on your career in medicine, or did you have other interest that were strong?

No, I think if you take medicine at university you are going to be a doctor. A lot of people aren't as it turns out, but at eighteen that's the way you look at it when you pass all your

exams. Other things that I could have done were possibly music, but that went out early on in grammar school. I took the academic avenue and even though I enjoy music now, I'm quite convinced that that would have been the wrong thing to do.

Do you find yourself an oddity amongst climbers; a career minded Doctor, an Art Dealer and climbing grade eight?

One thing about climbers is that nobody seems odd in it, it doesn't matter whether you're a Bank Manager, a Doctor, or a Dustbin Man, that all seems to be forgotten when you start climbing. It's one of the things that I really like, the characters of different people. I must say in defence of all this stuff, you keep reading from the older generations about 'things ain't what they used to be.' I think there's a better atmosphere and certainly a happier more enjoyable spirit amongst sports climbers now than there has been for a long time. Climbing got quite nasty about 10 years ago when it became very competitive and consequently very dangerous. Now people encourage others to do the climbs that they have already done.

Was that evident when you were taking up climbing or were you then obsessed by sheer climbing?

It's so long ago it's difficult to remember. Competition has always been there, how healthy it was when I started I can't remember. What has always been the same is that it didn't seem to matter who you were and what you did. I think that classlessness in a very class conscious country like Britain was certainly one point which made climbing quite special.

I've heard you say in the past that you like doing things well, why didn't you become a surgeon?

No, I had no aspirations to be a surgeon, I just wanted to do a reasonably good job. People think that medicine is a great vocation, I think a lot of people do it because that is the way it goes, it's a job that they are interested in, and want to do reasonably well. I'm not the best doctor in the world, but I'm not the worst. I think you can do it well but it is a job at the same time. It isn't something that is going to devour my whole existence.

Do you get a similar enjoyment from climbing or is it something very separate?

Very separate. I can't compare them at all. When I get out climbing I just forget everything that frustrates or stresses me in medicine. Sometimes you're thinking about climbing when you're bored in a dull part of the surgery. Seeing your sixth kid with a cold that morning; you may be working through the moves on a route listening to the chest! You have to watch that you don't miss anything!

Does it ever work the other way that you may be frustrated by your fifteenth week on a route and you get frustrated that you cannot do the climb?

Do I think about medicine when I'm climbing? No, not generally.

Does climbing ever frustrate you like work?

Yes it does, but if I'm climbing badly or I'm weak or fat or something like that I tend to think 'how can I get around that and do positive things to get around it.' You can in climbing because you're dealing with yourself. There is only you there and it's you that's too fat, you that's too weak and you that's a total bumbly. You can deal with those problems. But you can't deal with the massive bureaucracy which weighs down on you head in medicine. That's what frustrates me about work, the bureaucracy of it, certainly not the patients, I can cope with them. If I've got someone who is ill; or if I felt that someone needs a bit more care or was depressed, then I can see them again, I can deal with that. If I don't know the scientific answers or the medical answers to a problem, I can ring someone up and ask. What I find stressful

about work, is the fact for example that you can't get someones hip replacement done or you can't get a home help for someone who needs one – that sort of thing. So the frustrations are quite different. The frustrations that you can deal with yourself are fine.

Have you ever felt that your duty might be to do study more and devote your experience to helping climbers with their injuries?

No. I think the reason probably is that I'm more interested in Art and more interested in the art side of life generally. I'm not disinterested in medicine but I'm not interested enough to spend any more of my time doing it. You've only got one life. If I had twenty lives I'd probably spend one doing concentrated medicine. I wouldn't want to spend all that time doing one thing though, it doesn't interest me enough. I'd love to do a degree in art history but....that's life.

What things do you do in your life now, which are important to you?

Firstly it's wife and kids, they're the most important. I'm a full time G.P., we also run a contemporary, commercial art gallery. Now my wife has given up teaching full time to deal with the administrative side of that, and it is a great passion, we actually end up feeling quite responsible for both the customers and the people you represent because you're representing several painters and potters with international reputations and their income depends on the work they sell, they are good enough not to need us but at the same time we've got a good relationship with them and the more you do for them the better. Ultimately I'd like to be able to devote more time to the Art gallery.

Do you find any similarity between these artists and climbers?

They are both interesting people, which in reality 90% of people aren't. The people that are very good are absolutely single minded. Similar to Jerry or Ben, they have nothing else in their life, nothing else exists for them but climbing, and it's the same for painters. They work long and hard at painting and succeeding at what they are doing is very much their aim.

Have you had that ambition in either climbing or art?

No, not really because I'm always looking at the other side of the fence and that always appears a bit greener. At times I wonder just what I could do if I did nothing but climb. I can go for a fortnights holiday in France and I'm climbing better at the end of it – I wonder where I could take myself to. I would not be a Moffatt a Nadin or a Johnny Dawes, I don't think. But I could certainly be a lot better, I'd love to find out quite how much.

Do you feel that young climbers now who are attracted to sports climbing will be missing out?

Yes, because probably the things I've climbed in the past are so easy; but they didn't seem it at the time. A lot of people say that 'sports climbers miss all the days and the fun we had, crashing cars through gates, climbing in the rain and hitching till you were soaked to the skin.....' But I'm sure they have their laughs, hitch down to the South of France, do daft things and get away with it by the skin of their teeth. I think there is still a death wish in a lot of young climbers, I know a 19 year old sports climber, he's done things like soloing DREAM OF WHITE HORSES at Gogarth. It's not particularly hard but it's still inherently dangerous.

Have you done much soloing?

Not a lot. A modest amount, mainly on grit, nothing of note on limestone.

Is soloing to you an important part of climbing?

No. I wish I had the bottle to do it, but I don't think I'll ever get the bottle now. The few things I have soloed were fun but I found them too frightening really. I've got quite a vivid imagination and I can imagine things breaking off or things going wrong. Possibly at the time I did a bit of soloing I was working on intensive care and when you see someone who has fallen off a ladder from 10 feet and you're sticking a tube into him to ventilate him, it does actually affect you. I've seen some pretty horrible things in intensive care. You hear of climbers falling quite long distances and then you know that afternoon you'd been working to try and save someones life and they've really just fallen off a ladder, you pause and think.

Do other doctors feel that climbers are an irresponsible part of society?

I'm sure some doctors do but I'm sure half the population does anyway. You will always get people in society trying to make our very existence 100% safe. You end up with a ridiculous situation like in America where you can be in trouble for almost breathing in the wrong place. Where are we going in society if we end up like that? I think people should be entitled.....even down to cigarettes, I will encourage patients not to smoke, but if a patient turns around and says 'well I actually enjoy smoking, I know all the risks and I just want to carry on,' I do think, that is their privilege and right. I might not agree with it, but it is their right.

When you were 36 you did your first 8a+, did you feel that was a strike for pensioners?

Comments were made about my age, but only then did I suddenly become conscious of it. It made the ascent a bit more important, and it also made one or two good climbers open their eyes a bit.

Where in France has climbing been most enjoyable for you?

I suppose Buoux and Volx. Volx has got big holds....I just like France. It's a wonderful place, I like the climate, I like mediaeval villages, I like the ambiance, all the lyrical side of it.

What about the people?

I get on alright with most of them. We have a little house in Cereste and the villagers there are really friendly.

What about the future climbing wise?

I'd like to climb harder so I can do 8a's quicker.

Do you take your family climbing wherever you go?

Yes, we always go as a family. I try and get 26 hours out of a day because I do like to spend time with the kids when I'm on holiday. Working routes and red-pointing hard routes, absolutely suits me down to the ground because you can't saunter up hard routes, you don't climb every day like you used to. The rest days are good for playing with the kids.

Is it good for climbing that families now come to sports crags?

I certainly can't see it does any harm, for years I thought the feeling of climbing in France was great. You go to Fontainebleau on a Sunday and there is not only mum and the kids out climbing, there is grandma as well. It's great, it's a day out doing a sport like people might go out bike riding in the Peak. I don't see that can do any harm. I'm not suggesting that the cliff should be crowded with climbers, there is a dichotomy of what is best for climbing here. Large numbers of people climbing is never going to be a healthy thing in Britain. The solitude of it is a problem already say in Cheedale at weekends, but that's all part of the fun. It's great to be out with all the lads but I love to go down to Cheedale on my half day when there is Seb, Craig, Mark and Ben, and then a group of them walks off somewhere else and you're just left with two of you on a route.

Doctor Hart's own route THEORIA 8a+ tucked away in the corner of The Nook, Cheedale. A route with at least four dyno's, going up a 40° overhanging wall.

Nick Dixon

Born 24.2.63 at Middlesbrough, Nick did most of his early climbing on the sandstone outcrops of the North Yorkshire Moors. Alongside Ian Dunn and Paul Ingham he put up many new routes and set a name for himself as a climber who did bold leads. He then started a climbing journal called 'Rock Action' which only lasted one issue but nevertheless laid the foundation for Ed Douglas to start the now successful magazine ON THE EDGE. From there he moved to Stoke and became an activist on The Roaches in Staffordshire. He put up many E6 climbs such as CATASTROPHE INTERNATIONALE E5 6c, and A FIST FULL OF CRYSTALS E6 6b; which now have received excellent status. His finest achievement was the new route on Cloggy in Wales called FACE MECCA E9 6c, in 1989, which confirms his great reputation for climbing the bolder routes.

Interview 17.1.91 Dewsbury, Yorkshire.

Where did you get your first interest in climbing from?

Well as you know Dave I'm pretty old, and when I started climbing it wasn't really the kind of footbally sport that it is now, it wasn't the high profile sport that it is now and it had much more mountaineering type connotations. I think I became attracted to the sport really through hill walking - massively traditional. I went away hill walking with the school and with my mum and dad, and gradually grew to love the countryside, and being in the open wilds. I was looking for those things that I was good at which would take me to the countryside, and where I had a good group of mates around me. I think climbing was the first place that I really got to grips with that.

Had you always towed the line when you were at school or were you a rebel?

A classic cliche climber response – The Rebel? I don't think I was a rebel, I think I was a pretty timid kid actually in some ways, I think it would have looked from the outside like I was a bit of a rebel really at times, I was involved in some quite gnarly things but probably then I cooled down as I did my various exams. I don't think I was as much of a rebel as people thought, but, I was actually very easily influenced all through my schooling.

Did you do well academically?

I actually broke my leg skiing just before my 'O' levels and I think I would have done appallingly had I not done that. I was just getting into climbing, I'd read a book about John Gill the legendary American boulderer and was training like hell at the age of 15 to try and do a one arm pull up, purely because I'd read about John Gill, I didn't actually realise

that this didn't have a great deal to do with climbing. I was training like mad at school to do this one arm pull up and then I broke my leg skiing; so I had to jack in any physical activity for quite a while. That was the Christmas of my 5th year at school, so I then worked for probably about 4 months bloody hard, I didn't have anything else I could do really, I was hobbling around a bit but I couldn't go out cragging, I couldn't do what I wanted to do. I did well at 'O' level age, then did badly at 'A' levels, but I did enough to go through to Poly. By that time I was completely into climbing, it was the centre of my life. I went to Poly. entirely to climb, and was looking possibly to being thrown out at the end of the first year, I wasn't really bothered. I got involved with Andy Popp, Allen Williams, Steve Lowe and various other people, we had a really good group of people at Stoke. Somehow I managed to stay in college, I don't really know in retrospect how, I did very little work in the first two years, but I suppose that's why my climbing really became quite fruitful.

What did you end up with at college?

To begin with I ended up with a '2.1' in combined science which was geology and chemistry. I then went on and did a small amount of research, a year starting an M Phil. and then jacked that in at the end of the year. I worked for a year as an instructor which was part time so I was spending the rest of my time

climbing, and taking kids out climbing and canoeing and what have you. Then immediately after that I went to Oxford university to do a PGCE which is just a teaching qualification. That was getting into Oxford by the back door. There again I met some really good people through climbing, I think if I was to now put the greatest value of my climbing in retrospect, one of the really large things that it's given me is making friends immediately when I've moved to an area. I think that's quite important.

Have they always been hard climbers you've met?

Usually they have but I don't think that's necessarily anything to do with it. When I went to college E5 was hard and very few people climbed it. A lot of the people I met at college were E1 type of climbers, but that was the sort of people they were, they were really good people, really honest, really trustable, really genuine; and I think that's the most important thing I've drawn from my climbing life.

Is honesty an important part of climbing do you think?

I think it's incidental, you do meet very honest people through climbing for some reason. I think people are very honest not only about the things around them, but about themselves. I think it puts you in a situation where you have to trust people, and often you make light of things that I suppose could be quite serious. I think it brings people together and honesty is probably one of the great things that comes out of it; honesty with yourself, not necessarily with other people.

Is honesty within yourself a realisation which contributes to making you a very good climber? i.e. knowing how good you are at certain things.

I've realised that what I'm saying should apply to me, about all these honest people I've met, all these marvellous... Well really I don't consider myself to be very honest and I think another major aspect about the climbing is your ego. The ego that drives you to do ever harder routes, both for self fulfillment and recognition from other sources, the media, what have you. You actually start to develop a lack of honesty within yourself, because of the attention you get, not necessarily from the media but from your peers around you, the admiration for doing this route or that route. I think that you begin to not really realise what you are being honest about and what you aren't being honest about. Certainly I can think of times when I've not known exactly why I've been drawn into climbing.

Have you had long lasting friends from climbing?

Definitely, Andy Popp was an usher at my wedding and a very, very close mate. Allen Williams I still see, we all actually arrived at Stoke together, purely by luck. I don't see Steve Lowe often, but I can imagine bumping into him and instantly being good mates. I think even if I don't see these people month in, month out it doesn't really matter, they're very close friends and long lasting. I also met Tam in the hills, the girl who is now my wife.

Do they climb bold routes like yourself?

Certainly Andy Popp does very bold climbs and I always say Andy is probably one of the boldest climbers I have ever known. At one stage in his climbing when he was probably only leading E4, he was certainly soloing E3. I don't think that is necessarily admirable, in fact it's a bit foolish really, but there is no question that Andy is a very bold climber.

Does it worry you having such a good friend when you know exactly, how dangerously near the edge he obviously goes?

Not at all, but having said that, the only time it ever worried me was last summer (1990). In 1986 I did a new route down the Churnet called ONE CHROMOSOME IS MISSING which initially I gave E6. I think probably it's gone up to E7, it involves a few 6b moves probably 60 foot above the ground with no protection. Andy was there when I did the first ascent and top roped it back in 86, I know he was very keen then, he managed to top rope the route and was really keen but he decided that he wasn't in the mood to solo it. Last year he started going out there again early on and I knew he was going to do it, I'd speak to him on the phone and I knew he was getting nearer and nearer and that was the first time I've ever felt for anyone else. I felt a bit responsible because I'd sown the seed of wanting to do that route, and these routes are mental routes, you can't compare them with modern power routes, they're not the same game, it's about being able to perform when you're scared.

Is being scared an appealing part of climbing to you?

I don't think it's being scared, I think it's not being scared, when you should be scared. Beforehand you realise just how frightening the situation should be, or just how dangerous the situation is. But when you're actually doing it, and especially when you've practiced it, I find it a bit of a paradox. You know a route well enough to be able to flow up it, knowing the moves very well, being able to flow from hold to hold almost in safety: yet knowing you're on really hard ground and knowing that a fall could be a catastrophe, death or at least a broken leg situation. I think that gives you a really elated feeling, both while you are doing it and when you finish. The last 2 years I've got very involved in sport climbing which I really enjoy, I think there's massive positive points to it but the same paradox doesn't apply. You do feel the flow when you work a route really well, and know how to do it; you can really flow on those moves, really difficult moves. I feel the same flow, but I don't feel the same elation of doing it as when it's dangerous, and being so confident to be able to do it, when it's so dangerous. I feel you really have to peak that bit more.

Do you do any on-sight solos?

Very rarely, it's not my game. I try and avoid soloing, I always have. I had an acquaintance who got killed soloing, and I was around at the time. Certainly it made me decide that soloing was a bad thing for me, at the time the people around were making such a deal about soloing, and there was so much admiration for people who soloed hard routes that I felt very much, that if I soloed a route, certainly I shouldn't tell anybody, because then people might solo routes for the admiration and I think that is a disaster. I have done things in the past, purely because of the admiration that I would or wouldn't get. I think your ego takes over and if someone dies through that, it is very sad.

Is that ego in your life diminishing fast as you get older?

I've got other things in life now which perhaps I didn't have 5 years ago. I don't think it diminishes, but I think it changes. You become less bothered about what people think about you, whereas 5 years ago I was very bothered, though I would never have admitted it. I think now I am genuinely less bothered. If anything I feel that now I would like to do some bold climbing again, but all the time you have a conflict in your mind, you aren't really sure

Nick Dixon with Johnny Dawes at base camp, Pete's Eats in Llanberis.

why you're doing these things. If you take a famous piece of climbing like, FACE MECCA, which received a lot of press afterwards; I have to ask myself why was I so drawn to that route. It is very difficult for me to decide in my mind whether I was drawn to that route because I loved the line; I loved the moves; I wanted to do it; or I wanted to be the person up there doing it and couldn't have given a toss who knew and who didn't know. In retrospect now a few years on that is actually how I see it. At the time or a week later I would certainly have questioned whether I was doing it for the media attention. I think Johnny Dawes comes across this, I think a lot of people do, it's very difficult to differentiate what you're doing for the people around you, not just your immediate peers, but the whole climbing movement and what your doing for yourself.

By still climbing you've proved the point that climbing is something you do for yourself, do you think you will climb forever?
Yes I do, I don't think I'll climb competitively forever, but definitely hope to climb competitively again obviously. I'm injured at the moment and hope for that to clear. I will climb forever because I get so much joy from going out. I get so much joy from the friendships I've made through climbing, there is nothing else which gives me quite so much joy and complete gay abandon. What's going on in the world around you is of no consequence when you're up there, it's a gorgeous day and you can go for a swim or you can do a few routes, it's all there!

How could you explain Cloggy to the Limestone 'Bolt Addict' who thinks it is somewhere in the clouds?
Well I'd say 'it is,' your right! I don't think I'd try, I think if you go and feel it and know the history of the cliff, then you either feel it or you don't. To explain it is to ruin it; some people love it, others hate it. It doesn't matter, nobody's any the worst for either of those. I'm very proud of my climbing on Cloggy and I think my ego doesn't control me so much now, so I'm quite prepared to say I'm very proud of some of the climbs I've done on it. For me it's the centre of my climbing, not the routes but the place.

When you say the history, is it because of the people that have climbed well there?
Yes, It's also I think I've never been to Cloggy and not remembered everything I've done right the way through the day. Whether that's a reflection of how I feel about Cloggy or how Cloggy affects me, could be going in either direction, but there is an input from the cliff, and there's an input from me to the cliff. I'm not sure in which direction I can feel that, but

even the very first visit I went up there I can remember everything, every route, it's just a magical place.

Is there any point in linking it to your childhood?
No. But it can be linked with my very early climbing, I climbed in Wales with Squawk (Ian Dunn) and with Paul Ingham and old Adam, I can link it to that time.

Do you remember any particular days from those times or particular trips?
Well my first day on Cloggy I was climbing with somebody called Adam Haynes. I believe I led my first E4 pitch which was the second pitch of Great Wall, we did WALSH'S GROOVE, WEST BUTTRESS ELIMINATE E3 5c, SHADOW E3 5c, CLOGGY CORNER HVS, and also did THE BOLDEST E3 5c; all in one day and I was only climbing E3. so obviously days like that leave a massive impression on you, the cliff becomes very important. You have to walk up and walk down, there are the beautiful views and the sun setting just as you're walking down it's a magical place.

That magic touches you?
Absolutely no question. Often in hilly areas I'll spend a lot of time on an abseil rope working moves and I believe the achievement when you've worked a move is magnificent. You may go bouldering, there's boulders below Cloggy and you'll perhaps boulder for hours but I think to be in that place doing it, just makes it so much more fulfilling.

Is Cloggy your favourite cliff?
When I think of cliffs I think of climbing, and whilst Cloggy is my favourite cliff for it's atmosphere, it's climbing and where it is; it's views and feeling, I have other cliffs which I'm probably equally in love with. The place I've always loved is the lower tier of The Roaches at the left hand end but it's only a 15 foot crag, probably 100 yards long that overhangs 45 degrees. If I had to specifically pick a particular piece of rock, it wouldn't be on Cloggy, it would be there. I love the bouldering there, I love the routes there. Again there's places at Froggatt I really love; places near The Stanage Plantation I really love, Brimham, then there's places on the N. Yorks. Moors. I can look at it as a whole crag, and then we're talking atmosphere, friendships made, friendships to be made, we're talking about the whole place, and then for me we're talking Wales and we're probably talking Cloggy. On another level we're talking about bits of rock where I really love to be and where I love to climb, where you can just remember the smell... I can remember the smell now of the lower tier left of the steps, all the mosses, I have so many memories.

But isn't the excitement of being out there the most important part of climbing?
No, I think climbing is exciting but I think that it is only one percent of climbing's appeal, I think it's more to do with other aspects. I love the texture, the touch of rock, there are so many routes that I've had to memorize so well that you almost understand the geological makeup. There are so many places I can remember hanging on this hold or that hold, and even now I remember how it felt; I can remember how the lichen felt, I can remember how a little undercut feels or how this arete feels; how rounded it is, how to palm it, how best for your hand not to skid off; how the smells come together, how the whole place buzzes, it fills you. Now, I don't really think I've found anything else that fills me like that. Getting good at climbing is an entirely separate thing, the appeal of climbing is right across the board, true it has excitement, but that's only a way of expressing fulfillment to every one of those different aspects, not just adrenalin alone.

You do hard routes in extreme positions; is it a big psychological pressure?
Only in those last few days where you've found that you can do the route, that's because it's no longer purely a project. You've found you can do all the moves, you're starting to link them. You realise that now you're on a dead end course, you can't really turn back now. I'm talking about my two routes in particular FACE MECCA and TENDER HOME COMINGS. Once I'd completed all the moves on both those routes, I knew that ultimately there was no question to my going to have to try and do them. I don't know why, perhaps it's just conditioning from doing it so many times; I knew that I had to progress down the road of eventually being up there without a rope and trying them. I think it's quite a magical trip really. I don't think I slept very well the nights prior to either, partly out of fear but much more out of excitement.

Did you ever feel that after you'd linked all the moves on FACE MECCA, just to leave it?
No. I think had I not been able to do one move I could have done that, but I think I'd have never forgiven myself had I done all the moves, and not gone up and done it. FACE MECCA isn't death, in fact it's quite a safe route. It's a big lob and it's frightening, perhaps skidding down 130 feet of rough slab, but at the end of the day there is no chance of hitting the ground. I take my hat off to Johnny Dawes on his route The INDIAN FACE, to the right of it. I looked at that and actually climbed his route on a top rope, it's a much more dangerous proposition. The moves may be easier but the proposition is a far greater one in that it does risk death, it's a big difference some how.

Stanage Edge in South Yorkshire. The gritstone escarpment has collapsed, tumbling down the hillside and settling to create a climbers paradise – The Plantation Boulders.

The Addicts

'Is there a cure' – 'yes, more of the same' they cried, 'more, more, more!' The inclination, the urge, the bent, the mainliners; if the professionals were the pedlars then these are the addicts. Yet of what, it cannot be climbing for even though they are talented, they are not up there, God like and passing testament. They are down there deep in that spell of climbing, under it's uncanny powers, not always in the sense of doing, but the sense of breathing, living and thinking. There have been very few climbers ever addicted to simply climbing, and they most probably are the best, yet others seem to be caught in the web of self indulgence, enjoying the part of climbing that gives them complete satisfaction. It can be rock both hard and soft, big and small, adventure, seeking the unknown; it can be the abuse, the desecration and the abomination; and it can be the enjoyment of the ambience, the day out and the night in revelry. There is no cure but more, more, more.

Joe Healey

Joe is a very well known climber to those at the top of the sport because of his incredible natural talent on rock. Joe is one of the true characters in British climbing, his attitude has never been serious, except in his determination to have a good time, yet his talent and skill have kept him in touch with the top climbers for over 15 years. Joe was born 18.6.62, just around the corner from Pex Hill Quarry, St. Helens, near Liverpool, where he developed his climbing. He first came to fame in doing repeats of routes like LONDON WALL E6, LORD OF THE FLIES E6, when he was 17. Along with Phil Davidson, he developed Pex Hill on Merseyside to one of the most prominent bouldering areas of the early eighties. Over the past 10 years he has climbed a lot on indoor walls and is regarded as one of the best wall specialists in the country, as well as being a formidable on-sight climber.

Interview 6.1.91. Meersbrook, Sheffield.

What made you first start climbing?
I used to go birds egg'in years ago, into climbing trees and camping at Helsby, just South of Liverpool. We scrambled up the rocky gullies since my brother had done a bit of climbing. After that I went for a cycle ride to Pex Hill, a quarry just down the road when I was 14, then fell into it from there.

Were you naturally good at climbing when you started?
I was a natural, yes. I had no brain and was really light. There were other more powerful lads, I was better in building technique, more of a technician.

Did your interest in climbing grow fast?
Yes it did, I was into it straight away. I read every mag, every book; I even missed a few of my 'O' levels. On the day of the Art 'O' level exam, I went to Pex Hill as it was sunny and a really good climbing day.

Do you regret that?
No, not really, I'm sat here earning 500 quid a week, drinking beer with some good fellas, nothing wrong with that.

When did you leave school?
When I was 15, with 7 CSE's.

Did you go straight into a job?
Yes, youth opportunity, that kind of thing. I had about 20 to 30 jobs in the first five to six years, which was because I used to pack in and climb every summer.

In starting at Pex, was that good bouldering training?
We didn't see it like that, it was purely training for Wales, to do the big routes in the Pass, because in them days climbing was on vertical rock, the same as Pex, but it wasn't so good for

the head. Saying that, I remember that we were into soloing, but I wouldn't say it was dangerous, just a bit necky. Soloing things like Black Magic, a 30ft 6a route in 1983, was quite a big number in those days.

Have you enjoyed the bold side of climbing?
Years ago, yes. I personally think that when you're climbing well you don't think its bold, it's simply climbing. I used to get a good buzz out of getting above gear, I didn't consider it bold when I did it. Today they wouldn't be bold routes anymore, routes like LORD E6,6b were bold for the time; it never felt dangerous or bold because it just used to flow so well.

Do you think now that climbing would benefit today if the hard routes were bolder?
Not really, I'm quite happy with the state of affairs personally, I'm happy with them being

bolted up, and competitions also. Personally I don't think it will make any difference.

Do you think routes like LORD, should be bolted up?
No, not really, but I wouldn't say anything if anyone did bolt it up. I do what I want, and if someone bolted LORD up, it wouldn't affect me one bit.

Did you enjoy the English style of climbing?
Yes, but I think you've got to move on with the times. It's all sports climbing now so I'm happy to stay on bolts from now on.

The epitomy of British bouldering, Joe on 'Jerry's Block' at the Plantation Boulders Stanage.

The Green Traverse, Plantation boulders.

When did you first climb in France?
1979 I think, It was the 'Easter Bolton mini bus trip', the early pioneering days. Verdon, Buoux, St Jeaneat, Fontainebleau; me and our kid were the only mad ones on the bus. It was a yearly trip, along with the ever so sensible Bolton boys. I used to love it, a good crack, good wine, good food, sunshine, it was all you knew. In the old days bolts were amazing, I'd never seen a bolt before, it was just wicked to climb on bolts.

Did your 90ft fall off CAPITAL PUNISHMENT E3, in 1980 change your view on natural protection?
No, the reason was that I didn't put much gear in it was because I'd just solo'd SUICIDE WALL, E2 5c, on sight really well. I then went on CAPITAL PUNISHMENT and only put 2 runners in the whole route, snapped a hold off and then decked it. I went climbing three weeks later at Tremadog, head to toe in plaster. I did a couple of HVS's, I was so keen and not

frightened by it. The reason I don't do necky routes anymore is age, as you get older it's fear; I can't see the point anymore.

What other things were you doing then?
Nothing. Climbing, going to the pub and dogging.

Which order is the best fun?
Dogging, drinking and climbing, Well dogging and drinking equal actually. Climbing is a close third.

Where did work come?

It never came anywhere in those days, I used to work winters for 50 quid a week, then pack in a job and just climb. I never thought of work, ever!

Did you have a social conscience?

No, not one bit. I've got no morals what so ever.

Now you're working, did you see the light or something?

No, I had no money for so many years, never had a decent job. I've worked really hard at times for shit money in the past. Then all of a sudden, a really good job turns up that I enjoy, and with good money. I don't know of the future but I want to climb well again. I'm a bit confused with the climbing scene at the moment, but I enjoy the money now, so I can't see myself becoming a full time climber again.

When did you do RAIN DOGS, your only 8a?

A year after it was put up, I'd been working and dogging in Hereford or somewhere, in the winter. I went to Malham and Mark Leach had a top rope on RAIN DOGS, and said 'have a go at this'. I hadn't climbed for 6 months, and got to the third bolt, I was really impressed with myself. Leachy failed to get to the third bolt, got a sulk and went down the cafe. I then worked it for 7 days and did it. It was great to do because it was so much harder than anything before, it really was a big jump in standard. But for me it was going away from the side of climbing which I really enjoy which is flashing routes. That for me is the important side of climbing, it's pure. My style doesn't include going down to a pub and saying,' I've flashed a route, or done a boulder problem.' I always want to do it first go, and feel as though I've failed if I fall off something. RAIN DOGS was good to do, but it wasn't the same as flashing it.

Can the hard grade 8 routes be flashed though, Does bolt climbing allow that?

I think Simon Nadin's proved that. I go out to flash every single route I do, even if I go on something too hard for me, I go out to try and flash it. Simon does as well, and it shows. You improve and flash even harder, Simon flashing THE GROOVE 8a+ at Malham says it all, it can be done.

Do you think that climbing is going in the right direction?

Yes, I totally believe in bolts. I know that people say it's terrible and sports climbing is shit, but personally after 15 years experience of both sides, I see it as a very good thing. I agree with Dr. John Hart. Gritstone of course should be left alone, but that's bouldering anyway.

Have you thoughts of taking up alpine climbing?

No, I wouldn't touch it, it's not my cup of tea; TOO many people die doing it. It seems such a shame, especially as most of the time it's not even their fault, like it's avalanches or rock falls, seracs and that kind of thing.

Do you think climbing shouldn't be a sport where you need a screw loose?

There's two, if not three, branches of climbing. Traditional, sports and bouldering. If you keep them separate you don't get confused. They can't even be related anymore, they're so different. The sooner people realise that sports climbing is not even rockclimbing anymore the better, we can get on with it. Everything is different in sports climbing, the boots, gear, ropes, techniques, skills etc. When the old timers realise that, the better we can get on with it.

Do you respect the 'Old timers'?

Yes. I respect the other half completely, and I can understand them moaning about bolts, but climbing isn't that important. I go out to enjoy it, if I put up a route then it got bolted afterwards, it wouldn't affect me one bit. I don't know why people get so irate about climbing, if you take six months off, completely away its great. Nobody knows anything about Jerry Moffatt or Ben Moon in society.

The organised BMC climbing world doesn't affect you?

I don't give a fuck! I do climbing on RP's, bolts, etc. and if someone chops a bolt it doesn't bother me. I get a lot of enjoyment from being competitive with my mates, there's no bullshit involved, you've just got to do it, no bolts, no high side runners, controversy or crap; you just have to do it. Fontainebleau with the lads is superb. Climbing walls are even better than doing routes, I'd rather go to a climbing wall than even do a route.

Do you find conflicts of personality between the traditionalists, sports climbers and boulderers?

I get on with everybody, it makes no difference. No matter with that, even if they're a non climber, V Diff. to E7. If they're a fuckwit, they're a fuckwit; if they're alright, then they're alright, simple as that.

What is more important, quality of climbs or climbers?

Definitely the people, like for a good trip it's got to be the right people, right place; well not even the right place, climbing does come secondary. You've got to have plenty of totty, a nightclub, good wine and bars, lads who want to go into town dogging after a hard days climbing, go to swimming pools and dog. It's really important to have the right company,

I'm the kind of guy who wants to go into town of an evening.

Do people need time off climbing?

I think so, yes. That's where a lot of people go wrong. You get obsessed with it, you don't realise that there's other sports out there, other people. Lets face it there's nothing more boring than going into a pub and listening to someone completely rabbiting on about climbing non stop. I take time off, do a bit of walking, get clubbing it a few times, see how the other half live.

Have you always had as wild times climbing in France, as in England?

Yes, parties at Fontainebleau, parties. I've hitched to France. That was one of my greatest achievements I think, hitching to Buoux from Liverpool. It was tough not speaking any French, no money and not even a map, hitching to 'The Mecca.' That's one of my greatest achievements in life.

Was it daunting?

Yes, I was gripped shitless I tell you. Sleeping on the sides of the road, hitching actually on the motorway, I found that hard. Daralyn my girlfriend dropped me off at the motorway, I was madly in love at the time. It says something about climbing and the people who do it: no map, no money, and hitching 1000 miles to the South of France, purely to climb, obsessed with climbing, even though you might be madly in love. Climbing came first at that time.

How did you survive without any money?

I didn't drink or eat anything for three days, I nearly died. Like when I got to Buoux all the lads were nicking food and wine, but because I had a tent they used it as a wine cellar, they let me have free wine, we had some wicked times in those days.

Could you handle the serious climbers?

No, like going to bed at 9 o'clock was stupid. Like I was doing 7c's and quite fast, but for me having a few beers in the evening, listening to some music, eating loads of chocolate, getting totally shitfaced on tequilas, that was all part of the trip for me.

Did it affect your climbing?

Yes, I probably dropped a grade, but you have to ask yourself; do you climb 7c and have a good time, or climb 8a and be a Zombie. What's more important? I cannot see the point of not enjoying yourself.

Is climbing there now, as mad as it was back then in '85?

No, it's not got the same characters anymore. The old days were better for the wild and wicked things. Now its bed early, boring.

Gary Gibson

Writing any book is more often a labour of love than profiteering. Fiction can be fun, but to write a factual book requires immense hard work, necessitating many long nights. Gary on his own has written seven climbing guides, a monumental task, and one that all climbers in Britain should be very grateful. His climbing life began quite early and his preoccupation with putting up new climbs has become ever stronger over the years. He has now climbed over 1,600 new lines from atrocious to three star brilliant classics. His efforts with a bolt drill have been both liked and disliked, yet at the end of the day he supports his views and remains open to challenge and democratic mediation on any such issue. Unfortunately in 1984 he was very seriously injured in an abseil accident. He recovered from a coma eventually and with tremendous courage returned to the fore of new routing after two years. He has never been in the top leagues in terms of personal standard but has shown enthusiasm to improve and now has many E5 and E6 routes to his credit. By not being in that elite peer group, his new routes have always been regarded as pleasant and in consequence, by far the most popular new routes in places such as Pembroke, Lundy, and the Peak District.

Interview 9.4.91 Stoke, Staffordshire.

Did new routing begin very early on in your climbing career?
No, the first new route I did was in October 1977. No particular reason why, I did it with my brother at Willersley, but a little later I had a big argument with him, and as I had no transport I had to go to the Roaches on my own. As I'd done all the routes I could do there, I started to try and do the ones in between, so from there it really took off.
Were you at university at the time?
As you know I'm a Chiropodist, but I didn't go to university, I wish I had done because I'd have got more qualifications out of it. I didn't even get a degree out of it. Hazel my wife is also a Chiropodist yet surprisingly we met through climbing. We slogged our guts out to get the qualifications we needed, now they've made it a degree course over the past 12 months and don't do any different work. I've been qualified for nearly 9 years now, I enjoy the job I do; I enjoy it immensely. I enjoy the people I work with, I wouldn't do it if I didn't. I appreciate that I'm very lucky to enjoy my job. I have tried to change it and get a job with: Troll, Wild Country, BMC National Officer; but in retrospect I'm glad I haven't, because people in those jobs seem to have had far less time to actually go and enjoy climbing.

How many new routes have you actually climbed?
Over 1600 to date, but it could vary upon that, say 30-40 because a few have probably been done before. I've had aspirations to do certain routes and the majority of routes that I've aspired to do I've now done. So there's not many left, and all that remains for me to do, in my own mind, is to do more new routes. I don't know why, it's just got this attraction. The previous reason was fame, to get my name in the magazines and be known to everyone, now it's gone full circle and I feel the exact opposite. I don't want to be known, I just want to do new routes. People see you on the cliff and it holds a lot of pressure, because they know your name and expect you to be this great climber; which I'm not. I'm just the average climber who goes out every weekend.

So what made you start writing guidebooks?
I started to do a lot of new routes and sent them in to the magazines and appropriate guidebook addresses such as the BMC, and got an invite to go to a guidebook meeting from Dave Gregory, so from there I got involved in the Staffordshire guide. By the end of heated internal politics, having written three sections, I afterwards wanted my name erased from those sections. The main step forward was when Geoff Birtles asked me to be the new routes editor for High magazine. From that base over the years I've written 7 guidebooks almost single handed and been involved in many more.

Has that given you great enjoyment?
Yes, I think it has. I've put as much enthusiasm into those as I have into my climbing, undoubtably. I wouldn't do them unless I couldn't give them 100 per cent.
Have you not wanted to do the established routes at all?
I don't know why but my attitude is that if you get the new route done then the other routes aren't going to run away, yet the new route might. Even so, after doing most of the possibilities on a cliff I would leave it, rather than systematically go through the rest of the climbs, however Pembroke seems to be different.
Have you ever the desire to go and repeat one of your new routes?
I've been back to the routes that I've done and don't want to touch them, it's very peculiar. I have this opposite desire when it's been a great moment for me because you go back again and the feeling is very flat and almost strange. You remember the routes with the people as well so it's almost a breaking of that special partnership you had together, that great day out. It's also very strange how people have different attitudes to your routes, the classic one being QUIET WATERS in Pembroke, something I never rated then later it becomes a three star route, very strange.
What is your favourite type of climbing?
Wall climbing, just off the vertical, but I really look for new lines, more than what I particularly enjoy. It is strange though because at the end of the day I can't answer directly. I'm not

sure whether people know why they climb or what the attraction is. I don't know what the attraction of new routes to me is. Originally it was the fame and the magazines but now it's an obsession. I like climbing but I like new routing, that's my obsession, and the other side of it is secondary.

Do you train a lot?
No, not really. I've got a finger board upstairs and it just sits and collects dust. The most training I ever did was when I had my accident, I needed it to build up the muscle, I lost 2½ stone in 7 days. I don't know what happened. I assume that I was abseiling and something became dislodged and hit me on the head, then cut my rope, and I fell about 70ft to the ground. I don't know the exact facts, perhaps it's best that way.

Did that not put you off climbing?
When I actually became conscious of what was happening which was 3-4 weeks after, I aimed to go climbing again as soon as possible, not necessarily because I wanted to climb again, but I knew that if I didn't go climbing as soon as possible, it would have a mental and psychological effect on me. I had to do it, it's the same as driving a car, if you have an accident you must break that fear factor of doing it again, as soon as possible.

Did you come back again with the same enthusiasm and enjoyment?
My attitudes changed very slightly in the initial period, away from the new routing field. I was off work for 6 months and my attitude was initially to break the fear since I wasn't sure of even climbing again. Then in the period after that, the obsession came back. I've got as greater passion for it now as I ever have done.

Have you always been honest about new route claims?
Relatively; as ethical as most people. I had the odd rest point here or there that I wouldn't deny. The odd yo yo, but I think I'm probably just the same as other climbers of the time. My attitude is affected by what I've seen a lot of good climbers do and then claim all sorts of things. I've stood there and watched them do it, then spoken to them a couple of weeks later and they say something completely different. I could name names but there's little point in dragging THEM in the mud with me. Hazel and I have stood and watched a couple of very good climbers at Malham, get up to very dubious things but at the end of the day it's only cheating themselves. To be honest I don't believe in dredging up the past, there's so much hypocrisy in climbing anyway that what I try to do is to keep out of it, I try to keep myself to myself. Take the controversy at Pembroke over the bolts and drilled pegs. They took my drilled pegs out, and I was quoted in the magazines as being very annoyed about it. Well how could I, because whilst all this was happening I was unconscious in hospital.

What did you think of the CLARION CALL controversy in Cheedale when your bolts were removed there a few years ago?
I think it was quite a funny event. They removed the bolts and left them in the cafe for me. I collected the bolt hangers and wrote to Paul Mitchell and said that 'you've taken the bolt hangers out but you haven't repaid me for the bolts that are in place.' Then I got a cheque off him, but only for half the amount of bolts because he only removed half of them, so I got about £1.20. Then he said you'll have to get the other money off Andy Barker. I wrote to Andy but got no reply, then 4 weeks later Paul wrote and asked for the money back and said that he had made a mistake in giving me the money in the first place. So I didn't reply to him, either. It was all quite a funny situation. I don't think I had any bitterness towards them at all. I think if it had been Ron Fawcett's route they would have left it. The whole idea of the route was to stir up a hornet's nest of controversy, hence the name. Having said that I know a whole load of routes done in Cheedale at that time were done with bolts and nothing was said.
It's interesting about the Pembroke issue in that I had quite a few discussions with quite a number of well known climbers, about placing bolts and I can say that nearly all of them encouraged me to place the bolts. Then suddenly when I'd done it and after a couple of years when the issue blew up, one of those people in particular stood up and said I shouldn't have, which amazed me, I've known the lad for quite a while. Basically he stood up and stood with the crowd. Having said that, a lot of people have said to me that they liked repeating the routes and are very much for the bolts but won't stand up and say anything. What really disappoints me is their lack of strength in character, not being able to stand up and say, I agree with him; I find that very sad but that's climbing for you.
My attitude about climbing, and I'm talking about this in terms of my opinion of climbing, as a whole and not as how I go about my climbing; I think there's so much hypocrisy about, it's not true. Some of the older leading climbers are very hypocritical, and I find that very sad that they should stand up and be against bolts, after some of the things that they have done I find very dubious. One of the most whitest of white, or supposedly believed, whiter than white characters of British Rock climbing, I know to have done some dubious things, I'm not citing that as an aim to that person, I'm citing that as an example of what I think climbing is. Now climbing is a lot more open whereas in the past, I think a lot of people were untouchable behind closed doors.

What of the future as new routes are diminishing?
There not at all, I look at it this way. If you've got a rock face then you've only got one line. Then when you have a route on it you have two lines, one either side, after that you have three routes and 4 lines, and so on. (Gary chortling away). Yes, they are diminishing but there's plenty still for me. When they're all done I might just fade out of climbing altogether, but at the moment I doubt it, upstairs I've got a box full of bolts, and a lot of pegs.

Nick Harms

Nick Harms, born 7.1.65 at Leamington Spa. Nick is the first to admit that he is not one of the great climbers but his influence and energy has had a great impact on the Llanberis Slate Quarries. He is 5ft. 9ins. high and weighs in at 8st. 9lb., which is incredibly light. Nick often laughs at this and does point out that he has very little muscle also. He wrote the first guidebook to Slate and had climbed most of the routes in the North Wales Quarries, with a few of Johnny Dawes exceptions. Of late he has contributed new hard 8a climbs, which come into the classic status.

Interview, 21.11.91 Llanberis, Wales.

You grew up in Blackpool, had you climbed when you were at school there?
There wasn't really a climbing club or any thing like that. I went on a course at Pen Y Pass in Snowdonia when I was 16, I only climbed about once a month until I went to an Outdoor Education College in Liverpool when I was 18.

What influence did that have?
Well, as part of the course you went climbing. Every fortnight you went on a climbing trip for two or three days, alternating with canoeing, so I suppose it got me out. It helped me because you'd get away with other climbers for the weekend, which didn't happen in Blackpool, you could never get away otherwise, and there were only a few places to go bouldering. Eventually I had to go to Llanberis on a placement from college, a few months later in the summer I moved here and met a lot more climbers.

Did you complete the course?
Well not really – I did three years of it, then left, I just stopped going in the fourth year, the honours year, which unfortunately was compulsory really.

And you stayed in Llanberis?
Yes. I met Paul Pritchard at the same time, he needed transport and someone to climb with and I had the transport and no one to climb with so it worked out.

What were your first impressions of Paul as a climber?
It's hard to say really – I never had any preconceptions about what someone who climbed hard was like. We just struck up a friendship really easily, going climbing and getting drunk at night, and not really bothering too much about where you lived or how much money you had. It was a really good lifestyle at the time.

Did you accompany him to left hand Red Wall at Gogarth?
I went with him once when he went to do SCHITTELGRUBER, I think his first new route there. I had an absolute epic on that, jumared up half of it, then got absolutely gripped and climbed up the other half. Then I went with him to do THE BROCCOLI GARDEN. He took me down there, I saw it and wimped out, I wouldn't do it. Then we had to do an awful route to get out, it was just hideous! awful! it was like compressed talc, so that was the end of that, I never went back again.

Did that affect your climbing with Paul?
Not really, but it did in that he did a lot of routes at Gogarth which I wasn't really interested in, however we still climbed together.

Were you surprised that he stayed alive?
Yes and no. Yes in so much as the routes were not held together that well, he seemed pretty much out of control, that is in relation to the rock – what stayed on what didn't; which gear stayed or what held. But then he was so highly motivated that he could pull things out of the bag when he was at full stretch. I always trusted him when we were doing something bold, I always knew he'd come through.

Then you started climbing slate around that time?
Yes, it was a different scene then to now. You used to get a group going to Gogarth and a group going to the Quarries or Pen Trwyn. Everybody went there as a group, eight or nine people, where today it's only two or three. I went with Paul mostly to the Quarries, but

Nick Harms at the end of a six month spell, just before he finally climbed THE DARK HALF 8a, up in the abyssal, surrounding oceans of slate that make of the Dinorwic Quarries above Llanberis.

then I went with others, Mike Thomas and occasionally Johnny Dawes as well. You tended to hang around as a big group, socialise in the same group, and probably even lived with the same group.

Why do you think you moved to Llanberis?
Personal reasons. I moved away from Blackpool, there was nothing for me there. I met Paul and found a group of friends, a group of people I could live with, that was the prime mover. At that stage I didn't even realise that there was a group of climbers living in Sheffield, Leeds or Llanberis.

Was bolting completely accepted by then?
I think maybe it was, it depended who you were. MANIC STRAIN 8a, had been done which is a bolt ladder, MENOPAUSAL, had just been done. It still seemed that you had to have a big run out, or it had to be a bit sort of dodgy.

When did you do MANIC STRAIN?
1988.

And had that been chipped?
Totally, I can remember Johnny Redhead chipping it with a hammer and an angle peg, chiselling it out. It's a good route, he made a nice job of it.

Was that the first time you'd seen Johnny R?
It was probably the first time I'd come here. I was trying to dog my way up THE DERVISH E3, and this guy was there hacking away at this route. It seemed a little bizarre, nobody was trying to stop him, everyone was egging him on.

Having done the route was it worthwhile, was it a great route?
I really enjoyed.

Do you think it perhaps should have been left un-chipped?
It's hard to say. I don't think I ever saw it before it was chipped so I can't really say whether it would have been climbable or not, but I suppose it is quite tastefully done. A lot of routes since then have been chipped which haven't come close to being, as well made. Some Austrian bloke who came here last year didn't even know it had been chipped, they couldn't tell, which shows the quality of John's work.

Does the colour of slate ever depress you, it's sombreness?
I suppose it is sombre in a way, if you go around the museums and archives you get an appreciation of the quarries when they were working. It's a bit like climbing in the middle of a concentration camp, the conditions were so poor for the people who used to work there. Having to walk 40 miles on a Sunday evening to get to work for the next week. A friend of mine, his uncle or great uncle got hurt in an accident which took him months and months to recover, no sick pay. At the end

of it, he got presented with a bill for the tools lost in the accident, and his stay in hospital. It is sombre, but now when the trees turn, the colours seem more vivid against a dark background. It's not all grey, there are greens, reds and yellows, all sorts of colours, you just have to have an eye to look for them.

Does the sense of industrial working come across whilst you climbing ever?
Oh yes, you might be halfway up a route and you suddenly come across some bore holes for dynamite or something. When it chucks it down you can shelter in the old houses, it gives you a completely different feel to anywhere else. There are huts you can go up to in the top part of the quarries which still have boots on stools, and jackets on clothes pegs. It almost feels like people have just left them from working. Occasionally you meet the old quarry men, they go for a walk and see you climbing. They think it's great, someone is actually using the quarries and they're really quite appreciative, not of the routes that we've done obviously, but that there is a use for the place, other than just leaving it to crumble into history.

It's an amazing mark on the landscape, does that environmentally affect you?
Not the quarries, what does seem a shame is the visual impact of the slag heaps which cover twice the area of the quarries. I'm sure that there are plenty of land fill sites in Wales that you could fill in with the stuff, but I suppose it will never happen because there are no financial incentives. I think it's good, that the quarries are left, because it is a monument to what those people did, it's what created Wales, anybody who visits the quarries should go around Penrhyn castle in Bangor which was built almost solely on the profits of the quarries, it's an incredible neo-gothic place.

What attracts you about slate?
I don't know really. What does attract is the form of it, the shapes, and it's cleanliness. In general if it's got a feature such as a groove or arete, you actually climb it. Whereas on limestone if you have a groove you still climb it like a face route. I suppose it's the movement that really attracts me.

Does the friction worry you?
No, I think that the low friction is its strongest point really, that's what makes you actually climb the feature.

Does a chalked up slate route make a lot of differences?
If its over chalked its hideous, but you end up with just as many blind alleys on the slab routes. On the steep routes it does make it easier.

Is climbing hard important to you?
I like climbing generally, but as soon as I can do something I lose interest in it. If I'm doing a

new route I can work it; red pointing it seems a bit of a bore. It then takes me ages to redpoint them, I don't really ever feel the want for something I can do. Climbing wall problems are a bit like that, one day its hard then the next day you can do it to warm up, it doesn't seem interesting after that.

What are the great hard routes on slate?
I think THE CURE 8a, is the best slab route, it's the most varied. The first 20ft of it is typical Rainbow edge climbing, on-off in places. Then the middle bit takes the crux of the rainbow which is very unusual since your climbing up a slabby ramp which is at 90 degrees to the other slab. It's a lot smoother and really on-off as there aren't many holds, the last half is quite dynamic and powerful. The other great routes are QUARRYMAN 8a, THE DARK HALF 8a, BUNGLES ARETE 8b, THE MEDIUM 8a, BOBBYS GROQVE 8a+, CWMS THE DOGFISH 8a+ and WINDOWS OF PERCEPTION 8a.

When you led THE CURE, had you top roped it first?
No. I've not led The Cure, I've top roped it and its brilliant. It would be more pleasant for me if it had two more bolts, since it's quite run out.

Would you like to go and do it?
I would yes. It's probably the one slab route I'd actually like to do that I haven't done.

Can you ever see France envying Llanberis, taking a plaster cast of the quarries and putting it opposite Buoux?
Not really, I don't think it would be good to take or copy another area or another culture because then you immediately kill what you appreciate. It's the variety which makes climbing areas stand out.

How could you define the art of climbing on slate?
That's quite difficult to explain, for me it's the concentration and movement that stands out. On other rock you just seem to move over it, whereas on hard slate routes you seem to move around some part of the body. On BOBBYS GROOVE 8a+, you've got one foot that you must keep static, then you have to move your body around it to do the crux, the same on THE MEDIUM. Whereas on limestone you can often do moves in several different ways thugging past most difficulties. What I enjoy about climbing is movement, it doesn't really matter how hard the route is, I just enjoy climbing. The other sports I do: Skateboarding and Snowboarding etc, it's the movement and fluidity that I enjoy. I feel that climbing in the quarries has similar movement patterns. Limestone for me has always seemed superficial and stilted, I don't enjoy that type of movement.

Dave Turner

His commitment to Southern Sandstone over the past 10 years has been second to none. In the early eighties he remained a quiet youth, repeating in good style all the hard routes of the previous era, then in the mid – eighties started adding very hard routes of his own. All his hard routes have been major lines such as TEMPTATION 7b+, THE REPUBLIC 7c, COOL BANANAS 8a+ and CHIMERA 8b. Along with Gary Wickham he has developed the Sandstone outcrops of Kent and Sussex fully into the 8a grade. His guidebook to Southern Sandstone was very much a solo effort and today remains one of the best, and well presented guides to climbing in Britain. Injuries have plagued him over the last five years and unfortunately have made climbing at a high standard both painful and difficult. It is impossible to say how far his climbing could have developed, but one can only admire his enthusiasm and energy in South East activity over a decade.

Interview 6.1.91, Meersbrook, Sheffield.

When did you first go climbing on sandstone?
In 1980, I was at school and went to Harrison's Rocks, just outside Tunbridge Wells.

Did it become an instant grab?
Not really, I only went 2 or 3 times that summer. I was studying quite hard in the 6th form. I got my A levels then unfortunately failed the Cambridge exams, perhaps I wasn't good enough but I had got heavily into climbing by then, so who knows. I then took the rest of the year off.

Why didn't you go straight to university?
I didn't want to do what everyone else was doing, then after a year I went to Sheffield which was in 1982 and started a degree in Medicine. I only lasted a term and two weeks, it just wasn't me at all.

Do you remember any climbs from that time?
Yes, LEFT WALL. When I did it, it was almost too hard for me, and I was on my limit, it's such an intimidating wall and for years I'd read the history books about Joe Brown and Don Whillans. It was done with aid in their time so you thought you were brilliant when you did it free.

What standard were you climbing at the time?
E2! It was given E3 at the time, so it was an intimidating thing to do. I'd done CENOTAPH CORNER before, but that was a bit disappointing because it just doesn't have the exposure

of being on a blank wall like LEFT WALL.

Was LEFT WALL mentally tiring?
Yes, I was really psyched up for it. You needed to because there's quite a long hard bit at the top.

Did you know that was coming?
Yes, but I still wasn't really prepared for it.

In what way?
There's a hard bit in a wide crack low down and I thought that was desperate when I did it. Then I knew that the next bit was meant to be harder than that. You're thinking is it or isn't it, can I do it or not, am I being sensible in carrying on, will I be safe or not. Then to make it worse I'd used up all my runners lower down and could see myself in for a big fall if things didn't go right. That's just the situation, and it's so much more frightening than CENOTAPH CORNER.

Have you climbed any hard routes since then which have been as frightening?
In terms of danger yes! there have been, but actually as frightening no. LEFT WALL was the first time I'd been on a steep blank wall, a complete physical and psychological battle. Once you've been in that situation a few times you get used to it, even so it's still a stunning climb for the grade.

Is DOWNHILL RACER E4 6a, similar?
It's not exposed in the same way, it's gripping but it's shorter and you can see what you're letting yourself into from the ground, that's a big difference. I did LEFT WALL so much earlier in my climbing career, psychologically

it was much harder than DOWNHILL RACER. When I did DOWNHILL RACER I'd done a lot of harder routes on limestone so I knew I could do it, that's psychologically very different.

How do you cope with that psychological pressure in doing a grade that you haven't done before?
I need to have done a lot of climbs in the grade below, and not failed on any of them; that's how I went up the grades. I didn't have the confidence until I was never failing on any route in a particular grade, it held me back in a way, but it also mean't you've got the experience as well, rather than just shooting up what you're good at.

Whilst at university you made a very early ascent of ROOSTER BOOSTER 7c, how long did that take you?
I went on it one day and fell off on the crux, pulled my ropes and left the gear that I had in, I then got to the the very last move second go but I slipped off a jug. I went back a few weeks later and did it first try; very English style.

Do you kick yourself for not flashing it?
Oh yes, I kick myself for not doing it the second try, obviously the plan was to flash it but the crux is hard for 6b. I think it's the best way to climb although it is clearly impossible on a route that is getting near your limit.

What stopped you climbing seriously?
I was probably fittest in 1985, then I started having injury problems, necrosis of the finger-

pads, it killed the tissue inside the pad. Too much climbing, it basically crushed the life out of them. I had ultra sound, heat therapy all a painful experience. But my main injury was my forearm which started in 1986.

How did you get your injury?
I fell off and broke a bone in my wrist in late '85, so I had a long lay-off and was doing my exams, I had 4 or 5 months off climbing. I went back into climbing, trying too hard and I had problems soon after. I went to Australia with the ambition of flashing one of Kim Carrigan's hardest routes there, INDIA 7c+, but in turn the climbing made my forearm worse. I had physio and rested it, spent ages trying to get the problem diagnosed which wasn't until '89, so I wasted a lot of time really.

How do you view the concept that all guide books should be banned so that you go out and just climb, is there a valid point for that?
Yes I do. The other point in favour of not having guide books is to keep people away since places get trashed, but that is elitist so I don't really go along with it; although I did nearly rip up the guide at one stage. I had the feeling that it was going to draw much more attention to sandstone and it's in such a sorry state anyway, the guide wasn't going to do it any good. I think ego got the better of me; bar the typing up, I did enjoy it.

Do any of the routes that you put up on sandstone stand out in your mind?
The last one I did stands out, CHIMERA 8b, at High Rocks, because it was the last one, it was the hardest, and I really didn't think I could do it a few years ago. Cool Bananas 8a+, stands out because it's not powerful, it's sustained technicality which is extremely unusual down there.

In what sense?
Just really intricate moves, if anyone could do it on-sight I would be stunned, but when you've actually done it, you can usually do it again quite easily. The difficulty was working out how to do it, once I'd worked it out I did it fairly quickly. TEMPTATION 7b+, stands out because it was my first, and because a lot of people didn't think it was possible. Guy Mclelland, David Jones, were all capable of doing it but had considered it too hard to try. It's slightly competitive but more it's a sense of pride in achieving the first ascent of one of the best routes on Southern Sandstone.

Do you feel privileged to have been the climber to have done it?
No, because the era before was Guy and yourself's and there were plenty of good

Dave on his route CHIMERA 8b, at High Rocks. 20ft. of climbing leads to the crux section of getting into the groove, making an Egyptian, and squirming to the top.

routes done then. Before that was Gordon Delacey, Nigel Head and Boysen's period when they did FANDANGO 6c, things like that, it's just a matter of someone putting the effort in. Today there are still plenty of routes to go at High Rocks.

Do you think putting up new routes is an essential part of climbing? Does a climber need to do new routes to get things out of climbing?
No, there is so much else to do. However for me you do get a bigger buzz out of doing a new route, particularly when it's something new in terms of difficulty or at the limits of your own ability, but if it's just a good line that's been overlooked that's good also. I haven't done many new routes but the ones I've done have stood out.

Has climbing in the South East influenced you a lot?
Yes. Particularly because it's a backwater, people do it purely because they like it, it's not really trying to get into the magazines, in that sense I think it's quite good. It's obviously changing with competition climbing, because people can see making money in the future, it will definitely raise standards, although it hasn't done yet.

Do you have climbing plans for the future?
Yes, I went to Pakistan in 1989 and I did two rock peaks with no real snow plodding at all. I liked it and would like to do more, but it does take a lot out of you. It's time, expense and commitment. I liked going somewhere completely different, somewhere that other people don't go. I'd also like to do some proper dogging and lots of bouldering.

Andy Goring

Andy Goring, often known as Mad Dog. Born Sheffield 10.7.63. Andy was one of those climbers who drifted into sports climbing and drifted out again without really anyone knowing. He did over 10 routes of 8a and just broke into the 8b grade before giving up. His ascents were in good style and well deserved.

Interview, 16.1.91 Beauchief, Sheffield.

What did you do after leaving school?
I worked for about a year and a half, had three different jobs. I then went into the Infantry in 1980 until the end of 1984. For the last year I wasn't enjoying it at all, partly because where we were stationed in Gibraltar, it wasn't a very nice place really and what, with getting married as well, I decided to leave.

Why did you join the Army?
It was something that since leaving school I'd been interested in. I had nothing else, family wise, attachments or otherwise. I really enjoyed it for three and a half years. But it's not the job you do unless your totally committed.

Did you learn a lot from it?
I guess you learn a lot from anything in life, but you don't realise it at the time, it's only a few years later. I think you learn a lot physically about yourself, and mentally what pressure you can handle. Being cold and wet for days on end, you realise that you can either do it or not. You're tested physically, and mentally to an extent, but you don't really learn much else, since you're told to do everything and don't have to think for yourself. That's why since I left, I've been mainly involved in physical achievement sports, I had it with climbing and now from doing Triathlon events. I don't like to go in at the bottom level and gradually work up, I like to go in and get to the top as quick as I can.

Did you enjoy the thinking part of hard climbing?
I don't think I really thought about it when I was climbing. If I was physically fit, it was a matter of getting the hold and pulling on it; that was the way I used to climb, if I was strong enough I'd get up the route. Mentally rehearsing the route never seemed to work, I'd keep doing it, and doing it, until I eventually succeeded, it was like beating it into submission. I couldn't be negative about a route, it was always, I will do this route at some stage. I did get a mental block on MECCA 8b+, which was the time I started to pack up climbing, my motivation had dropped a little bit, and I started thinking about it too much.

You did AUSTRIAN OAK, top end 8a+, a good achievement. Did you feel that the big time had arrived?
No, I never really thought of the big time because you're climbing with people like Ben Moon and Jerry Moffatt, so you don't kid yourself, in power terms they are just so far ahead. You find your limits, understand your improvement curve and it's not on the same level. Nowadays some people think that they're big time, they kid themselves.

Did you not feel like making a name then, soloing the routes?
I can't understand why people do solo. I suppose they might get something out of it, but I look at climbing as a physical workout. Not even as you're trying to beat the route, but more as, if you're physically fit enough to do the route. With soloing your standard is a lot lower, because you can't solo as hard as you can climb. I look at people soloing and think, that's not for me at all. There is a certain level I'll strip down to, harness and rope is compulsory, top rope preferably. Leading to me didn't even make a difference, if top roping had counted as an ascent then that's what I would have done. All these ethics and things. As far as I'm concerned I haven't got any ethics. My ethics went as far as getting from bottom to top unaided, no falls or rests. Chipping of course was a no no. Why cheat yourself, it's the same with drugs, also.

Being involved with athletics heavily in competition you're aware of drugs. Have you seen any of the top climbers taking drugs?
No. You obviously hear rumours. I wouldn't be surprised if people are, because there's money involved in it now. You can't really say though. I train in Jerry Moffatt's cellar and am very close to the scene, and there's nothing around. But worldwide you don't know what's going on, top stars stay within their own small groups. If somebody was doing it then it would be very individual. It's come in every other sport, so I would say it's only a matter of time.

With your interest in training and in depth knowledge what effect would drugs have?
I would have been awesome on drugs, but so would everyone be in real terms, so there's no point. You don't know what the Eastern bloc countries are doing, especially as it might get into the Olympics. If it does then it will speed up that's for sure.

It'll get in the public eye a lot more then, will that help?
It will be a change. In the past they've looked on us as weirdos. I'll never forget Rubicon Wall, I was hanging on a bolt having just fallen off and Joe Public came up to me and said, 'what are you doing, looking for fossils.' A lot of the time you think like turning round and saying "Why don't you fuck off".

Did you?
No, I'm always conscious that I am out in the countryside, and swearing your head off when Joe Public is about, is not very good, or for the sport in general. People don't like it so there's no point. You just smile and say something amusing or polite. It's hard, you've fallen off something for he 10th time, you can't do it, your fingers are cutting. You get very close sometimes.

What do you hope to do now?
I still don't want job, but I'm a bit more realistic about living and feeding myself. The trouble now is that, it's the same with Triathlon. I'd sooner train than do anything. I'm studying Recreation and Management Tourism, I don't know why.

Quentin Fisher

Quentin Fisher, born 9.7.65 at Chesterfield, Derbyshire. I first met Quentin at Windy Ledge, Stoney Middleton. We both used to struggle up the start of KELLOGG, which always seemed to be hard for 6a. His reach was fantastic and made me struggle to keep up. Now he is 6ft 3ins, so on reach problems it's no competition. More remarkably are his new routes for they all have small holds on the crux's. It's amazing that anyone weighing 13½ stone can pull on the size of holds he manages. His heart is just as big and warm, and he remains one of the most helpful and jovial climbers around. There are few other climbers around so enthusiastic as Quentin when it comes to bouldering. Along with Jerry Moffatt he has developed Cressbrook Dale, with problems like CHEROKEE LANE, LIFT OFF and BRAIN POLLUTION, all around English 7b.

Interview 15.12.90, Beauchief, Sheffield.

What got you interested in climbing?
When I was 14, I went on a poaching trip to the Peak District. We camped beneath Birchens Edge, I walked up to the crag and just started soloing in my pumps. The first route I did was TRAFALGAR CRACK and it started from there. I solo'd up to VS before I learnt to climb with ropes.

What motivated you to climb?
I don't know, I guess its sort of addictive, you see the lists of routes to tick off, I've no idea at all. I think the trouble is that, if you start thinking of a reason for it then you're likely to think up all sort of bullshit reasons, which aren't necessarily true but are just your excuses for having a good time. I've no idea what makes it so addictive.

Did the danger of soloing worry you?
No, not at all. I never ever considered that I could hurt myself soloing, it never crossed my mind.

How did climbing affect your schooling?
I got very keen on it but still managed to get 4 'A' levels.

You got another in your year before going to university!
Yes, I took pure Maths but that was just something to do because I was then going climbing every day.

Did you feel career minded?
At the time I used to argue with my parents because climbing was really important to me and I wanted to take two years off, then I could concentrate better on university when I got there. I had this sort of naive impression that the climbing would go out of my system after doing it for a couple of years, and would then

be totally bored with it. Then I could work like hell and have a good career afterwards. In many respects that was true, since in the first two years at university I was really lazy and got terrible results at the end of my second year, which counted a lot to my 2.1. Then again, climbing just doesn't go out of your system so I think my parents were wise in forcing me to go. It became practical since they wouldn't support me for another year, I compromised by picking the university closest to the Peak District, Sheffield.

Was that an important choice, did you need to climb as well as study?
My choice on university was totally linked to climbing, I only put Sheffield on my UCCA form.

Did your standard improve at university?
Yes, definitely in the first two years, but not comparatively to the other lads who were climbing full time. It improved, but not to the same percentage of the rise in standards over those three years.

From 1987 you haven't done any routes, why not?
I've done a few routes, but bouldering interests me far more than doing routes. A lot of the time it feels like its good training, for what I don't know, maybe doing harder boulder problems. Generally the moves on problems are so sick compared to anything on routes. Take things like GEORGES'S WALL dyno for instance, I tried that every time I went to Stoney for 3-4 years, I got really obsessed. I can remember leaving nightclubs at 2 o'clock in the morning, staying awake till five, then driving out so I could try it really early in the morning, when it wasn't greasy. There's just something about, doing something which is so hard and powerful. You get so strong but it's also uncertain, whereas if you go on a route which is say an 8b stamina route, it's just a certainty that you're going to do it. I don't think bouldering's the same. It's not a certainty, on a lot of problems you're either strong enough, or your not. Somehow I like that, a lot, lot more.

Does bouldering entail any mental strain?
Oh God yes, the nervousness is just horrendous, when your really close to doing something, it's just beyond, it's just like going into an exam. I remember when I used to play a lot of chess, going into a match, I had an unbeaten record playing for the school and it put a hell of a lot of pressure on myself, every time I went into a game I was nervous. It's the same when you're about to do a boulder problem, a

Quentin's partners in crime, Jerry and Ben at Burbage South in the Peak.

lot more so than I find on a route. Something that you think you're very close to. For me especially the problems at Cressbrook when I knew I was close to doing them.

Who do you boulder with?
Jerry Moffatt, Ben Moon, Sean Myles and Ben Masterson of course.

Is there any competition between you?
Oh yes, really friendly. I can't think I've ever ever been at the bottom of a boulder problem, where we all are about to do it, and someone has thought, I hope he falls off. I've never ever done that, it's friendly competition, you heckle more, it's fun even though I often end up losing. As soon as anyone bets anything it's a

sure thing to make me fall off, Jerry's got more beer out of me than, well I think I still owe it.

Now you've started a Ph.D. at Leeds, does it give you more time to climb?
No. I really enjoy that sort of work, it's a bit like climbing, a bit competitive. I really enjoy it, doing things before other people, its good fun. It's a challenge in thinking of new original things, I'm studying Mud Rocks, it's quite scientific and hard to explain in laymans terms. Generally it's reactions both chemical and microbiological, which happen due to the transformation of muddy sediments into shales and mudstone.

Quentin in mid flight at Cressbrook Dale, completing LIFT OFF 6c. The 'Plank' behind is used to brush holds with a tooth brush, before attempting these desperate 'sick' problems.

MOFFATTROCITY 6c, a classic traverse done in 1983 by Jerry Moffatt.
Cressbrook Dale one of Britain's premier bouldering areas.

Does that involve working with other people or is it very solitary?
Yes, there are other people in the laboratory, but it is very solitary, there are so few people doing that sort of work and those that are, are too busy to talk, it is a very solitary thing.

Is bouldering solitary?
It's good going out with a team, but I guess climbing is a very selfish thing, climbers are probably the most selfish bunch of people I've ever come across, without a doubt. I go out bouldering on my own a lot of the time, since Jerry and Ben are often out of the country, and my other friends are busy, so it is a very solitary affair.

You've done soloing in the past, any projects for the future?
Yes, at the moment I've got really close to soloing CAVIAR. I've touched the hold, got my fingers round it and not quite hung it, 8a+ would be pretty good.

Have you seen different characters of people who boulder, to those who plod up V Diffs?
I don't know too may people who go and plod up V Diffs to tell you the truth, you don't see too many at Cressbrook generally! Climbers in general though, do seem quite similar I guess.

What qualities make a good boulder?
I've no idea, just determination I guess. It's the same with anything. I can't say that I'm a brilliant boulderer, I'm not naturally stronger than Joe Public. It's just the determination to push yourself further.

Do you think soloing is an important part of climbing?
I've always enjoyed it, even at any grade, all the old classic's on gritstone are superb. In a way its really relaxing, especially if you're working hard. It's impossible to think about work when your soloing, so it is a good break.

Do you need more concentration, soloing than bouldering?
I think you have to! When you're soloing you have to concentrate, and you do concentrate obviously, because your life's at risk, whereas it would be nice to be able, to concentrate that well when you're bouldering. You try to but probably never can.

Have you had any bad injuries from bouldering?
A few years ago I pulled a tendon at Cressbrook, Jerry was about 20 yards away and heard the crack. I couldn't hold a pool cue for weeks afterwards. I couldn't climb for 6 months, but time off and sensible training made it stronger than ever.

How can you see climbing developing in the 90's?
I think the big explosion in the mid eighties was down to the dole, people caught on to the fact that you could exist without working and take up full time climbing. It doesn't seem now that there are many good climbers coming through, so it's hard to see forward.

What do you do to relax?
I treat reading like work, so that's not relaxing and consequently I've only ever read one fiction book. Climbing is really the thing I do to relax, because it is very different. Even so, I do listen to a lot of classical music, I even go shooting occasionally.

Paul Pritchard

Paul started climbing in the Lancashire quarries in the early eighties. His tall and very lean physique lent itself to climbing and after a very short while he was repeating some of the hardest routes locally. Mark Leach and John Monks were climbing the hardest physical routes at the time but with his long reach and thin fingers he felt at home on the more unfriendly routes without protection. This continued when he moved to North Wales where he became one of the main pioneers in bold, dangerous climbs. His addition of routes such as COME TO MOTHER E7 6b and SUPER CALABRESSE E8 6c, give an indication to a wild zest for almost suicidal excitement. Miraculously he survived, and has gone on to climb many classic climbs on slate, and for the record books free climbed THE SCOOP, E6,6b,6a,6b,6a,6b,6b,6a,6b,5b, at Strone Ulladale in Scotland. What is quite exceptional is that Paul has also proved himself on hard technical routes as well, doing new routes such as BOAT PEOPLE 8a on the Orme, and CURE FOR A SICK MIND 8a, on slate.

Interview 3.4.91 Llanberis, Wales.

Why did you choose Llanberis as a place to stay?
The people; the weather as you know is hardly the greatest recommendation. I started coming to Llanberis in the summer of 1986 because I'd heard about great climbs being done on the slate quarries. So I came down here and started repeating a lot of the slate routes like, RAPED BY AFFECTION E7 6b etc. There were loads of people here like Trevor Hodgson, Johnny Dawes, Nick Dixon, Nick Harms and Stevie Haston. It was such a wild bunch. Lots of wild things were happening, doing great routes in the day time, and then everybody would be in the pub that night recounting tales of the days happenings. After you would party all night, get up the following day and do something else wild; quite an exhausting lifestyle but really exciting. I met all these people and knew that I could equate with them.

Were routes like RAPED giving you a hard time?
Those routes were the same standard to those I was previously doing in the Lancashire quarries, I found them OK. It was August 1986 when I first went to Gogarth and started doing harder things than I'd ever done before.
What were your first routes on Gogarth?
The first time I went there I did POSITRON E5 6a, which turned me onto the place, it's such a fantastic climb. I did a couple of the other main cliff routes but then one day I went to South Stack Red Walls, I did MEIN KAMPF E5 6a, which turned out to be the second ascent but I didn't know it at the time. It was so loose, I'd never climbed loose rock in my life before and I just hated it, I thought it was horrendus, it made me vomit actually! Then we had two days reminiscing about the days adventure and it started to sound a lot more fun than it felt, right at the time. I started going back there, and then learn't to enjoy it more immediately. It was gradual, within about a week.

Was Gogarth more impressive than anywhere you'd been?

In a lot of ways yes, I'd already spent a lot of time in France at Buoux in 1984 and 1985. I'd climbed in the Alps on places like the Eiger, Monch and the Jungfrau when I was 17, I'd seen a lot more impressive things but Gogarth is unique.

What was the fascination of THE RED WALL area at Gogarth?

I felt competent there, in fact more competent than in any other aspect of life. Also it suited my style, which was big runouts on small edges.

Do you enjoy climbing in the considered DANGER area of the sport?

Oh yes!

How do you mentally prepare yourself for an E8 climb?

What the books call visualization really helps, mentally climbing the route again and again, all the time and succeeding on it in your brain, and in your mind, because that's the same as succeeding on it physically, so your body thinks that it's totally capable of it.

You find that method works?

Yes, it's been proven to work.

You wouldn't go on a route if you couldn't have that kind of approach?

You do sometimes and it feels a lot worse, like COME TO MOTHER, Johnny Dawes and I turned up to do that, we didn't know we were going on it until half an hour before hand. It feels much worse, you're a lot more shaky on the rock, well I am. It's on Left Hand Red Wall and it fell down three months after we did it.

What attracted you to it?

We thought it looked easy! We abseiled into the base and tried this other route, a big corner. Both of us had a go but backed down, it was just unbelievably scary; we tried to climb over this massive block in this corner and it just kept moving, in the end we had to climb down it it was so dangerous. As an escape we saw this huge overhanging arete that looked like it was covered in buckets, we thought 'let's do this it looks fantastic', We eventually climbed it in two pitches, all these buckets that we saw from the bottom were completely loose, it was like quartz blocks you get in rockeries, they just sat on sloping ledges and stuff, the gear was appalling in the soft talcum powder rock. It still is, the most scary experience for Johnny and I, because we were totally unprepared for it.

How could you cope mentally on the lead?

I was just relying on everything that had gone before, all you're climbing experiences.

Was getting to the top a relief?

Yes, that was just a massive relief, no sense of pleasure or achievement. Johnny led this first pitch, 90ft. and a fall to the ground was on the whole time, the arete was falling off and everything. He got this belay in a crack that went up and back down from this big roof, which recently has fallen off. I climbed up which was gripping enough, then had to do a 60ft traverse off this belay, with no gear at all on the lip of this overhang. If I had fallen off, it would have pulled the belay out with Johnny on and we would have both died for sure, it was ridiculous.

Did you both have confidence in each other?

At the time we hadn't actually, it was before we'd done a lot of things together. That route is what gave us a lot of confidence in each other, to go for other things like THE SCOOP on Strone Ulladale.

Does climbing a route with someone build a confidence?

Oh yes, I don't want to be sounding too romantic, but it does build up a definite relationship between two people that is quite special.

Does the more scary the route add to it?

It's not just like doing multi pitch routes anywhere with someone, it's somewhere you are climbing that you really have to trust each other and you're both going to die if something goes wrong, you both rely on each other, the situation demands it!

Chris Plant on, THE CURE FOR A SICK MIND 8a; one of the scariest hard routes in the world. Johnny Dawes (left), tried to on-sight this and fell off slightly lower down, consequently falling 100ft. He stopped just off the ground, nasty scare factor '10'!

When you've done a climb like that do you want to go back for the same experience or something new?

Something new yes, in a way harder and more serious! It's probably more addictive than a lot of things in a way. What I'm doing is, searching for that feeling that comes when you get yourself into a very bad situation, and you've got to rely on loads of different senses and strengths to get through it. It's a very peculiar feeling to get, I think it just comes from adrenalin, but it's different to adrenalin; like if you've done a bridge jump then the adrenalin you get is just a steep buzz. But, if you've got to really pull it out of the bag to get up a piece of rock, then it's a very different feeling, it's an unbelievable feeling.

Do you think that someone like a prime minister in an election would feel the same?

No. It's a very different, instant risk. I may be wrong but I don't think a prime minister has to make personal life saving decisions in half a second. It's essentially a very physical thing, and of course mental, but very interconnected. I've tried to put a lot of thought into why I do things like that, and it's almost inexpressable.

Does the concept of technical strength appeal to you on rock?

Yes, very much so, it's just the same, that's what people don't understand. It's just the same, not the same feeling but it's rockclimbing which is very enjoyable, some people are really bigoted on both sides on that.

You would enjoy either?

I do enjoy both styles of climbing, sports and bold leading. I think it takes a lot less commitment to accept only one style of climbing.

Do other peoples standards affect you?

Yes, when I see somebody doing really hard things it's great, it makes me want to climb harder, it's like a big family and everyone gets psyched up by what each other does. It's like that in Llanberis anyway, but for me it's like that on a national scale, I hope it is for everyone.

Do things like the Eiger North face excite you?

Oh yes, looking down to the White Spider and seeing footprints in the snow was really exciting. At the time I actually hated the exertion of walking up massive hills, but as you get older your body strength gets better and now I feel I could cope with it a lot better physically and mentally. It is something I have to do, to keep things as diverse as possible.

Would you go to the Alps now?

I don't have the draw to the Alps because there are too many people, and that's one of the main reasons for going to India and being inexperienced in alpine type climbing, and now going to Patagonia. I'd rather improve myself in more remote places, even in India there were lots of expeditions, so in future I'm looking for even more remote places.

Do the long term ambitions of climbing hold anything, or is it a very short term, immediate?

For me it's very short term, and it used to be a hell of a lot shorter, day to day. But once you start doing big trips you have to start having annual ambitions.

Is travel an important part to you?

Yes, it's very important, I don't know why really but it is. Travelling around India is very adventurous, and it's not easy either.

How successful was the India trip?

In climbing terms it was pretty awful, but in learning terms it was very successful. I learnt so much from that trip which should stand me in good stead for future trips.

In what way would you say you learnt a lot?

I learnt a lot about my body's ability to cope with altitude in climbing, physical things like that; also coping with other people in really stressful situations that are prolonged. You go rockclimbing with someone and that's not a prolonged stressful situation. But when you've got 40 days in the mountains under severe stress, it's very interesting to watch what people reactions are on quite simple things.

Do you think you will ever find anything better than climbing?

Not with the same feeling, no! I do a lot of writing which gives me tremendous satisfaction, when you have a day of finding a good way to express yourself. But that actual ridiculous feeling you do get in climbing, you can't describe.

Two Tier Buttress lying deep in the Cheedale valley. The river Wye passes beneath, meandering as it gurgles through the stones and the trout swim peacefully in the shallows.

The Hustlers

To Hustle, to have impatient energy perhaps, but in this case it is to deliver the goods, 8b's. They get put up as test pieces, classic hard routes and the Hustlers come and shoot them to pieces – 8b if they're lucky. They take no prisoners, there's no dainty ponsing around in this division, you either come up with the goods, or you get your arse kicked right out of town. They come in every form, deceiving the onlooker: thin and spindly, big eater's, city slickers, duckers and divers, rough and unshaven, right off the plains and shooting from the hip. The performance is staggering, everyone looks on in amazement, the Hustlers leave the smouldering crag – deliverance. Others may try to Hustle, the graduates, the punters, the boys; don't bother, you're gonna get roasted.

Chris Plant

Christopher Plant, born 14.1.58 at Heanor, Derbyshire. Known to most of his friends as Plant Pot. A climber who developed slowly and has always been in the shadow of the stars and able to retain his very quiet but likeable character. He has also helped with guidebook production and has a knowledge of British climbing right across the grades. A first ascentionist of late, adding classic hard routes such as POWER PLANT 8a, in Cheedale and BATTLE OF LITTLE BIG ORME 8a+, at Pen Trwyn.

Interview near Llanwrst, Wales. 1.11.90

What did VECTOR feel like when you first climbed it in 1980?

I don't now, I just went and did it, we read about it in Hard Rock and just went off and did it. It was surprising because we were HVS climbers going out on weekends. Nobody climbed extreme in those days really; apart from a few people you read about in magazines.

In 1982 you went to America and climbed NAKED EDGE and HALF DOME, were those hard routes at the time?

They weren't over here by any stretch of the imagination. But in America nobody did NAKED EDGE, it was quite a big thing that people were actually on it, if you weren't named then you didn't do that route. HALF DOME'S a different thing altogether, that's a big aid route so its different and a lot of people had done it. We didn't really know what we were doing. I tried learning to jumar on the 17th pitch which was funny, I had two 9mm ropes and put one jumar on each rope, set off for about 10 minutes, then the ropes went tight and I did the splits. Its the only time I've ever done the splits. I led all pitches after that. I climbed the rest, by what was then known as French free, where you dyno from tape to tape and just pull up.

Do you think climbing has benefited from losing Aid climbing?

I don't have an opinion on it really, the people out there were doing really hard aid climbing, I never did any of this A5 type stuff, its just too serious.

Did pictures of routes like SEA OF DREAMS A5, and ZODIAC A5 inspire you at the time?

Yeah they did, you were impressed by the rurp belay on whatever route it was, all these people were crazy and it inspired me to want to climb El Cap, even though I never did it, mind you I got inspired by everything then because they were within your capabilities. You weren't inspired by E5's because they were just not in your capabilities, you didn't climb that grade unless you were mega famous, but aid climbing didn't have that aura I guess. I'd still like to do a big aid route on El Cap like THE SHIELD, you think about TROLL WALL but it's too cold, I don't want to do that.

Had MIDNIGHT LIGHTNING been done then?

Yeah, that's ancient. That was just something John Bachar did, he was a legend, he was right up there. Nobody ever did that, I never even tried it, I was climbing E3 and had no pretentions of climbing anything hard at all, I just progressed through the grades. They were them and I was me, I wasn't in there league, I was never going to be in there league.

Do you regret not having a job over the last 10 years?

I regret having a job over the last three months! No, not at all, no way. I wasn't going anywhere with a job, I'm a labourer, I'm always going to be a labourer nothing else; maybe if I pulled my finger out, but I'm too lazy. I mean what's the point, you might as well be on the dole. you can be anything you like when you're on the dole, you're just unemployed; whereas when you're a sweeper-up, you're a sweeper-up, a jobs just money, isn't it?

Do you have thoughts that you're sponging from society?

No, not really. I mean I do work, I take advantage of the situation as far as I can. You can get the dole so I get it, but if I couldn't I'd just work when I had to. You can still work, get enough money and climb. You don't need to climb all the time, it's not necessary, we never thought about it either when we started. When we were on the dole I always used to justify it to people who said "don't you think you're sponging on society". This was in '81, unemployment was so high then that people were very sympathetic if you were on the dole, you'd occasionally get offered jobs and people would so "Oh it's really bad isn't it". If they got a bit stroppy you'd just point out that someone who really wanted to work was doing the job that you didn't really want to do. You didn't want to do it and a lot of people had to be unemployed, so it might as well be you who had some gumption of what to do with it. A lot of people just have to work, it's their ethic, they're lost without it, they feel really degraded, so it's better for them to work than for a load of lads who want to climb, have no responsibilities and who don't want to work. Maybe that's a lame argument but I've used it for years.

Has the idea of a family life ever appealed to you?

No, I couldn't imagine it, I wouldn't be able to support it, I'm just too lazy.

Do you think that might change ever?

I wouldn't imagine so, unless she's rich!

Chris on the crux of YORKSHIRE 8b at Water Cum Jolly's Cornice. Moves involving undercutting a hideously tiny hold, with feet smearing on nothing.

Do you thinks it's important for climbers to travel?

I don't know, I guess it depends why you're doing it. I think you get a lot more out of it if you do travel, you're going to see a lot more places and your climbing career's going to be a lot longer. You've got variety and you're meeting people – climbing is still down to meeting people, I think it always has been. There's always been the camaraderie and everybody is on equal terms with it. The class that people climb, they're all pretty similar - they all tend to be reasonably educated, to a degree and down to my sort of level. Mostly they're bright, so you can relate to them. In the past everybody went to the mountains but I don't think it's quite so now, but you still meet a lot of different people if you travel, there's no point in just going to Raven Tor all the time.

Does seeing litter at crags bother you?

Yes, I think it's an indication of what sort of people are climbing these days. It's just not necessary.

Do you find that English crags are tidier than French Crags?

Yes, but I'm not sure who that's down to - it's probably down to the Germans. British crags are getting to be a right state, they never used to be, you'd never see a speck of rubbish. Whether or not its the sort of people that it's attracting. There's more and more people, and a lot of places like Stanage are getting a lot of groups, it's a lot of young people and they're not so bothered, many of them don't want to be there and a lot of rubbish gets chucked that way. Ravens Tor is filthy but a lot of that ain't nowt to do with climbers.

Does it bother you that Rubicon Wall was once filled with nice green bushes and plants at the bottom but is now trodden down?

Well, Rubicon used to have a tarmac road going past it, there was a wall the other side of the road before the lake and there were road workings so I guess it's sad that the greenery has gone but before it was part of the mill, part of the industry. The thing that is more offensive to me is that giant spiked iron gate, that's absolutely appalling. Greenery soon grows – I wouldn't like a tree to be chopped down but greenery is a bit different.

Do you think of permanent bolts as detracting?

It's not very good really, pieces of tat are more offensive to the eye, they are more noticeable, they are horrible and shouldn't be there. Bolts are worse in the fact that you can climb anywhere with them so there's more littering. But I've never really thought about them to be honest. I couldn't say I find them terrible, I climb on the things and I've placed them so I'd be a hypocrite to say otherwise.

In 1987 you started climbing a lot harder than you had done previously, and you did a fast ascent of WHORE OF BABYLON, How long did it take you.

Five and a half – six days I guess. I think Basher had done it in five days and Mark Leech had done it in two. So it was comparable to Gore's and Bashers ascent. I was quite pleased with it at the time because other people were taking 10 days so I was quite chuffed. That was all down to going to France and starting red pointing.

So that had a terrific influence on your climbing?

Grade wise yes. It's down to flashing grades because you don't climb in the same style now. I'm stronger now, I've got to say that, but because you don't climb in the same style as you did, it's hard to directly compare the two. Placing nuts and hanging in there and flashing something or red pointing something – one you do is E5 and one you do is E7 but at the end of the day, you're probably less worn out when you get to the top of the E7. Although you've spent more days on it, it's obviously a harder route, but it is hard to compare grades directly.

Does red pointing make climbers stronger?

It's bouldering with a rope so I suppose they will be stronger and they're actually trying harder routes than they would have done in the past, It makes climbers stronger but I don't know whether it makes them have better stamina.

Chris having fallen off SWIFT UNDERCUT 8a, on the Vector Buttress, Tremadog; swinging out, trying to get back into the belay.

In 1988 you put up POWER PLANT 8a, and you also did STATEMENT OF YOUTH and ZOOLOOK establishing yourself in the 8a grades. You also on-sighted HARLEM DESIRE 7c at Buoux, was that your hardest flash?
Yes, that was on sight which I was very pleased with definitely. I have always been pleased with them and they stand out in my mind.
What made that huge jump in on-sight ability?
It wasn't a huge jump. I'd on-sighted POKA DE RINGO in 87 which is like top end of 7b+. I'd always on-sited, that was just a natural progression.

Did you ever notice a jump in your climbing career?
I think in 84 I had a bit of a jump because we went on various strict stupid diets and lost loads of weight and got into real stamina climbs. We were just flashing left, right and centre. We'd go out and flash for example: PUMP E4, COCK BLOCK E5, and QUANTUM JUMP E5, and something else in one day.

People weren't often doing E5s even then, so that was a bit of a jump. And then in '87, there was Red Pointing, another jump. The rest has just been a natural progression. I generally climbed with people who were about my own standard and didn't boulder, didn't really train very much, so it was just down to the rock, down to doing a lot of routes.

You've climbed in America, Germany, France, Norway, Australia, etc., are those countries comparable to British climbing?
Australia is dead laid back, I mean they're all asleep, it's just ridiculous. When I got there I was running around frantic and everybody thought, who is this guy. By the end of the trip you'd got your climbing partner and were looking round the campsite for a third person to go climbing with. It's just that sort of atmosphere, you go there and hang out on the belays and mash tea while you're sat at the bottom, make little fires and mash tea. I had a good time in America but I think I met some untypical Americans a lot of the time. They're

very intense people and they don't like it when you say you're not very good relatively, because they can't accept that as you're better than them most of the time. They're very much into themselves. In France they're just geared to sport climbing and are getting more geared to competitions. They've coined the word on-sight, I mean what was on-sight a few years ago, it was just how you climbed. You went there, nobody top-roped, I always led everything, you'd never second anything. The only things you ever seconded were things that were well protected, you'd never second anything that was dangerous because you'd have to lead that, it was psychological. I didn't climb very much in Germany, I always climbed with Englishmen so it's hard to say about that. Norway, a lot of French influence is there, they are not very far along, and they're really into a very intense little climbing scene that they've got. They are over interested in what other people are doing really, rather than climbing for themselves.

Do you enjoy climbing on indoor walls?
No, I hate it, I've never liked it, because of the competition. I was never good at it, you've always got your wall expert who is always going to walk up and try and burn you off. It's just not a very nice atmosphere.

Do you like bouldering on the crags?
Yes, I'm really into it these days, I'm not very good at it but I'm getting stronger at it so I'm really more and more keen on it. It's very enjoyable, you go out with a group of mates and everybody is encouraging everybody else and it's a good laugh. I'm in a bit of an odd situation where I climb with the people I like climbing with. They are a lot stronger than me bouldering wise and so it's hard sometimes for them to share the same enthusiasm which is natural really when you're doing something that they warm up on. They are encouraging, they are a really good group of lads, but it's that thing, it's the same as trying to encourage somebody on easier routes, there's just not that edge somehow. But I'm going to do a lot more bouldering. It's a lot less hassle than ropework.

Which is your favourite rock?
I love gritstone, I've always like gritstone, it's just my favourite rock. It lends itself to interesting movement. It's what I started climbing on. You are limited to the time you have on it, since gritstone eats fingertip skin. Admittedly though limestone lends itself to harder, more powerful moves.

Ben Masterson

The first impression you get of Scottish Ben is a typical laid back and dishevelled rock addict. Then to see him climb on an 8a+ and believe the transformation to a powerful, clinical sportsman, is more than impressive. His wry grin afterwards suggests that the satisfaction of climbing is more than a vagrant pastime. Born 23.12.64 in Belfast, then brought up in Scotland. He moved to Sheffield in 1984 and four years later consolidated 8b, with routes like MISSION and ROSE AND THE VAMPIRE at Buoux. He has always put tremendous energy into his attempts and climbed most 8a's in a day. His preferred style is climbing on-sight, or in a day and consequently has never managed to really break into 8b+.

Interview 20.1.91 Nether Edge, Sheffield.

What made you start doing a degree in Business Studies at Sheffield?
I've always had the ability to do a degree. I did well at School and then tried to do a degree in Physics at Strathclyde University. That I failed by virtue of going climbing all the time. Today the future for professional climbers is not very good. You need a job, and I don't particularly want to be a sales rep, not that there is anything wrong with that. I don't want to work in the professional abseil game for the rest of my life either; so you have to find an actual direction to go in. I feel as though I've been economically forced out of climbing. I was professional but not earning enough to think in terms of any kind of future. I had to do something, and in the same way as I like to do climbing well, I like to do anything well; it seemed logical to do a degree, get into business and hopefully go further.

Is doing this degree as satisfying as climbing?
Doing a degree is not remotely satisfying although some of the work is interesting. I hope that as I get more specialized it will become more interesting, but most of it is not, and from that point of view, not particularly stimulating.

What was stimulating about climbing hard or even just climbing, is there a difference?
Sure, climbing is just great fun. It's really fun to move like that, getting excitement from being high up, being out from gear, being on for a fall, being in nice surroundings; anything like that you can get excitement from. That's something anyone gets out of climbing, or that any climber good, bad or otherwise will get out of climbing, at any level; whether it be a level you find hard, easy or what, there's always that kind of satisfaction. As for climbing hard, that satisfaction is the excitement inside, of doing something well, or as well as you can.

Do you have any regrets standards wise from leaving climbing?

I definitely could have climbed harder, I was getting better all the time, as does everybody, but that's not a regret in itself. I don't regret not having climbed as hard as I possibly could have.

Of your climbing career, doing MISSION 8b, TABOU ZI ZI 8b, THE ROSE 8b, all in 1988, was that a reason to bow out?

I think I know what you mean. I really did want to quit whilst I was ahead, but in fact I probably didn't really do that, I quitted slightly after I was ahead. I was still trying to hang in there in 1989, and certainly in point of view in competitions. I had some good results but also some bad ones, so I didn't really succeed in quitting whilst I was ahead.

Does doing hard routes give you lasting satisfaction?

Not from the point of view of hardness. There are some routes: I don't know whether it's because of the particular way I had to go around doing them, the particular trouble I had in actually doing them, actual moves or beauty of the routes themselves; for those reasons some of the hard routes I've done will stick in my mind for the rest of my life, not from the point of view of hardness, more from the way I had to climb them.

Do any stand out in particular?

I think the ROSE AND THE VAMPIRE, I found it hard partly; I spent a lot of time falling off the last move, and also because the moves themselves were just so perfect. From any other point of view, aesthetic or anything like that, I guess its chipped and horrible.

Is getting to the top of routes a very important part?

Yes, I mean I wouldn't have said you've lost everything if you don't get to the top, it's just an important part of the whole procedure.

What was it initially that made you move from Scotland to Sheffield?

It's really difficult to say. More than anything I just got sucked into Sheffield. I like Scotland, I think its a great place, I'm glad I was brought up there but I visited here to climb, and just got sucked into the enthusiasm of it all, then it seemed logical to move here.

What was the enthusiasm, was it the anarchy, or the will to climb?

The fact that everyone really seemed to be into having fun. You can climb anywhere I suppose, anywhere there's rocks; but everything down here seemed to be worked out to having fun which is good. Also for me, it was the first time I became totally independent from my parents, which is a step everyone has to make.

What was your idea of having fun?

More than anything, you'd get up in the morning, decide what you'd wanted to do, and do it. That was something I hadn't really experienced before, prior to then it was a case of fitting things in around other people.

Is that freedom of doing what you want to do important within climbing?

I think within climbing it is, It's one of the most important things in climbing itself. I've climbed for an awful long time and some of the climbing I did, I felt as though I was forced into; training for particular competitions, doing competitions themselves if I didn't feel like competing. That to me was as frustrating as being stuck in a city on a nice day and not being able to climb. So I'm very aware that freedom is one of the most important things.

Does the freedom of Alpine climbing appeal to you?

Alpine climbing appeals to me. I've done a fair bit, but I wouldn't say there's any more, or any less freedom involved in that.

Have you ever approached alpine climbing without consulting guidebooks?

I've never owned an alpine guidebook. In a sense, I've followed given paths and given routes, so from that point of view I've followed guides as much as anyone else.

Do you think guidebooks should exist in climbing?

It's hard to imagine a world without guides.

Is the course your doing now, searching for a break from climbing?

No, not at all. I think that breaks from climbing are important. I've always had breaks from climbing, either to work and earn money, which you have to do whether you like it or not; or short breaks to do something different. I've been into skiing, travelling, going to the Zoo, things like that, going and seeing my family. I think they are really important, it's a really important part of the overall balance. For me going and doing what I'm doing now, has got nothing to do with having a break. It's simple, for economic reasons I have to have a job, and if I'm going to have to have a job, I want it to be something that I enjoy.

Had you been tempted to look for a job associated with climbing?

I think it depends to what you mean by associated. I now work in the access game which you can say is related, particularly as a lot of the jobs, require physically climbing things, more so than abseiling; but it's like scaffolding, a job that anyone can do. A lot of people think it logical for climbers to get into; but for me I think its a business, just like any other business. The climbing equipment business doesn't particularly interest me either. At the time I was involved, a couple of years ago

now, the market seemed to be booming. It seemed to be full of enthusiasts rather than business men, manufacturing the equipment that they wanted to manufacture. I don't think this kind of challenge is what I would be looking for.

Does competition in business or climbing interest you?

For a start competition in climbing, since this is about climbing. I wouldn't like to pass a judgement on whether I personally think that competition is a good or a bad thing. It may well even be a bad thing, but for me, I enjoyed it because it enabled me first to make some money, and second to do the climbing I wanted to do. It gave me an opportunity to develop myself, and it gave me an opportunity to compete with people. Everyone competes with each other in climbing, in a sense by doing the hardest routes and so on; maybe not everybody but a lot of people do, and it gave me a chance to compete with people on what I felt were my own terms. It was also the way I liked to do things, like a one off burst to do something, rather than just a case of who gets bored the quickest working on a hard route.

Is that feeling of excitement important to your life?

I think I get bored easily, so anything I do, I have to do all the way so as not to get bored. If I do something at an easily attainable level, or at a mundane level, I get dissatisfied, so I tend to pursue things that way.

If that encounters danger does that worry you?

Assuming that it is only danger to myself. I wouldn't like to make decisions for other people that involved danger. I think you have to look at things from, the point that there's a risk getting into your car, hopefully a small one. But you just have to make a decision on that strength, if the reward seems to justify a risk, you take a risk, if the rewards get bigger, then you take more risk. I'm not opposed to danger at all, you just have to look at it in a broad minded way.

Has soloing appealed to you in that sense?

I've done an awful lot of soloing. I used to solo madly, good solos on the gritstone, and used to have solo circuits of stacks of, what at the time, were hard routes: BITTER FINGERS E4, WEE DORIS E3 at Stoney Middleton and routes at Buoux. I've solo'd a lot of ice climbs, because that's the way for me to move in the mountains. It's fast and that's the way to get the most out of them. Going to the limit soloing rather than just doing it for freedom is not for me, not where the penalty is certain death or very serious injury. The risks outweigh the benefit.

Are achievements and goals quite important to you in climbing?

Not for the reason of climbing in total, but when I used to climb hard I used to have levels, like parameters, in which I would want to perform. Below that I'd be saying, that's too low a standard of achievement to justify what I'm doing. If I can't do that then I'm going wrong and I'll have to think again.

Does the form of a rock face hold anything for you?

Definitely, I think it does for everybody. The best routes are the ones that look good too. There is no doubt about it. When I first saw Ravens Tor, the first time I came to the peak, I thought wow! It was really important for me to go and do all the routes there. Also area's like the Gunks in New York State, which are like a better version of gritstone; again the features are very important. You see things and then don't look at the grade, you just go and climb them. Then places like the Verdon Gorge in France, where one route seems to be the same as another, a vertical slabby wall with a few holds that may or not be chipped; that to me is far less attractive.

Has loose rock ever appealed to you?

Not at all, I've needed stiches before from pulling loose holds off and hitting myself in the face with them; I find very little attraction in that. It can be that a route is so good that you can excuse a few loose holds, about that there is no doubt. I would never exclude a route because of a few loose holds: but there are climbers who climb just pure, pure garbage all the time, and that is simply not interesting.

Can you relate to them?

I really don't know, I don't know many people like that. I probably could relate to them as human beings, but I don't know if I could relate to their activities.

Is it important for you that climbing does have such a broad aspect of interest from loose rock to soloing?

I don't know because, if we were to bring in the whole spectrum of things we would be bringing in things which really don't interest me, things which might be very important to other people. It's important to me that everything's there that I'm looking for in climbing. As for being ultralistic, and hoping for what everyone else looks for, will be there too; that doesn't come into it.

Can you see anything that's going to stop you climbing?

Serious injury! No, It's something that I enjoy doing, so long as I'm able to do it. Circumstances have kept me away from it at the moment, I'm in a particularly busy part of my life, but I intend to fit recreation in. I enjoy climbing, and I will try and do it as much as I can along with other things.

If you can't climb 8a, does that matter?

No, I'll enjoy climbing when I'm an old man and I'm sure then I won't be able to climb 8a.

Chris Plant on the last move of YORKSHIRE 0b, so named by Ben Masterson because 'The route is only 8a, which is the equivalent of all the 8b routes in Yorkshire!'

Dougie Hall

Some climbers go down in the record books as great pioneers of free climbing, others for conquering Everest, others for soloing; yet Dougie must go down in history for pioneering convenience climbing. Following the stars around, watching them struggle to put up new routes, then popping in to do the second or third ascent, quickly, efficiently; and most importantly for Dougie, enjoyably. His skill as a climber could have easily made him into a new routing superstar, yet a relaxed character of unselfishness, has given him at the very top level a great opportunity tp go out for a day on the crag, and simply tick routes. The title convenience climber is indeed a bizzare accolade, but Dougie should be respected for climbing the very hard routes of the 70's and 80's in such pure style. In many ways doing second ascents of the hard routes of the day was physically harder than the first ascentionist because you had to climb them on sight. His success in this style along with other climbers like Chris Hamper, Phil Davidson, and Kim Carrigan, really helped the on-sight ethic survive at a time when it was threatened by the introduction of bolt protection and domination by the new redpoint ethic.

Interview, 17.1.91 Royton, Oldham, Lancs.

You left school at 15, what did you get a job as?
An apprentice sheet metal worker and that's what I'm doing now to this day, well I'm not an apprentice any longer.

At what age did you start climbing well?
I didn't start until I was 21, then after about a year I was climbing E3, E4, it's quite a long time ago like!

When was that?
It would be 15 years ago in 1976, days when we used to hitch out to Stoney every week, we used to all stay in the wood shed and just doss there, Animal, Dirty Derek, lots of funny other names.

Can you remember any routes at the time?
KINK E5 and KELLOGG E4; they were the Stoney routes. All the hard routes were at Stoney Middleton at one time, we used to follow in Tom Proctor's footsteps really. The routes there used to stay unrepeated for a few

years and then once one of the gang did one, we used to all do them.

Did you see Tom climb there at all?
Yes, he was very impressive and very powerful. I guess the days before proper stamina routes became the norm, Tom was really good at what he did.

How come you got into climbing so late?
I used to go sailing and my brother came home from the army one weekend, took me out and from that moment I was hooked. Three months later I packed my job in and went to the Alps, I used to like snow and ice climbing. If the conditions were any good in England I'd still do it.

Did you notice any jump in you climbing ability?
I was climbing about E4 and doing Tom's routes and then I went to America for about 9 months. I climbed virtually everyday and when I came back in 1981, I was climbing top E5 I guess, and whatever E6's there were in the country then. Ron Fawcett was on the scene and it was a case of trying to repeat Ron's routes, things like SARDINE E5 at Ravens Tor.

Were you repeating Ron's routes fairly easily or finding them absolutely desperate?

No, I was repeating them all in a day, but that was the year you could repeat routes in a day, just because you repeated a route in a day didn't mean a lot really.

Do you think it's a shame that people spend more time on routes than a day now?

It takes a little bit of the enjoyment off it. When I go out climbing now I tend to look for routes that I can do in a day, but often I can't. I go on them if I have to, if there's no other routes, but preferably I'd stay on 8a and 8a+ routes.

When Ron was putting up the routes at the beginning of the '80's did you ever feel that you should be there, putting up the routes?

No, not really, I've never been into new routing in any way. If there were routes that hadn't been free'd, then I'd go and try to free them, but I'm just too lazy really, too busy ticking routes. To me it's just a waste of a day if you have to abseil down and clean something.

Do you thank the people who have put up the routes?

Yes. When Gary Gibson was climbing a lot I used to slag him off, all in fun because I like him. He said to one of my mates "Doug must be really thankful for me, I keep him going on all these routes," which is quite true, I've always admired him because he puts up stacks of routes you could go and repeat. The type of routes he was doing you needed four or five a day, to keep you going, they weren't easy but they were like E5 and mild E6's; you can do a few of them in a day.

Where do your best abilities lie in climbing?

Bold routes which need a bit of finger stamina I've quite liked.

Are you disappointed to see British climbing going towards bolted climbs and away from routes like LORD OF THE FLIES?

No, I look at it as a new avenue in climbing really. I'm disappointed that a lot of people don't do both types of routes but I'm not disappointed that climbing is going that way. Sometimes I think, I must go and do some bold routes, or something a bit different because you're not getting the full feel of British rock climbing, which is quite varied. That's why I like climbing in Britain.

What made you do a route like THE CLOWN E7 at Gogarth?

For the experience really, and to get some ticks. I haven't got that many ticks left on limestone, therefore I have to go to different places just to get some ticks. If I go to Malham now I'm stuck on 8b's, and it slow's you down a hell of a lot; getting a tick once every 20 weeks is a bit demoralizing!

Is getting the tick important or is it actually climbing different rocks?

No, just getting routes done, I like getting a pile of routes done. I like different areas as well, that's important. I love going to areas were I've got loads of routes to go at.

Does it worry you to do routes like THE CLOWN with a family?

It could be dangerous, but it's only as dangerous as the amount of pre-checking you do on it.

Do routes like INDIAN FACE hold any interest?

No I don't think I'd go that far now, you're just going onto the suicidal fringe there a little.

Do necky routes ever appeal to you in your climbing?

I've done necky routes quite a lot. I used to do a lot of the bolt routes without the bolts when they started putting bolt routes up. A lot on the Cornice I did without bolts when they were first put up, but they had one or two bolts in then, a lot of Gary's old ones; that was before bolts were accepted.

Have you enjoyed climbing abroad as much as in England?

Yes but mainly because of the travel and the adventure. I still like the climbing in Britain more than abroad definitely, because you can have the variety; whereas if you go to France it's all bolt routes which can get a bit monotonous after a bit, but I really enjoy going on holiday.

When you go on climbing holidays do you go with the family?

No I don't, I go with my friends, I don't involve my family with climbing really at all.

Is that's important for you?

It's not fair on the family. It might work with some families, but when I go away with my wife and family, I forget about climbing totally, it is better for her, she can enjoy herself then without me nipping off every other day going climbing, she wouldn't accept that, and it works better that way.

Which 5 very hard routes that you've done, really stand out in your mind?

It tends to be the routes that you did last year that you remember but lets think... I liked EYE OF THE TIGER because it's E6 and there's not a lot of E6's without bolts on, necky limestone. It was done just before bolts were introduced, if it was done today it would have 5 or 6 in. It's a hard route because you have to put runners in, it would only be a quick tick really with bolts in, and that really stands out in my mind. I did it on-sight, as I do all my routes. Yes I fell off the start, placing some runners but if there had been bolts to clip you wouldn't have fallen off and probably wouldn't have remembered it, when you just miss the floor you remember routes quite a bit more!

A Stoney route perhaps?

I really remember KINK at Stoney Middleton, I had to go about 10 times before I got that ticked, because every time I went to do the jam over the roof I ended up with a big hole in my hand so I'd just try at the end of the day and at weekends, I was only climbing E4 then so that was a step up into the E5 and one of Tom's Routes. It's one of the few routes in those days which took more than a day, it was a hard route.

What's the best gritstone route?

I enjoyed doing SCOOP DE GRACE E5 7a, at Running Hill Pits. It's my own route it's in the Chew Valley area, that took me about 17 different nights to do it. I was learning to drive and I'd go up there in my car with my L plates on and try it for an hour, it's really fingery and you just didn't have much skin on your fingers after an hour.

Best route in Wales?

MIDSUMMER NIGHT'S DREAM, again it's something I did only six months ago. I tried it about 10 years ago, I was trying a second ascent and took some big falls off it because there wasn't a peg in it then. You almost hit the floor if you fell off. I enjoyed doing that, it's a different proposition with decent boots on, when I tried it for the very first time, I found a pair of boots at the bottom of The Cromlech on the boulders, and they were about a size and a half too big, but that's the type of thing you climbed in in those days, well our band of climbers did anyway. With good boots and that peg in, I enjoyed it.

Did you think of doing Nick Dixon's route - FACE MECCA?

I intend to do some of those routes next year, but I'm not into E9/10. Around the grade E7/8 I'll do them if they are necky, but the harder route need a lot of rehearsing, and I'm not into rehearsing that type of route. I don't mind rehearsing bold routes but I wouldn't rehearse something like INDIAN FACE.

Your final route?

THE GROOVE 8a+ at Malham, a modern bolt route, just a big trip which goes on forever, you keep going, it's tests your stamina.

How long did that take you to do?

It took 5 days which is quite a long time really, but some people take 20-25 days over it. A lot of 8a+ routes I can do in a day, but not a big stamina job like that, there are just too many moves to remember, I was getting the sections mixed up as I was going, even when I had it dogged!

Dougie on TEA MONSTER 7c+, Water Cum Jolly's Cornice, Peak District.

Is that a technical problem, remembering routes?

Most short routes I can work out quite easily and remember the sections, on THE GROOVE it took two days before I knew where I really was on the climb. It's been flashed now by Simon Nadin, but there are no hard moves on it. I could do bolt to bolt, more or less straight away, but rehearsing it for stamina is desperate, he must have had so much in reserve to flash that.

Have you any ideas for the future in climbing?

I just want to go on as I am really just enjoying myself just keep ticking! One good thing about me and my climbing is, that I have never once got bored, or lost my enthusiasm. I could go out everyday and climb and not get bored. I've done it for one or two years, never had days off or got bored. A lot of people want time off don't they, even the superstars have a couple of months off, but it has never bothered me.

Mick Lovatt

There are lots of climbers who fly up a few hard routes then chuck in the towel because they are afraid of finding their limit is just around the corner. Mick is of the other breed who keep on in there, battling away, week in and week out on the hard routes. The rewards are there and Mick has now climbed 15 routes of 8a and above, his best ascent being PREDATOR 8b at Malham. Being 6ft. 2ins. makes it difficult on the very powerful hard routes yet consistent dedication to training and application has made Mick one of Britain's consistent grade 8 climbers, and his two recent new routes at Malham: VOGUE 8a+, and ENERGY VAMPIRE 8a+, bear witness to this.

Interview 2.2.91 Preston, Lancs.

What were your first thoughts of climbing?
It seemed quite a natural thing for me to do as I enjoyed being outside, and the whole idea was pretty exciting. When I first went it was with these army fellows who were pretty square army dudes, as they usually are. They had no real idea about climbing even as it was then, but it still appealed. I don't really know what else my first thoughts were, except it was obvious from the start that I wanted to climb harder, I instantly understood what grades

were, and there were competitions between mates, who could do low level traverses without falling off.
Did you see climbing developing any particular way then for yourself?
I think early influences were things like Don Whillan's book 'Portrait of a Mountaineer', I read that, and Don became God. Obviously you picked route names out from the book and tried to tick them.
Did the alpine or Patagonia concept come over?
We used to rock climb as training for climbing in the Alps, that was the ultimate aim, we had this idea of climbing the Eiger by 1980, we started climbing in 1974. We set our goal as the North Face of the Eiger by 1980 which never materialized, although we did have several summers in the Alps. The first I think was in '76 when I did Mont Blanc, we were really gob smacked about the size of the place. It was always planned that summer holidays were going to be alpine. I think the harder we could climb on rock in this country meant that we were going to be better alpine climbers, which is probably a totally false idea. In 1978 we had a really bad summer in the Alps and had read that article 'Yosemite Shorties by John Sheard, in Mountain magazine. That was it, we wanted to go to Yosemite.

What affect did the trip to Yosemite have on you, did Yosemite come up to what you expected?
Yes, more than what we expected I think because it was bigger than we imagined. We were 18 years old, first time in the States, we got to San Francisco late at night and didn't know what we were doing. We just dossed down on the bloody street, anything could have happened, we didn't know where we were and the reputation America has for weirdos and things, thankfully never materialized. Next day we caught the bus into Yosemite and had designs on climbing THE NOSE. I was with a guy called Frank Pearson who looked out of the bus window and couldn't see the top of it; you pass within 300 yards of the base. He was straining his neck, looked across at me and said,"Fuck that!" I ended up trying THE NOSE with someone else later in that trip. We got stuck in a queue one time, stormed off another, wasted so much time that we stuck to the short things after that. I think it definitely had a big influence on us.

Mick on THE GROOVE 8a+ at Malham Cove, Yorkshire. One of the really classic hard modern climbs, 150ft. long stamina test with apparently no hard moves!

Were you disappointed on not doing a big wall?

Yes! because it was the thing to do. You go to Yosemite where there are 3000 ft. walls, and you're doing 80-90 foot at the bottom, it was pretty outrageous for us back then. Having an Alpine background for the previous three years, if you didn't make it to the top you had failed. At that particular time I'd been climbing with a guy called Gordon Tinning, he lent me this haul bag to go out to The States and he said "take that up to the top of THE NOSE, that will be the 3rd time it will have done it". Pete Whillance used it first, then Gordon had done it, and I was supposed to be the third man to take this bag up to the top. We didn't get past 1000 feet, so I think I was disappointed that I didn't do a big wall. I went back the year after to try another, but it was then I had the fall, the accident where I damaged my leg. That was five weeks on my back on Yosemite, not so impressive!

What happened?

It was on CRACK A GO GO, 5.11c (E3), all my runners ripped out. I had a friend at the bottom of this left hand crack, then four wires up it. It was a typical British style of ascent, you'd go for it and it doesn't matter if it's mid day at one hundred degrees. I was steaming up the crack and I got to the jug, all I had to do was stand on the jug and rest, but I was greasing off so badly that I couldn't even take a hand off to put into my chalk bag, so I just said take the rope because we'd got into falling off a bit by then. He took in the rope and I dropped onto the top wire, that ripped and the one below ripped etc., etc., I just kept on going and hit the tree at the bottom, the 'friend' runner stopped me hitting the floor when I fell out of the tree. I had a severed artery in my thigh and was losing a lot of blood; it was Steve Monks who actually saved my life, he plugged the hole with a scarf and Roger Whitehead got the rescue.

Do you think with that British care-free attitude, if you'd carried on alpine climbing you would have stayed alive?

I think something had to happen. Take my best route of 1980 which was R & S SPECIAL E4 6a, on Raven Crag, it's lost a runner placement since and has been up graded now. There's that sort of attitude that, whatever runner you put in is fine and they will hold. They did several times on other routes, the wire held and they were good, we got a lot of confidence

until that happened, and it took three years for me to get over that. I know it sounds pathetic compared to the bolt stuff now, but E4 then was quite a big number. I came back to being like an E1 leader, for the next three years I'd look at runners in cracks, they'd be absolute sinkers and I just thought they were going to come out, I could see them jumping out at me.

Did you get over that in the end?

I got over that, because for whatever reason, John Monks picked up on me, I don't know why. I used to go on Bolton climbing wall and it was January '82. I then got involved with the lads on the now legendary mini bus trips to France from Bolton. I went and that was the first time really that I broke away from the Preston climbing scene. I started climbing a lot with John then, he had so much enthusiasm for climbing, whether it be leading, seconding or bouldering whatever, he was my driving force in climbing.

When you were getting really into climbing, did you look back and not want to go and do the Eiger?

For me it's still there now, I haven't totally put it off. I really have an urge to go and climb something like the Dru now, maybe more so than the Eiger. There are great rock climbs on it but I'm not into floundering in snow filled gullies. If I can maintain the fitness to climb hard rock routes I'll continue doing it, and when the enthusiasm falls off I'll go back to climbing big mountain routes.

You've climbed some hard routes with John Monks, did that affect you when he gave up?

Yes very much, I don't really know why he gave up even to this day, he was into marathon running all of a sudden. In his first marathon he did it in 2½ hours so I think he realised he could do well at running and just backed off. Also he was always the better climber and in the last few months, I had led some things that he couldn't at that time, I think I realised that I had a long reach and maybe that put him off a bit.

Was it a natural progression to go onto the hard bolt routes, as opposed to things like THE BELLS E7?

Yes, we'd done stuff like RIGHT WALL, LORD OF THE FLIES, so we were into doing E5 or E6's, they were big routes. John being the leader said we should concentrate more on the Peak the next year so we started climbing on the Peak limestone, which was steep and more often dry than anywhere else. We started climbing on Ravens Tor and Rubicon which had peg and bolt protection. That led us into the Pen Trwyn boom in '83 when it was being drilled to death. I think we were following the trends because although we weren't at the

cutting edge of putting new routes up, we were just bubbling under, repeating a lot of the stuff. It was an extension of the Easter holiday with Pen Trwyn being the Buoux equivalent in England.

Does climbing bolt routes ever compare mentally with leading routes like Right Wall?

I suppose they do mentally, probably it is as hard. I think it's the way you approach it really, on a dangerous route you climb well within your grade and the mental strain is on the danger factor, but it's the amount that you can handle. On a bolt route you are attempting a route that you might or might not do that day because you are on your complete physical limit, again you choose to set that. Both are mentally straining, but for me I push myself to the limit of what I can cope with in both.

Do you find that you need danger or excitement?

I need excitement, I drive fast cars and I climb. I don't solo, I never have very much. On a bolt route you often run it out, you might be 100 foot off the ground and run out 20 feet, it feels a hell of a long way out when you take a 50 foot fall. Take SUPERCOOL 8a+, Bashers route in Gordale, you're a long way out when you're on that top wall and you think it is exciting and that is what you're doing it for. But I think if there was crap gear down there, or you were going to die if you did blow it; THAT WOULDN'T be exciting.

Do you think it's nice in climbing that you don't get many deaths?

Oh Yes, definitely. Gordon Tinning, my partner, died when I was in The States, that had a big affect on me and it still does, because he was like a real hero for me that I looked up to. The less deaths, the better. If you want to go and solo something that's fine, you take your life into your own hands, you have virtually nothing to do with anybody out climbing, mentally it's on a different planet to sports climbing. Poor fixed gear in particular, doesn't appeal to me at all. If it's there, then it should be good, as on the first ascent.

Has the scenery and environment always been important?

Yes. I think I was brought up to that by a school teacher that started us climbing, a walk into the crag was part of the day out. You'd walk up to Scafell in the Lake District. You may only do one route and then walk down a different way, which is fairly ridiculous by today's standards but you were taught to appreciate the country you were in, and the surroundings. It is a very important part to climbing.

Mick Lovatt 'in bulk' on the top section of PREDATOR 8b at Malham. The belay chain is in sight, but definitely out of mind; concentration being the key to the moment.

Tony Ryan

Many climbers like Tony have remained in the background over the past few years but are constantly improving and becoming more involved in competiton climbing. At the end of 1990 Tony came 10th. in a World Cup event with a full field. His lightness of 8½ stone and 5ft. 6ins. frame allows him to levitate on small holds easier than most. In 1986 he put up the route CAVIAR 8a+, at Rubicon Wall, Peak District, which today is one of the major testpieces of British climbing.

Interview, 14.1.91 Chorlton, Manchester.

Did you start climbing at a very early age?
Not that early because at school I was good at football and coming from Manchester it was an important part of life. My father initially took me climbing when I was about seven, and it was from then that I became interested, but I only climbed very occasionally. If I'd have been good enough at football then I would have liked to have played it professionally but the major problem was that from 14 or so I was too small for a potential professional player. I played for schools and a Sunday league club, then had a trial for Manchester boys but it became clear that I wasn't going to make it. So at 14-15 I started to climb more seriously, and on a regular basis.

How did your footballing friends at school accept your interest in climbing?
It became a case of suddenly developing a new group of friends since up to that age most of my friends were footballers and they had no understanding of climbing. I made new friends and lost nearly all of what I considered were my friends before.

Did you always live here in Manchester?
Yes, I lived here and did my 'A' levels then went on to do a HND in Business studies at the Poly. in Manchester.

Were you not tempted to go to Sheffield?
I considered it since by then I was climbing a lot of the time with climbers from Sheffield but I've always preferred to be on the fringe of the major climbing scene. I think its a bit too intense in Sheffield and you can easily get drawn in, A lot of climbers are very intense for a short period and then give it up or find something else. In staying in Manchester I felt freer to do my own thing, and besides which I like Manchester anyway. I thought about studying elsewhere but I enjoyed climbing in the Peak District, and Manchester is very central to all the other climbing areas.

An HND in Business Studies, did you envisage a career?
Yes I think business does interest me. Since the end of the course I've always worked in the

Gary and Tony Ryan, brothers alike; big chip eaters and both 8a climbers.

climbing trade in shops, and now for the past few years with distributors. The business side of climbing interests me, but still comes second to actually climbing although I intend to develop my interests in the future.

Without the career would you have been a better climber?
I don't think you can just attribute that to choosing a career, or work over climbing. I think that if I'd applied myself more in say the past 10 years I could have climbed harder but I don't think I've reached my peak so far anyway. Because I've climbed so reguarly and consistently without pushing myself too hard, I don't feel that I've burnt myself out at all. I feel I cam still climb harder and harder each year, you learn a bit more about climbing all the time.

When you were at Manchester Poly. what climbing interested you?
Traditional climbing, well that's what I think you call it nowadays, even so things like hangdogging were just coming into the sport, but most of the hardest routes in those days were steep limestone and granite, hanging around placing wires and yoyo'ing if necessary. Routes like LORD OF THE FLIES E6 6b, in Wales, and TEQUILA MOCKINGBIRD E6 6b, in the Peak.

Was leading LORD a lonely experience?
It was really, something that you don't get so much with todays limestone routes. Lord is a much slower experience because you have to hang around and fiddle about with a lot of

technical nut placements and so on; Whereas generally if you climb a bolt route today you would be concentrating purely on the moves. Most of the time on LORD is spent looking for the protection and placing it. You can get pretty lonely on some bolt routes mind you, but generally they are much quicker to climb and only half a rope length so you can lower off. The lonliness on something like LORD, is being over 100ft. away from your belayer and knowing that there's a lot of stretch in the 100ft. of rope out so you're going to fall quite a long way, and you're too high to yoyo, so you don't want to fall.

Has it ever worried you?
Yes, but as you become more experienced it becomes more enjoyable, probably the first few experiences of lonely routes are more worrying than enjoyable, but as you become more experienced it becomes very satisfying.

Did you ever consider routes like Lord to be bold?
Not really, no. As far as I'm concerned, if a route is well protected even though the protection might be spaced, when you fall off you're not going to hurt yourself. You might take a reasonably big fall, but it's not really what I consider as bold climbing. The type of climbing I don't like is where if you fall off, you can seriously hurt yourself, or if you are not in complete control of the situation, like on loose rock. Big leads on good runners are safe because you're in control and that makes a difference.

Rubicon Wall at Cressbrook Mill, Derbyshire. CAVIAR 8a+ takes a line up the darkest central part, with DANGEROUS BROTHERS 8a just to the right.

Do you regard that bold climbing in Wales as a fringe activity, like THE BELLS, THE BELLS?

I think the climbers that do it are very fringe really, because it's only small group of climbers who are really keen to do that sort of climbing on a regular basis, and they make it there sort of number one activity within climbing and tend not to venture further afield. It doesn't surprise me because there are so many different types of climbing to choose from, but I personally wouldn't do it, it's too scary and too dangerous. It depends to some extent to what you want out of climbing but for me I would consider that bold climbing is becoming more and more fringe as the safety of sportclimbing becomes more widespread.

How has climbing changed since you did LORD OF THE FLIES in 1983?

I think say 10 years ago climbers started to look more at the physical side of the sport and started to train more effectively, improve their strength and so on. It was a logical conclusion that they would look for more physically difficult routes. With this there becomes less opportuninty for it to be a dangerous route as well. It just becomes unjustifiable to confront that danger if theres a lot of physical demands on you. If this is not so, then you can cope with more stress from loose rock and bad protection. Safety has become more paramount in climbing and it's because the routes are physically harder. Were not machines, we make errors so it has to remain a fine balance to stay a challenging sport, it's not Russian roulette that most climbers are after.

Did you have any premonitions then of sport climbing then?

I actually thought it was a good idea because the part of climbing that I enjoy most is bouldering, redpointing is a way of breaking a route down into boulder problems and then linking the problems, so for me when I saw it coming I was very interested to take it up but I never felt it was a threat to traditional climbing. It has changed the nature of climbing, in that now you have a lot of climbers who choose to hang dog whereas in the past there wasn't the choice. ie in the past you mostly did a route without falling off or you yoyo'd it. You won't find many people choosing to yoyo a bolted route nowdays. It's probably a good thing in that with todays redpoint concept, it allows you to compare performance and gives you a clear cut answer which says you have done the route. In the past with yoyo's people never used to lower down to the ground, or take marginal rest places and get into very dodgy concepts about having done a route.

Has climbing bolt routes been enjoyable from day one.

Yes, I think climbing bolt routes has always been enjoyable, but not all the time. It does depend on the frame of mind you're in on the day, and the type of route you're on. Just because a route has bolts, doesn't mean that it's going to be an enjoyable route to climb and vice versa. Some routes where you have to hang around and put nuts in are still enjoyable, even though it breaks up the flow of the climb. What interests me more than ever is the art of climbing in the physical movement, and bolts allow you to explore that more.

Is there a mental aspect to bolt routes?

Yes, the mental aspect is a part which most climbers don't realise, it's a very big part of bolt climbing. Perhaps most climbers do realise it but it's hard to understand it and improve on it. Having the right mental attitude is just as important as having the strength and technique. There hasn't been so much research done on the mental training for climbing so it's still in a very under developed state.

How much strength do you need to climb 8a?

8a is just a grade really, it could be a very physical or technical route which requires specific strength, like fingertip or upper body strength, but its hard to quantify. Certainly a lot of people have the strength to climb 8a and don't climb 8a. I certainly don't think strength is a limiting factor because it's one of many. True, on specific routes you can quantify, for example a steep overhanging route on small edges you can quantify, or if it's an overhang on big holds you can quantify it. Strength is not the only or even key factor. I personally don't think I am any stronger now than when I first started climbing, but I know how to use my strength much more efficiently.

But can you do a one arm pull up?

Normally yes.

And is that any use to climbing?

Yes, I think it is. A lot of people say it isn't, but I think now days routes are getting more and more physical and most people climbing at the top standards can do a one arm pull up, so it must have a bearing on the type of strength you need. On a lot of the overhanging routes you are trying to do a one arm pull up as one of the moves. Even if your feet are on the rock quite often the assistance is very minimal and it certainly feels as if you are trying to do one, sometimes 2 or 3 on quite small finger holds.

How do you endure the pain of small holds on routes like CAVIAR?

What Pain?

Don't lie!

I think I've always had fairly naturally strong fingers and wouldn't say that my fingers are any better at enduring pain than other peoples. Maybe because I'm light I don't suffer so much on small holds as the heavier climbers but I don't have a high pain threshold, and if a fingerhold hurts then I very quickly let go of it. There's no special secret.

What made you put up CAVIAR 8a+?

I'd always like bouldering at Rubicon Wall anyway. One day I was down there with a friend from Manchester and we just deceided to have a play at the start, I worked a problem up to about 15ft then realised that it might be possible to climb this bit of the wall. It was very steep and the flattest part of the cliff so it was a bit of a surprise. It didn't take long to climb as it's only an extended boulder problem. Up to that point new routes hadn't interested me at all, and to some extent they still don't. Partly because I'm quite lazy and I can't be bothered to spend the time cleaning and bolting them.

Did you think at the time, I could solo it and make a statement?

Yes I did because originaly when I abseiled down I looked for some nut placements and I thought it was just about possible to do it without bolts but it would have been quite scary as the holds are quite fragile. At the time most of the Peak limestone new routes routes were being bolted, so it seemed appropriate to bolt it.

Could that ever spill over onto gritstone?

I hope it doesn't. Certainly if people did there would be a backlash because gritstone has the purest ethics of any rock in the world, and there's no need. Most of the really hard test pieces, if you havn't got the ability, then it's quite easy to top rope them. That is what will keep bolts off gritstone.

Have you ever top roped a route that later on you became good enough to do on sight, and felt that you had spoiled it?

No, I can't think of any, but I'm sure there are some. I wouldn't really regret it because if I chose to top rope it at the time, it was probably because it meant something to me, to be able to top rope it. I would never just top rope something without a reasonable justification. It would be a challenge at the time, you can't save every route for the future because then you have no routes to improve on.

Do you get pissed off and go out for a day without getting up a route?

No because there are many days like that, often I don't even try routes, I go and boulder or solo some easier routes. I enjoy climbing without having to use a rope very much. I certainly don't need to do a route to gauge whether I have climbed well on a particular day, nor have a satisfying day.

Do competitions excite you?

Yes. I think competition climbing has made me appreciate on-sight climbing, through the discipline of the competition you are forced to train by on-sight climbing and then see the benefits of how important and satisfying the success of an on-sight ascent is. I try to on-sight everything that I climb nowadays. I went to America last year and climbed about five 7c+ routes at Smith Rock and Colorado on-sight.

How far away is 8a on-sight?

For me. I hope not more then a year away, thats one of my big goals. I think on-sighting is something which I've begun to realise is very important in all styles of climbing including bouldering and sportclimbing. Even when I first started climbing I very rarely went on routes that I didn't think that I could on-sight. I've never been the sort of person who goes on a route knowing that they have no chance of getting up it first time.

Ed Morgan demonstrating without difficulty, the crux of CAVIAR 8a+, on tiny holds with negligible footholds.

Ian Vincent

Born 16.1.64 at Ilkley in Yorkshire, Ian started climbing at school on the local gritstone outcrops around Bradford such as Shipley Glen. He did well with academic studies and went to Sheffield to study European Business. This took him to Germany, and then eventually studying at the University at Aix-en-Provence and hence spent a lot of time climbing at Buoux and the other crags in the South of France. He has climbed many classics such as CHOUCAS 8a+, AUSTRIAN OAK 8a+ and TABOU ZI ZI 8b. He suffered from tendonitis badly on THE ROSE AND THE VAMPIRE 8b, at Buoux and now spends more time training than climbing. He recently worked as a management accountant, but now as a market research analyst.

Interview 9.1.91 Hounslow, London.

What made you choose to study European Business at Sheffield?
Quite a lot to do with the fact that I wanted to go climbing, and Sheffield at that time had the big aura of the climbing crucible, everyone was climbing there and it was a big scene; it had quite a reputation. Also the course I wanted to do was in Sheffield so it was partly academic. It was a business studies course but it was a language course as well, During my year when I was re-taking my 'A' Levels I also learnt German, whilst living in Germany for a bit studying. I just thought a language would be a good thing to have, it was something which I thought would be quite useful for the future in terms of occupational prospects. Also my father was quite keen on me learning a language, so I thought I'd get out and have a couple of months in another country and Germany was the choice at that time.
Had you thought of France at that time?
Not really, I think if I had thought of France it wouldn't have been anything to do with climbing, I would have just gone to learn the language. When I finished college, I went to France and at that time I was actually ready to go climbing, whereas before in terms of climbing, it would have been just wasted in France.
Do you regret not starting limestone climbing when you were fifteen?
Not really because I don't think it would have changed the way I was actually climbing. It was only when I went to Poly. that I put any effort into getting good. If I was climbing at 15 I would have been just pottering around and I would probably have gained a lot of ideas that would have held me back at a later stage ie. attitudes towards certain types of climbing, I might have been a bit more conservative or reactionary.

Because climbing at that time was conservative?
Yes, Probably also because of the people I would have been climbing with. At that time most climbing was wires etc., etc., and there was a certain view of what climbing should be and it would probably have rubbed off on me. At that stage I was just a boulderer. When I actually started climbing seriously I didn't have any preconceptions about what I thought should have been the done thing.
Do you think that's a good thing or a bad thing?
The way I view climbing is that it should be what I want to do. I don't really want to go out and risk my life on something. What attracts me to climbing is the gymnastics of it and the physical effort rather than any sort of psychological side. So the attitudes I'm bringing to climbing, suit what I want to get out of it.
Did you pick those attitudes up from working and climbing abroad or at a later stage when those ideas had been readily accepted?
I Think because they were readily accepted in France and Germany it became easier for me to consolidate my attitudes. I wanted to climb reasonably hard routes and didn't want to be risking my neck in trying. Because the French and Germans were doing it, the concept became readily acceptable.
Did you finish and pass your course at Sheffield?
Yes. It was a degree, three years in Sheffield and one year on industrial placements at

various places, six months of which was in the Frankenjura, which is of course the prime limestone area in Germany, that was nice.
Were you climbing hard then?
I was starting to climb reasonably hard, I was just bouldering initially because it was cold during the winter. I went down to France and I was climbing well on-sight, I came back and broke my wrist so I was out for about 4 months.
How did you break you wrist?
I was bouldering at a crag in the Frankenjura, my feet were about 2 maybe 3 foot up, and I slipped off backwards landing on the flats of my wrists. I broke this very small bone which take ages to heal so I was in pot for three months. It was quite sickening but very nice because I got to know a lot of people in Germany and a lot of crags. Once I actually did start climbing again I knew where to go.
How did the German scene at that time compare with the English scene?
Germany was quite strange in a way because although they were climbing on bolts and things, there was still quite an old-fashioned attitude to climbing. There wasn't that many people trying to climb very hard routes, just Wolfgang Güllich and one or two others. Most people were just prepared to worship these guys, Wolfgang was just a hero, he was idolized. The scene was quite friendly but a bit different in that they'd all be climbing and go for coffee and cake. Even people like Wolfgang were wolfing down big bits of cake which you

Ian, high up on the final overhanging section of BULLET 8a, the left hand side of the big main buttress of Kilnsey.

partners, we used to go out quite a lot during the week and also at weekends.

Was it a good social scene in Aix?

There wasn't a climbing social scene, France is quite different I think. In Aix there isn't actually that many serious climbers, most of them are mountaineers or Alpinists and they just go out now and again and go down to the French Alpine Club. There was a peripheral climbing scene with committed climbers and I managed to get in on that.

Do the French Alpinists accept the French climbers compared with the British Alpinists?

More so because the French Alpine Club was organising competitions and actually sponsoring crags getting bolted up. I think the French Alpinists were a lot more open to innovations within the sport. I didn't really have that much contact with Alpinists because I was a rock climber but I think there was a lot more cross-fertilization of ideas. A lot of the sports climbing ethic was actually getting brought into the Alps as well. In France at places like Chamonix, there's an awful lot of sports climbing routes on the big mountains so they're more open to progress or change.

Does that make climbing in France nicer than Britain?

What makes climbing in France nicer than Britain is the weather. I think climbing in France is a lot more of a surf culture, it's more akin to that sort of thing. You are just doing it for the movement, it's safe, stylish, and people are there to enjoy themselves. Britain sometimes, it's a very masochistic sport because the weather is bad, you're cold and wet. It's quite retrospective a lot of the time. You're just doing it to be climbing, whereas in France it's an all round enjoyable experience - you have all the different things working together, the weather and the safety etc.

You did TABOU ZI ZI 8b, in 1988. Did you feel it was very hard?

Sort of, but it gave me a lot of confidence to do other 8a+ routes like CHOUCAS and NUIT DE LEZARDS. I went to Germany and did a little climbing there but I got quite bored with climbing and came back to Britain, thinking I was climbing 8b. I then went out to do the ROSE AND THE VAMPIRE at Buoux, I had a real hard time on it, it was just a different standard to something like TABOU ZI ZI. I got a bit of a shock really. Unfortunately I got quite bad tendonitis from trying it and that was the end to that French trip.

Did that hard style siege approach appeal?

I think it is quite strange but I never really aspired to trying anything really, really hard because I didn't think I had the power to do

don't expect after the Stoney Cafe scene. It was also a lot more affluent, they were all travelling around in GTI's.

When you came back to Sheffield and finished the course, did you work after that?

When I finished the course I went to France and didn't have any intention to work. I was going to France and wanted to learn another language so I went over and studied French for a year at Aix-en-Provence. So although I was climbing reasonably well at that stage, I'd done a couple of 8a's, I went over there and it's really where it all started, I got a lot done.

Did it worry you going to France for a year on your own?

No, because I really wanted to go. I was used

to going away, I'd lived in Germany for 6 months and it didn't really bother me that much, I'm self sufficient in that way. Whatever you do, if you have an interest there's always people with a like interest, so you can always find people to meet and to talk to. If the worst had come to the worst and I hadn't been able to speak any French or meet any French people, there was always Buoux where there's always a load of English people.

Did you climb with French or English in the end?

Most of the time I was in France I actually did climb with French people. After the initial period when I got to know people, I actually got some quite consistent French climbing anything that hard. Also I just didn't have the staying power when I thought about people being on routes for 30-40 days, it's just something I couldn't do myself, so I stuck to more middle grade things. I could do 8a, and 8a+ reasonably quickly, but anything longer just didn't have as much appeal.

Did you not want to give everything to trying the hard routes?

No, which was different to a lot of other climbers. A lot of people dropped out of their courses and it became like a craze, a bit of a trend one person did it and there was an avalanche effect, I always thought it was a waste of time. Personally I didn't think it would be worth giving up everything like that unless I thought I would be number 1. I couldn't understand why many of the people did it because they weren't going to be number one either, so it just seemed really short sighted to pack in a course for a couple of years, climbing when you don't *need* to have 24 hours in the day to train and climb. You can do other things and in fact, I need other things because when I've been full time climbing, like during the summer holidays, I've actually found myself going backwards, I just haven't had the focus.

Do you find it hard getting motivation to climb?

Sometimes I do, sometimes I just get burnt out because when I do get into it, I get quite intense and I'll be doing a lot of things and trying to pack a lot into a day. Then I'd lose interest for a week or two and during that time it's really hard, but I try and keep up some regime of training.

When you've been on a route for a couple of days, do you get more tense on the climb?

Sometimes, but I'm not really bothered if I don't get up a route or not, in one way I've tried a lot of routes but I don't have that many I've actually finished. I don't actually feel the tension because if I don't do it, that's tough. If there is something that I really do want to do I try to take the pressure off myself by saying I'm not going to do it, and if I'm in a more relaxed state I climb a bit better. It's one of these little strategies, it tends to work quite well. Because I'm not that bothered about getting up the thing, then that pressure is not so intense anyway.

You said earlier that you got stressed when you were training, more than when you were climbing?

It's strange because when I was in Sheffield we built a cellar in our house, a big climbing wall and I used to get more psyched to go down to the cellar than I did to go climbing. We used to have all these problems that I was working on down there and I used to go down there really, really keen. I didn't really bother about going out climbing at all, it was much more interesting for me to go down and try these things in the cellar so it keeps coming back to the same thing, that physical involvement being more important than the 'Climbing experience'.

At the Leeds International competition you came 5th beating people like Edlinger and Glowacz, was that a shock?

I think initially. Some of them didn't climb as well as they might have done, perhaps if I had found a hold where I fell off, then maybe I could have got higher as well, but it's exactly the same as everyone else. Climbing competitions are quite interesting things, there are so many different variables that you can sometimes just hit it lucky. I went into other competitions and didn't do as well but I felt I was climbing better at Leeds which gave me a lot of confidence in my own ability. Competitions are the area of climbing which I thought I was more suited to. I didn't actually feel I could do the hardest routes, but I felt in terms of my mental attitude and also the level of my fitness, the climbing in the competitions was something I could be reasonably good at.

Who were the climbers in your climbing times in France and England that did impress you?

When I was in France people like Didier Raboutou were quite impressive. The most impressive French climber I think was Antoine Le Menestrel, he hasn't actually done much in terms of gaining the media coverage but for his time he was probably the best climber around, his record is incredible.

How does someone like Wolfgang compare with Antoine?

It's like beauty and the beast. People like Wolfgang are very strong and they just typify German climbers, very muscular with no technique. They get up things just by brute force. When I saw him do CHOUCAS it was just horrible, whereas Antoine has such a natural style, it's not forced. I Can respect Wolfgang and people like that, also Mark Leach for being very strong, but I can't see them as being wonderful climbers because it's something else.

Have you ever seen anyone flash an 8a?

No I haven't. I've seen people get quite close.

Is it exciting?

Yes it is actually, It's quite depressing as well when you've spent a couple of days on a climb and you've had to work very hard to do it, then someone comes along and falls off very, very high and you just think..my God....why can't I be that strong.

The Frenchman, Didier Raboutou at Malham, experiencing the cold, miserable British early summer! One of the world's great Masters, who has won numerous competitions and came second behind Simon Nadin in the world cup, has flashed 8a+ on sight, and made the second ascent of Ben Moon's AGINCOURT 8c, at Buoux.

Pete Gomersall

Pete is living proof that greatness is achieved with age, his recent success on four 8b's: THE MISSION, PREDATOR, TABOU ZI ZI and WELL DUNNE FINISH, show this well. At 34 he is still enjoying climbing and seems to have plenty left in him, adding daily to the list of 40 or so 8a's to his credit. Pete has remained in the limelight of the very top stars over the years, but has been involved in putting up major new climbs, from technical masterpieces to complete horror shows such as Yorkshire's first E7 in 1980, DEATH WISH on Blue Scar. By 1988 he had consolidated in the 8a grade and lately has been adding some really excellent routes at Kilnsey: BULLET 8a+, SHOWTIME 8a+ and URGENT ACTION 8a+.

Interview, 3.2.91 Cononley, Yorkshire.

Do you see yourself as a controversial character? I don't see myself as that, but it seems to have turned out that way over the years. In many respects it was right from very early on, influences placed on me with various climbing partners in the past. A lot of people have said that since I spent a lot of time with Livesey, a lot of his traits have rubbed off onto me, some of them have and others haven't.

Looking back, the route Mongoose you did had a lot of controversy attached to it? That was a weird route actually, I would never have looked at that and seen it as a really controversial route. The only thing that we did was to top rope it before we lead it. The risks involved in falling off at that time were unjustified, so we traversed across to Void which was 5 ft. to the left and protected it with a side runner, which was totally acceptable on grit at the time. After that it got a lot of publicity for certain things, people were claiming that we didn't do it properly. I think it was a very fair ascent, let's face it the joke of that time was The Berzin's claiming a subsequent ascent of RIGHT WALL, they belayed halfway up the route on the girdle ledge, that's what I call a joke ascent, maybe they like picnics or something. Two years later I did go back and climb MONGOOSE without the side runners anyway.

You'd obviously been climbing for a long time by then? Yes, that was in 1978, I'd been climbing 8 years then. I first went climbing in '69. I started at secondary school and before that I had been into soccer, I played for Yorkshire Schoolboys at a reasonably high level, but preferred climbing. The first extreme I did was two years later, WHITE SLAB on Cloggy. I'd been up one day and was so impressed with the place that I

couldn't actually climb, I went back up the next day and decided I had better do something. I was with a friend of mine who really wasn't up to it, we took about 10 hours.

Was WHITE SLAB a trade route by then? It had a lot of ascents and wasn't a desperately hard route, but it was certainly regarded as an impressive extreme. Cloggy had a very forbidding atmosphere and was very impressive. I really enjoyed it at the time.

What sort of impetus did that give you? At the time I just wanted to do more, better, and harder routes, improve my own standard. That's what I was into from that early time onwards, my whole life revolved around climbing.

Did you set yourself any challenges after that? I think my aim was to do what was then, the established hard routes such as VECTOR E2, traditional Brown-Whillans routes in Wales and a lot of Austin's routes in the Lake District. I ended up climbing with a guy called Graham Summers for quite a while, he was actually better than me in terms of what he could climb, but he was desperately dangerous because he had no regard for safety.

What was climbing like in the early 70's? It was all on-sight climbing, things like stoppers and hexentrics had just come in which

were an improvement on the pro available at the time. There were slight advances in technology but only very slight. Being on-sight meant that there wasn't really a great deal of frigging going on, those types of things started to happen at the end of the 70's.

Was there an attraction to Mountaineering in the 70's? At that time in the early 70's there was a natural progression from doing rockclimbing to mountaineering and in fact most people did this. In my first alpine season which was when I was 18, I hitched to the Dolomites, did some hard routes including soloing a hard artificial one. Then went to the Western Alps and did the American Direct on the Dru, and the Walker Spur, which at that time were the routes to aspire to. I had one or two other subsequent trips but even after that brief association with alpine climbing it was obvious that it was a totally different activity to rockclimbing and there isn't necessarily this link that people say there is. I thought that the technical involvement in those routes was absolutely minimal, and therefore the consequent interest and challenge was not there. It was all very brutal plodding away. If you kept going then you got to the top. It was all retrospective the enjoyment that you got out of it, it was very mundane and hence I gave it up.

Kilnsey Main Buttress, Yorkshire. The main overhang to the right is MANDELLA 8b, whilst SHOWTIME and BULLET take the left wall and overhang.

Do you feel that you had to do it?

Yes, I did, it was important. I felt that was what you had to do at the time, I would also never say that I would never go back to it since they are the routes and type of climbing you can do in middle age.

Did you climb much with Livesey in the 70's?

No, before '75 I was involved with Ron Fawcett and friends because they were locals; we went around in a bunch. There was quite a lot of peer group pressure to improve and aspire to a certain standard. Obviously that's why people in this area got better and better; because they had something to work towards. I went to college in '75 and Livesey was one of the tutors there.

What were the routes being done then?

I had done SPARE RIB at Tremadog, Ron had done MARATHON MAN E4 6b, and then in '78, Livesey and I started working through routes in the Lakes. We had repeated lots of Cleasby and Matheson routes and then really discovered Raven Crag Thirlmere. We had lots of wild, day excursions there culminating with the first ascent of DAS KAPITAL E6 6b a couple of years later. Livesey had already attracted a ruthless reputation, well sort of. Ron and I knew he was chipping holds because we had abseiled down MOSSDALE TRIP and seen these chipped finger slots. The first experience of having to actually be with Livesey when he chipped some holds I remember well. I agreed to meet Livesey and arriving at the crag saw he was already up there, practicing the moves where we previously had failed. Later he managed to lead the pitch, and he said to me that I could do the top pitch 'it's only about E3,' I got some gear in, made some moves up the wall and fell off. We retreated and inspected the headwall, it was certainly harder than E3. Livesey decided that one of the holds needed improving. We came back a week or so later, and then Livesey actually abseiled down with a hammer and chisel and chipped this hold. He spent a while chipping it, not making much headway, so after he was knackered I had to go down and finish the job off; that was the only incident where I was involved with chipping a hold out of blank rock.

Did that bother you at the time?

Yes it did, I wouldn't have done it, but you never know do you.

What do you think made climbing ethics swell up, was it just Livesey?

There were lots of things. Initially it was yo-yoing, that was fine but then a lot of routes were done using an adapted type of yo-yoing technique, where the second was tending to

Pete Gomersall on the crux of TECHNICIAN 8a+, Kilnsey.
Pete added an 8a finish to the pitch to give SHOWTIME,
a great route up the left side of Kilnsey main Buttress.

give you a lot of support from the rope once you'd got a bit of gear in, taking some of your body weight while you were actually having a blow holding on the holds. That was done a lot. Livesey's repeat of LONDON WALL was done like that on the top half. That was one example. Next it was heavily cleaning routes, I think Livesey believed that adding some holds to a route would produce a very good route, irrespective of the fact that it was chipping it. In the end Livesey's routes will stand the test of time; they're all classics aren't they.

Did you see at the time that climbing standards would perhaps rise, so that they could be done without chipping?
Yes, I think everybody knows that standards will rise and some of these could have been done without. It's a little naive of people to think that routes will never be done without this and that. When I first abseiled down a line of mine that became URGENT ACTION (Under the thumb) at Kilnsey I thought that I wouldn't be able to do this move at all. I had said to a lot of people that I would bolt a hold on there because I thought that it would be appropriate. However I was looking from an abseil rope, and when I cleaned the thing it was obviously possible. Once I put a bolt in and practiced the move it became relatively easy. If Livesey had bolts he might have seen things differently.

In 1980 you did DEATH WISH E7, was that a big step up?
Yes, definitely because it was the first E7 and a definite step up in boldness. That summer or the summer before a group of my friends had been to Blue Scar, and when you see it from the road it is a very impressive crag; just a completely vertical white, limestone wall. In the guide book at the time, the '76 Yorkshire Limestone Guide, it mentioned this great white wall unclimbed. They had been to look at it, abseiled down it and told me that they could do it, but they would need a bolt on it. I wasn't sure at the time what to do so I went and had a look at the route. I saw it would go free and that became CENTRAL WALL E5 6a. I was drawn to the wall to the right an impressive vague ramp line, I looked at the big blank section, and there was no natural gear. At the time and because John Eastham had refused to use a bolt on the line of CENTRAL WALL I did likewise and I hammered a wire into a crack, but it didn't look any good. It's 6b climbing, that's for sure, and if that wire failed, it's hitting the ground from 80ft.

Climbing with people like Livesey and Faw-cett, did they seem better than you?
Yes, but it didn't annoy me at all, I just felt that it was a really good challenge for me to get as good as them. At times I thought I would never get to their standard or catch them up, but the longer I climbed with Livesey the more I was closing the gap. It got to the point where we had alternate goes on a route and then me doing pitches he'd fail on. With Ron I always felt he was better, he was improving right through until 1985 when he stopped hard climbing.

Has climbing new routes been very important to you?
Yes, it'a been important ever since my first new route in 1974, USURPER E1 on Lower Falcon in the Lake District.

Do you think by doing new routes it was a good escape from trying to compete with the top people?
Maybe, but I was also repeating the hardest routes at the time. Essentially I saw doing new routes as something different. Apart from Livesey there weren't that many people doing new routes so you had a good selection to pick from. In reflection I've only done about 50 new climbs but there's only 2 or 3 that are poor, most of my new climbs are good, and most of them are 3 star which is important to me.

How can you tell that a line will be good?
Half the thing about doing a new route is whether it has a good line. It can be rather arbitrary but there is a certain quality derived from where climbs go and also their relationship to other routes. I can tell by just looking, where good climbs will be.

What about the lines of modern limestone routes?
It's different on limestone because you can climb anywhere with a bolt now, but the good climbs still follow natural features. The better climbs like THE GROOVE at Malham, THE THUMB at Kilnsey still follow natural features. Therefore these route's are in a different class to some of the others that just go up a blank wall; ZOOLOOK is a superb 8a, but it doesn't have a natural line. I think that even younger climbers who haven't any real experience can still see the difference.

Are you glad that you were involved in doing the new routes?
Yes definitely, I believe that I've got the most enjoyment from doing new routes. I think that my climbing background has given me a broad overview about what climbing is about, and what one can benefit from climbing.
What can be benefited?
It's difficult to say precisely. Certainly climbing has given me a certain perspective on life in general, it's also has given me the possibility of climbing most of the year without having to do those boring jobs, it's enabled me to keep on doing what I like.

You've got so much out of climbing through new routes, can a young climber today get that same satisfaction?
It's very difficult because what decent new routes are left are going to be very hard, so it will take them a long time to even do them. It's difficult to see how people coming into the climbing scene will be able to do that.
Would perhaps by not using guidebooks and just going climbing get anywhere?
Oooh, unfortunately I don't think so, let's say that 99% of the people involved in climbing couldn't do that, they certainly wouldn't take the risk. There aren't many who are confident of there own ability to be able to just go to a crag, and climb as they wouldn't know where they were going, they'd be frightened.

Hasn't modern equipment allowed more flexibility?
Modern equipment allows you to be safe, but it doesn't mean that you're competent about your own ability, and know your limitations. I don't think that there's that many who believe in there own ability, you only have to look at the numbers of people who do serious routes. That's what we're talking about here, doing a route where you don't know what's coming up, and what you have to do is to analyse whether you're are safe or not. Just look at the number of people going on serious routes where the risks are high if you make mistakes, you could count the number of people on one hand.

Would you ever do that?
No I don't think so now, I've done my share of life threatening routes. Now I think that everybody wants to do routes that are safe and established. At the top it's commercially necessary to do certain routes, professional climbers have to keep there reputations going don't they.

You were born in 1956, do you feel as though you've peaked?
I think I can do harder routes but I will need to put proportionately more effort into doing them now. Obviously you get to a certain age where it takes longer to recover from training and you're prone to more injuries, also there are more psychological problems of boredom in training, so from those points of view then it is more difficult. However motivation is the prime mover, if you want to, you probably will do.

If you were born 10 years later would you be climbing 8c now?
8c? Didier Raboutou is similar in physique to me, so it should be possible, but 8c is in the mind. I really don't know, that's the great thing about climbing.

Mark Pretty

Mark Pretty, better known to the climbing world as Zippy. At Stoney Middleton in the early eighties he was one of the group who inhabited Windy Ledge by day and the Old Woodshed by night. The group consisted of those characters of yesteryear; 5c Mark as he was known then, Chesters, Little Smeg, Dirty Derek and many others. In those days the concept was very simple, go on the dole so you can climb all the time. You had so little money that the likelihood of getting fat through overeating or drinking didn't come into the equation. The big step forward came with the Hunter House Road injection of Jerry Moffatt and Andy Pollitt. The whole buzz of hard climbing accelerated quickly and 5c Mark became 6c Mark very quickly. Mark, to his credit, made early repeats of the big routes like BODY MACHINE 7c and WHORE OF BABYLON 8a, at Ravens Tor. This was particularly impressive as his miniscule height of 5ft 6ins meant he had to develop all his own ways of climbing 'Big Ron's' routes. In the mid eighties the scene shifted to Europe and Mark consolidated in the 8b grade with ascents of routes like CHOUCAS 8a+, MISSION 8b and TABOU ZI ZI 8b at Buoux. He has a fair few 8a first ascents to his name with DISILLUSIONED GLUE MACHINE on The Cornice, Water Cum Jolly, being perhaps his best contribution.

Interview 21.11.90 Llanberis, Wales.

At what age did you start climbing?
About 12 and a half, some friends at school wanted to go climbing on a school trip, I went and I liked it. I then joined a climbing club with my dad, climbing one day a week, and gradually more and more, I got sucked into it, then suddenly you're there 4 days a week or even more.

Did you like sport at school?
No, I hated it. Cross country running I liked a little bit, and I really loved football as a kid. But the other sports you had to play as a team I reacted against instinctively. I don't like games where you're playing with other people.

Do you think climbing is a very individual sport?
I think it certainly is at the higher levels, like the top thirty or so climbers. To get to that sort of level you have to be fairly egocentric and individualistic, not necessarily in a bad way but you are doing something that you want to do for yourself. You need other people around, but the group effort isn't there, I don't feel the

want to be part of a rugby team cheering hurrah about beating somebody, that just bores me. You do something that is really deep, intense personal pleasure for yourself, you don't need anyone else really. It's nice when people are really pleased for you, when you do something, it's not essential though, it's just within yourself.

Would you say that people who do a 9 to 5 job or work in industry, can apply better to team games like football and hockey?
I think it's a bit of a generalization but most people are team game orientated, fairly sociable. They're also scared of being alone and out of the pack, so they tend to stick with there fellow people at sport, or socially.

Is that individualistic nature common only to English climbers?
Perhaps, it might be my own personal slightly xenophobic idea, but I do think the way that climbing has developed in Britain with traditional techniques like wire placements, danger, mountains, that sort of scenario, has rubbed off in the past with people. Now bolt clipping is almost the opposite of what climbing is about really, its like the mass production of routes, take France, Germany and America where everything is bolted and everybody bangs away at the climbs, not using talent or anything, just like pure pig headedness. They're the group animals of climbing I guess. But in Britain you still find that people are going out and doing other things. People like myself, an ardent bolt clipper will still go out on gritstone, do a few routes with nuts and things, which keep you in touch with it all. Perhaps the English people in general are more individualistic.

Would you say climbing in the English way reflects the mad syndrome of English life like Isle of Man TT racing?
There are very few places like Britain; in general most of the world is into clipping bolts. Britain it seems, just likes doing its own thing totally. I think its definitely true that people who live on islands like England develop a sort of different mentality. I'm convinced, I mean Britain and Europe, there's them and there's us; were sort of a lot like them, but in a lot of ways we're not, and I think there is something to be said that our climbing is very British and theirs is very European. They sort of intermingle a bit, there's some common ground, but there are a lot of differences as well.

How do the characters of the top climbers compare, such as Ron Fawcett and Ben Moon?
They're actually pretty similar, they are pretty strong characters and know what they want to

do and are getting on with doing it. Whereas, all the insecure characters, go down to pubs, get drunk, go dogging women and stuff like that. They just don't need it, they potter along and it sort of shows in the climbing some how. They have set goals, work at them, and do them, not erratically but just a constant output. Ron was so regular at producing mega routes in the early eighties, and like Ben is now constant at either repeating or doing new routes. They're very different because what Ben is doing is so much harder than Ron, but still in his time what Ron did was amazing. It's psychological in many ways, like Ben made the break through for everyone else doing AGIN-COURT 8c. A lot of people could have done AGINCOURT if they had realised in their own heads that they could do it. It's the same with Ron when he did NEW DAWN 7c and ZOOLOOK 8a at Malham. We looked at it and couldn't imagine climbing it, Ron just took the bull by the horns and did it, that led the way for me, Ben and everyone. Ben is now doing the same for the young lads of the 90's. The psychological barrier is the really important thing. Jerry Moffatt's the same, he was just going all around the world, putting up hard routes everywhere because he had so much self belief, he could see that things were

possible that no other person could see. People then tried and found out that they could do them, that's not as hard as having to do it first of all.

Did you sense that Jerry would be the climber of the 80s early on?
Yes, in 82 he was already repeating all of Ron's routes, doing new routes like ROOSTER BOOSTER 7c, he was well above us. He was climbing E6 and we were at E3, that's a massive difference. There were things like going bouldering that we didn't understand, Jerry realised that if you wanted to do hard routes, you had to be strong which Ron didn't seem to realise or wouldn't let himself do. Jerry said to himself that he wanted to do a route so he would go and do these boulder problems to get strong first. He refused to be beaten by any bit of rock going, he got so much stronger than all of us, then set it onto the routes, and the rest is history. You could tell then by the routes he did that he was something special. What we didn't realise was that the bouldering he was doing, was going to make him that more special. His natural potential was good but not that much more than Ron's on basic stamina and plodding along. He just drove himself, which is something that Ron in a way, never really did, I think he missed out.

Over the years what has meant more, climbing with people, in countries or up through the standards?

I think people, different types of people, who I have met by coming through the grades. The countries I'm not really bothered about, I like going abroad but its no big deal. Coming up through the grades is really good, when I started climbing hard and did an E5 I thought the next year I would never be able to do one again, it was a one off, then the same with E6, I just couldn't believe it. Whereas with friendships you don't notice them so much because they're constantly there, but I think that's the same in all walks of life, the friends disappear and you have memories, then you remember the routes that went with the friends.

What makes a good climbing friend?

I don't know, the ones that buy you drinks Dave! No, I think people that take an interest in what you're doing, actually appreciate your attempts. If I'm climbing with Jerry or Ben they're really keen, psyched for you to do well, and in turn your psyched for them, it's a good feeling at the crag, and that also helps you climb better.

Can Jerry cope with coming down to your level?

It's not that, like we're usually on the same boulder problems, it's just that he does them and I don't! It's good because your sussing all the bits and pieces which is a team effort, but it's really a team effort to get an individual (usually Jerry or Ben!), up the problem. I just go back for a few more weeks and might get it or not, it doesn't matter.

Do you think Mark le Menestrel missed out climbing in Britain?

I think anybody who doesn't go out and do bold routes misses out, because I think its such good fun, its competing with yourself as much as the rock, which is what it's all about. Having said that, he's spent his time putting up routes in France which are all time classics like MINIMUM 8b+, perhaps he would have never done those things, he started young and got strong. If he did what I did, ticking routes on Cloggy, stuff like that, having a lot of good fun, he might have missed out on the things that he has done.

Did you ever meet Kim Carrigan?

Yes, in 82, He was a right cheat but a really good cheat as well. It's like all those people then, Ron and all of them, they used what toady, we would consider really naughty tactics; they were a bit naughty even then. But, the routes they were doing were big psychological tests. Routes like CAVE ROUTE at Gordale, Kim was doing them on Dougie Hall's gear basically, Dougie was doing all the work then Kim would bag the ascent. You're fighting psychological ground all the while, because no one climbed on routes that steep and intimidating. You walk into Gordale and almost wet yourself these days, in those days the thought of going in there was ghastly. So for all the jiggery pokery, he did some great repeats of routes and was one of the best around at the time. He went around Britain and blasted it totally, he did the same in America and back in his native Australia, he was the best.

Who of all the top climbers is the most natural?

Johnny Dawes, he's the ultimate natural climber, he's always out of shape but just goes on total natural strength and feel. Ben and Sean are similar but they've had to learn, it's not totally natural.

Can you sum up the Peak district?

Short, sharp and intense, the Peak is almost only jumped up bouldering. Virtually anything in the Peak is overhanging, very small holds and really intense. Consequently it produces some weird but really good climbers as well. It's a bit like Frankenjura, you get these really strong thugs who can't climb more than 20ft, anything longer and they get into serious trouble, they wonder what the hell is happening. People outside look on the Peak as quite weird. I find this hard to relate to since I regard it as normal, it's normal to me as a little eccentric micro sport, the land of extended boulder problems. Take HUBBLE 8c+, its really only a very hard boulder problem, with a 7c stuck on top to make it even worse for you, they're not exactly like routes.

Are there any routes in the peak that really stand out in your mind?

REVELATIONS 8a+, ULYSEES E6 6b, MASTERS EDGE E7 6b, BASTILLE E5 6b, MORTLOCKS ARETE E4 6a.

I can understand REVELATIONS, why ULYSEES, is it actually hard?

Too bloody right! It's desperate, it's hard on a top rope let alone on a .... solo. What Johnny Dawes did was just amazing, on-sight. I don't think its been done since, and is definitely one of the best things he's ever done in climbing.
Were you there?

No way, I'd have run a mile if I'd seen him on it. It's such a perfect line and looks unclimbable, one of the best bits of natural sculpture in Britain.
MASTERS EDGE, should it have bolts?

No, you don't need bolts on it, not unless you jump off going for the tricam holds. If anything, you should fill in the tricam holes and make it a total solo, that would be mega. Its lucky that the shot holes are there, that's like an act of God in itself really.

BASTILLE!

That's a great historic route, I tried it early on when I imagined all the holds to be the size of match sticks. I went on it in 1983, cranked away like a little fiend, and did it. Typical early eighties limestone, bumbly type, vertical but quite small holds. At the time it had the aura which REVELATIONS has now, it was THE ROUTE you had to do, and so for me personally, I have the memory of climbing something special.

If you were a young climber today, would you come up with the same list?

I'd like to think I would but I doubt it. Probably it would be just 5 bits of grot in Cheedale. I really love bolt routes but, I hate what people are missing out on. I climb mostly bolt routes now, but you can still remember and appreciate how good other routes and other rocks are. So many people who only climb on bolts are so boring it's just untrue. They are the sort of soulless masses of climbing. You find all the top bolt climbers really appreciate what Johnny Dawes and Nick Dixon do. The punters think you're stupid, they can't see any reason. They're very much like French climbers, they think that anyone who climbs a dangerous route on Gogarth must be an idiot, they don't appreciate what your putting into it, let alone what you're getting out of it.

Does getting to the top of routes count?

Yes. If I don't get to the top of these hard routes, my life won't be shattered by it. But to have done them is fantastic. You know that Ben Moon could do the routes all day and night if he wanted, he works out on The Rose 8b, so it's no big deal in the eyes of the world. But it's a really good personal satisfaction to set a yardstick for yourself, and actually know you've reached it.

Do you think Francois Legrand will come to the Peak next year and solo HUBBLE?

Nobody will ever solo HUBBLE. No way. I'll put a lot of beer on that definitely. Francois is totally obsessed with climbing on walls and most probably won't climb on rock anymore. I look at him as the first of the true competition climbers.

The crux section of BEAU GESTE 7c+ on Froggatt. As the pebbles to pull on slowly dissappear, the route gains further popularity as a top roping problem.

Andy Pollitt

Andy Pollitt. Born in 1963 started climbing at school and was one of the main pioneering climbers in the 1980's. His incredibly fast metabolism and light weight made him the envy of many climbers during the eighties. He started climbing with Jerry Moffatt at a very early age and put up many new routes in North Wales such as MOONWIND E4, at Craig Y Forwyn, and CAROUSEL WALTZ E5, in the Crafnant. His standard took off when he moved to Sheffield in 1983 and joined the Hunter House Road mob. His determination across the whole range of climbing is always impressive, repeating THE BELLS E7 on sight; his routes THE HOLLOW MAN E7, another death route, and WHORE OF BABYLON 8a, were remarkable for the time. He has done some of the finest modern routes with considerable style. The best and most often repeated route must be OVER THE MOON 8a, at Pen Trwyn opposite Llandudno Pier. His character is always full of enthusiasm and he now enjoys climbing in Australia most of the year.

Interview by correspondence, late at night by the campfire, Arapalies, Victoria, Australia. 2.1.91

Why in 1983 did you move to the Peak?
I was climbing in Wales at Tremadog and Pen Trwyn with the lads, it was Jerry Moffatt who made the move to Sheffield first. Tim Freeman, Chris Parker and I, all planned to follow as soon as we could. Tim and Chris got a place on Infirmary Road, which was a filthy hovel, so I took on a job at Blacks in Liverpool for three months. I spent summer '83 at Paul Williams place in Penisarwaen, working at Pen Trwyn and climbing in the mountains and on Gogarth. I then moved to Hunters Bar, Sheffield in Oct. '83 and took an old room at 84 Hunter House Road. By this time Tim and all had taken over 124 and wrecked the joint. Climbers soon took over in '84. Jerry moved in with me and the two remaining girls baled out. Zippy (Mark Pretty) and Basher (Martin Atkinson) moved in, to what was to become a very intense household indeed. Jerry left after a

year or so and Chris Gore moved in. Various people came and went. Pete Kirton, Spider Mackenzie and Nick Plishko; a great house that. Winter 83/84 we spent training madly in the Poly gym, Red lane and Broomgrove Wall. I got terrifically fit and had plenty of fun along the way. By this time climbing was a full-time thing, money came from the sponsors in 1984, dole, rent allowance etc. etc.

Why didn't you go with Basher to France?
1985 was my year out of climbing due to shoulder problems. 16 months inactivity. At this time he and Gore spent an extended period in France with Jebé Tribout and the Le Menestrels. They embraced the French Red-point ethics, competitions etc., and I was at home waiting to get better. When I got better I did THE BELLS and then CHIMES OF FREE-DOM 8a, the latter took 13 days. It was to show

Andy's route CHIMES OF FREEDOM wa 7c+ originally, then a block under the roo fell off to give a very hard route of 8a+, firs done by Ben Moon. Here Neil Gresha makes the hard clip in the middle of the cru roof section.

them that you can climb hard routes ground-up. It then had numerous 1 and 2 day repeats Redpoint style, my ethics changed overnight.

You mention THE BELLS, has Gogarth always been somewhere special?

Gogarth has always been, and always will be, precious to me. Lets face it, I've always stared death in the face, felt and smelt it there on more than a few occasions. Can't beat being on the main cliff or North Stack Wall for me, – not Auz, Buoux or anywhere. My early exploits are memorable but in '84 especially. Doing MAMMOUTH free was an all time high point, Ron and John Redhead had whittled away at the aid and left one and a rest point. Steve Andrews was fun to climb with and belayed me on my biggest and best new route of the time SKINHEAD MOONSTOMP E6. Today it's still hard but I went on it on-sight all the way from the bottom. It's a 300ft route and I was carrying a big peg hammer and lots of pegs. The second hard pitch was a really frightening flared crack without any protection, you couldn't hang on to anything even to place a peg. I kept on going up, running out 30-40ft on lead and

Quentin Fisher testing the possiblity of Knockin on Heaven's Door.

looking at an 80 footer, then loosing confidence and scuttling down the flake which was even more frightening since Steve couldn't see me or the 80 foot loop of rope until I was at the last point of the reverse move off the flake and pumped to kingdom come. I eventually got sorted out and led up the wall, across POSITRON, a rest and straight on up the final overhanging headwall. I was really pleased with that one. Obviously the North Stack thing has been the most influential thing in my life, just about everything has been said about my affair with that wall. I simply got hooked by it's unique charm, situation and reputation. I remember doing THE CAD E5, in '81 (or '82) with 'my dad' – Paul Williams the 5th ascent or something like that. I did THE LONG RUN E6, 3rd ascent and that only left THE BELLS, THE BELLS E7!! It took a few years to psyche up for that one, other than that, I simply adore the place and would happily end it all there.

Why do THE BELLS?

This route, more than any other, seemed to sum up bold climbing for me, I simply HAD to do it. I waited 3 years until I felt good enough in my head to go for it on sight. I Had a real gripper but it was worth it. It was technically pretty hard and certainly harder than I'd expected, it was an incredible effort by John Redhead in 1980. I felt particularly good about this ascent, I still do in fact.

Do you ever get scared?

Of Course. But if I'm psyched, say on KNOCK-'IN ON HEAVEN'S DOOR E9, at Curbar in the Peak, I fell pulling over the top, easily looked like dying but caught a sloper below my feet on the way past. I can turn it around and feed off the adrenalin rush. Likewise on THE BELLS, when my fingertips burst way out from the peg. I hated life for a minute or two up there, but if you're looking at the 'final big one' it's amazing what you can do!!

Is dying a worry to you?

To be brutally honest Dave, yes it does worry me, but if I'm psyched for something then it just inspires me more; If I'm facing the 'final big one.' Climbers are forever putting themselves in a 'death situation' - soloing easy routes; you just don't let it even enter your head. It's only occasionally when your foot slips, or a finger hold feels greasy or when you get a surprise pump going, that you realise your situation is potentially fatal. I have in the past, often courted death premeditatedly, and although it can be terrifically scary, it is the ultimate BUZZ!!! I certainly don't want to die a horrible death, a quick fall and a bump on the head will suffice – thank you! Be nice to be cremated and tipped over the edge of North Stack Wall at the end of the line, I just hope the updraught doesn't carry my ashes, and dump them in Tzunami Zawn or something God awful like that though!!

Why go to Australia?

A combination of reasons really. I had seen so many stunning photographs of the place. Working with Glenn Robbins for a couple of years around Britain. He was returning to Melbourne for a year and I decided to meet up with him and we'd get some stuff done out here in Auz. I Had done pretty well everything I wanted to do in Britain and thought a big adventure in Auz would rekindle my enthusiasm for climbing. It did!!

What kind of lifestyle is it in Australia?

Extremely laid-back on the whole, especially the climbing scene. The Auzies are just like you see in films and on TV. G'day, fair dinkum and all that. Really friendly most of them too. Living 'in the bush' is brilliant. Kangaroos, Emus, Koalas everywhere you look. Amazing reptiles – up to 6 feet long, spiders and snakes galore! Incredible sunset's and just vast open spaces. City life is great fun too. Millions of brilliant restaurants, mostly cheap to eat in and excellent, varied food.

Do you enjoy eating?

On the whole, food bores me, and I feel uncomfortable after eating meals. I can eat sweets, smoke, drink lots and booze forever, but my weight never changes. I frequently eat out in restaurants – especially here in Australia, where they're so cheap and varied: Thai, Vietnamese, and Malaysian especially, Melbourne has to be the eating capital of the world. Other than that I don't touch food, it's 'NOT' for dieting reasons, I simply don't like the stuff.

Will you stay in Australia now?

No. I'm happy with 6 months here then back to Sheffield for a few months. I always take a couple of months off climbing every year, I enjoy working for Technitube, access work with plenty of friends, and my family in U.K. It's as though I've got 2 lives, one here and the other in Britain; a whole new set of friends and a surrogate family here too.

What makes climbing addictive to you?

Many things make climbing addictive but adrenalin buzz is probably the biggest thing, also the amazingly good feeling of climbing something, really hard and totally in control. It fulfils you mentally as well as physically when you climb well.

Will you ever climb bold routes again?

Possibly, but only if it's something totally awesome though. That was a very important phase in my life but now I am far more inspired by much harder physical routes, and by working out desperate problems on wood, on my boards and roofs in my garage, and on friends boards.

Ben Pritchard on Andy's all time classic OVER THE MOON 8a at Pen Trwyn, Llandudno, Wales. No small holds but alarmingly overhanging.

Chris Gore

Today Chris is one of the leading business climbers of the eighties. His success at representing climbing firms in outdoor marketing and sales, has left him with less and less time to climb. Even so, ten years of climbing at the very top level has paid dividends and he still is be able to go out and tick off the 8b routes without too much difficulty. Chris has always been slim, light and tremendously fit and it was perhaps due to a wrist injury that he missed out on going to the very top on the competition circuits in the late 80's. He has never concentrated on new routes, yet his fast repeats of the test piece climbs are very impressive, 2nd ascent of ROOSTER BOOSTER 7c, NINTH LIFE E7 6c, LITTLE PLUM 7c+ and VERBAL ABUSE 8a. More recently he has done ZEKE THE FREAK 8b and the fastest ascent yet of PREDATOR 8b at Malham, in just two days. In character both as a climber and as a business man, he remains astute without any loss of generosity.

Interview 24.1.91 Hunters Bar, Sheffield.

Has it been important for you to remain at the top of the sport?

I think if you talk to any top climber, ask them why they started climbing and the majority of people I know will have tried a lot of sports. They've gone through everything, tried this, tried that, jumped and jumped until they have found what they are good at. Generally you will find that they have done tennis, sailing, canoeing, but not team sports, so they have wanted to find something that they are good at. They are naturally good at climbing or that climbing is such a minority sport that it's easy to be good at it. When I started it was just easy to be good at climbing, now it's harder, there are a lot more people in it and we are getting the people that are naturally strong. I'd never say that there's a naturally talented climber, The nearest thing that we get to a natural talent, is someone who has greater body awareness, someone who has good balance, they could go on a pair of skis, a skateboard, etc., and they could do that. I think that counts a lot more, that's as natural as you're going to get.

What made you choose rock climbing as opposed to mountaineering?

Primarily because you're in Britain, you don't have much choice. When I started climbing I quickly quitted school in the middle of 'A' levels and just went rock climbing with the North London Club members, hitching off to Wales or the Peak District every weekend. Then I started working in the climbing shop Alpine Sports and saving money, climbing then was to go abroad. You practiced in Britain

to go and do something in Chamonix in the Alps. I'd had one weeks winter climbing and it was awful, it was bad weather, you had to wait, you got cold and miserable, I thought 'I don't like this.' I had the choice of going to Yosemite in the USA or to Chamonix. So when I was 19 I went to Yosemite for three months and I'd been climbing for two years. That was when I realised that things were coming together, because then I was flashing 5.11's. That was 1977 and it was 'on-sight' climbing. I flashed all the hard routes I went on and probably did one of the first complete ascents of NABISCO WALL via BUTTERBALLS (5.11). I only found out years later talking to Ron Kauk that it was an early ascent. I did a couple of Walls which you might put in the mountaineering category, El Cap, The Nose, Half dome, the things you read in the books.

Did the Big Walls not capture you enough?

No, Big Wall climbing was a tick, and a very enjoyable tick at that. You read all the early Mountain magazines and it was all the El Cap update, Charlie Fowler doing the SHIELD A5, and the ZODIAC A5, there was a lot of history there and I think that was important. You get it today but I can see climbing loosing it. I remember someone talking to Ben Masterson and saying Pete Crew wouldn't do that, and he

said 'who's Pete Crew,' and you consider Ben to be one of the older climbers who's been around a bit.

You did many early repeats of routes like PROFIT E5 at Curbar and RETICENT MASS MURDERER E5 at Cratcliffe, did you consider your climbing style to be higher than that of the first ascentionist?

Yes absolutely. It's always easier to do a subsequent ascent in better style that the first ascentionist. I always felt it was being competitive with the first ascentionist, proving that it was possible to repeat something that was meant to be hard.

Is it that competitiveness which immediately took you to competitions, or was it the style of on-sight climbing?

No it was the competitiveness. You always like to think that you know how good you are, and competitions will either prove or disprove that. Fortunately, I was a person that had the outlook or say manner that however I climbed on the crag, it was the same that I could do in a competition. Someone like Ben Moon has had an awful lot of problems, he knows how good he is, but he can't necessarily prove it in competitions because of his approach. He gets nervous and it's stopping now, but when he first started it was hard work for him.

Ben Moon making a very early ascent of Chris's route ENTREE, on Two Tier Buttress, Cheedale. Seconds later Ben was 20ft up and Sean, deep in shock at Ben's power, had to quickly give a traditional waist belay. Ben was a hair away from flashing the route, before downfall....plop!

When you first went into competitions did you expect to win them?
No I never expected to win, I went into them and wanted to be in the top ten, and that meant, 'the top 10 in the world,' along with climbers like Tribout, Edlinger, Glowacz, Atkinson, Cortijo and Marc le Menestrel. The standard was high, but now standards are higher and there's a far greater number of good climbers.

What stopped you from carrying on in competitions?
I was bouldering at Red Rocks near Las Vegas. I had spotters and it was on a problem that I'd done before and I relied upon them. Well, I fell off, they missed me and I landed on my wrist which broke and trapped the nerve which needed an operation. Then for 4-5 months I had no feeling in my thumb, first and second finger of my left hand. You cannot

begin to imagine what a disadvantage that is; I could top rope to keep fit but I couldn't feel a thing. So in a leading situation when your on say a poor hold, you start slipping so you increase your strength; but when you can't feel your fingers you fall off. The operation that they did, was a decompression operation which basically involves cutting the ligament across the hand, there was a 50% chance of loosing my grip strength, 'between the devil and the deep blue sea.' I took the chance of loosing my grip strength, fortunately I didn't.

Do you think you could cope with giving up climbing?
A difficult question. At the moment in the winter, not being in the sunshine it feels easy but I couldn't cope with being unfit. The ambience of being at a cliff though is... well I don't think anyone who's done it for a long time could give it up easily.

Has that built up over several years in travelling with other climbers?
Yes, very much so. I'm not someone that can just go out and say 'Oy, you hold my ropes'. I have to go with somebody, someone who I enjoy climbing with.

Do any trips stand out in your mind?
It must be the trip to the states with Jerry Moffatt in the winter of 1982-3. I went to the Gunks, Colorado, and various areas in California like Joshua Tree.

Was that competitive?
In some ways yes, and in some ways no. I think the bouldering was more competitive than the climbing, but as a trip it really does stand out because it was so enjoyable, purely climbing. Then I went to Japan, again with Jerry in 1984, I had just recovered from breaking a wrist and ankle at the same time. I was on an easy route Psychophant Roof E5 at The Orme, climbing up to the first bolt, about VS standard and a block came out, I fell crashing to the ground breaking my left ankle and right wrist. Martin Atkinson was trying to chat up these two Irish nurses, and was impressing these girls, "come and look at my mate, he's one of the best climbers in the country," and all this chat, typical Basher. They promptly came and saw me fall off and break my wrist and ankle. So they, totally unimpressed, walked off. Martin eagerly follows after them, and they say "Well don't you want to see how your friend is" so he comments "Oh, yes". Runs back and asks me how I am "well I'm not very well Martin" oh right! see ya! and runs off after the girls again. That's what I mean, the ambience of climbing.

Does the dangerous side of climbing appeal to you?
Climbing dangerous routes! I think that you'll find this with a lot of people, that psychologically it's not really climbing dangerous routes. If you thought that you were in danger, then you wouldn't do it. I used to do an awful lot of soloing on gritstone and every route I solo'd I did on-sight. I had a thing about on-sight climbing. If you top rope something, then you can top rope it until it becomes the grade you want it to be. Not so much with today's

gritstone routes, but it is the case with the older ones. I remember doing EDGE LANE E5, CAVE WALL E5, HAIRLESS HEART E5, ODE-PIUS E4, DOWNHILL RACER E4, all on one day in 1980. I've solo'd LEFT WALL E3 and PENAL SERVITUDE E4, in North Wales which are big impressive climbs which if you fall off, you are going to die. I remember soloing THE KNOCK E4 at Burbage, well it's E4 5c because it's badly protected; and I was looking for places to jump from the top. You talk to people and it's common, you'll have them up at 70ft., looking for somewhere to land and it's just ludicrous. I did that when I was soloing LEFT WALL, I got to near the top, was traversing on those friable flakes and thinking, 'one of these might break, I wonder where I'll go, I wonder where I'll land,' not thinking of dying, but thinking where's the best place; it's bizzare, you'd be a complete sandwich. The majority of people I know, unless there going on a suicide trip or something, won't see danger in what they do.

When you were soloing the PENAL SERVI-TUDE on Suicide Wall, there were people who didn't want to look. Did that bother you, or is it none of their business?
Yes, absolutely, I do what I want to do. They don't have to look, they don't have to like what I'm doing. OK if I did land, I might spoil their day. It's an arrogant attitude I know, but then again if you're doing something like that, then you can't think about other people. You just have to concentrate on what you're doing.

Does that spread over to climbing ethics generally, you do just what you want to do?
No, I don't think so at all. Obviously it does in that you have to consider what you're doing is right, so if I'm soloing I consider that right. But when I'm climbing there are things that are considered right, it's a different subject really. There are these unwritten rules 'thou shall not chip', 'thou shall not put bolts on gritstone', etc. But in the end in climbing, I think that you're proving to yourself that you can do something.

What other pastimes do you enjoy?
As a kid I used to really enjoy sketching, drawing and I was reasonably talented, but with climbing the dexterity goes a little bit so photography took over from that. I like watching dance and gymnastics, not necessarily for the flowing movement but for the physical manipulation of the body. I always think that a practiced routine is so much nicer than something staggered and not well thought out. The same applies in climbing if you're flashing a route. If you do it nicely, then it can be the ultimate experience; but if for other reasons you have a hard time, it can be enjoyable for very different reasons. Take a worked route

where every move is hard and you're pushed, but because you've practiced it then you can push yourself through each move, that once again is nice.

Take a worked route like MAGINOT LINE 8c, isn't that very similar to gymnastics?
No because, yes you've got Maginot Line which is a sequence of moves, and you practice the sequence like you do on the rings, but then you go onto AGINCOURT 8c, and it's a different sequence of moves. The moves on the rings remain the same, yes they might come in a different sequence, but every time you go on a route you are likely to come across moves, completely different to anything you've ever come across before.

Does searching for that constant difference appear in your everyday life?
Yes, I always look for things to enthuse me, routine is boredom. That's what I found so good about competitions. In 1986 I had done the majority of the the hard routes in Britain, so when competitions came along it was new, something to go for. Now since having a few years off in Europe there's a stack of newer routes in Britain.

Do you feel that there is anything that you can put back into climbing through teaching climbing to youngsters?
The appreciation of it, where it's come from, what they can get out of it.

Can you ever get the enjoyment from climbing now with all the gear hanging down around your waist. Can that ever be seen again as like the style?
No. It's a pain in the arse, I mean look, there's my climbing gear, it's a rack of biners. Maybe, I shouldn't say that, it's wrong to say that. I know so many climbers that do not know how to place nuts, and I think it would be sad to loose that. But the other thing is that people can go to a gym and come out climbing at E4 without ever having touched rock. I know some young lads from Rotherham College and they just climb on a cellar wall and they're good climbers. They don't go near routes with nuts, they just go on bolt routes. It's difficult for me to say. it's a part of climbing I really enjoyed, but at the same time I can see what a hassle it is, and maybe because of my standard I won't go back to those sorts of routes; maybe in a few years I will. For me climbing is about enjoyment, if I go don't enjoy doing something, I don't do it. I don't feel pressured into doing things that I don't have to, I think it's important, in the end you are climbing for enjoyment.

Dave Pegg

Dave is one of the younger top climbers who has established himself as an 8b climber. Born 4.2.67 at Leeds. His climbing started whilst at school, going out to the local gritstone crags of Almscliff and Caley. Then after spending three years at Sheffield University he returned to Yorkshire and saw a great new line at Kilnsey. On this he succeeded to give YORK-SHIRE RIPPER 8b, which is considered as a modern day classic route. His gritstone explorations led to Brimham Rocks and Earl crag where he put up two more hard climbs respectively: THE BOTTOM LINE 8a, and MIND BOMB E7. Recently in 1990 he climbed a very serious route on Esk Buttress, arguably the first E7 in the Lakes, FIRST AND LAST AND ALWAYS.

Interview 11.5.91 Kilnsey, Yorkshire.

In 1989, what made you look at the line of The YORKSHIRE RIPPER?
A lot was happening at Kilnsey then, it was the period when Martin Berzins, the anti-bolt traditionalist, had gone away to The States, everybody was putting up loads of new routes at Kilnsey. I was climbing quite well and thought I had better grab a line before they were all gone. I'd been going to Kilnsey since I was sixteen and had seen the scooped wall right of BIOLOGICAL NEED 7c, it was really, really obvious. I was in a state of panic for about a week because I thought somebody else was going to bolt it up. I'd just done things like THE AUSTRIAN OAK 8a+ at Malham, but when I bolted it on abseil I could see that it was quite a bit harder.

Did you doubt in your mind that it might be too hard for you?
Not really because once I'd got the bolts in, I'd actually done all the moves; and I think once you've done all the moves then actually doing the route is academic. It might be two weeks, it might be two years, but if you've done all the moves, you're going to do the route. You start to worry when there are two or three moves that you haven't done, then it's back to the gym.

Is it excitement doing the route completely, or is it an anticlimax once you've got the moves sorted out?
The two best bits are: first when you go on the route and you're working out how to do the moves, and then when you actually do the ultimate redpoint. The intervening twenty days or whatever, are a complete pain in the arse. When you do it, you always think it's easy, you can't believe it, you doubt in your own mind whether it's 8b at all; because it only feels hard

when you struggle. On THE RIPPER, if you struggle on one move then you will fall off the next. So eventually you do it, and find it easy.
Was finishing your university degree, as good as doing THE YORKSHIRE RIPPER?
No. Not at all.
Isn't it similar that you're practising full time to do the final thing, just like an exam?
Not really. There is so much more involvement with a really hard route. You walk around and you may even be studying for you finals, but that's just something that you have to do. With a route it's always in the back of your mind, tweeking at you, you've done all the moves and it's just a matter of linking it, if only you were that little bit fitter you could do it. I've always been very obsessive about things like that, I don't think I've ever been on a route and done all the moves and not redpointed it. If I've done all the moves I can't walk away. I might be sat at work, I'll start to day dream and I'll have to go back and do it, it just eats away at you until you do it.
Was going to university a cop out from becoming a full time climber?
Not really. Obviously climbing was important to me otherwise I wouldn't have gone to Sheffield, I wanted to climb and do something else besides which, in those days only Ron was about, and Jerry Moffatt was only starting to

become quite well known, but there wasn't really any concept of a 'World Circuit', or professional full time climbers.
Did that change whilst you were at university?
Yes, I seriously considered dropping out. In fact I took a month out of the course, walked out, I said 'this is it, I want to be a full time climber.' I was living in Hunter's Bar, and everybody in the house at one time had been a student; eventually I was the only student left.
What made you finish your degree?
My mum, basically I was cajoled into finishing, but now I'm so glad that I did. Then I moved back to Leeds for two reasons: I wanted to climb in Yorkshire, and because I couldn't afford to live, except with the support from living with my parents.
Were your parents sympathetic to that?
Yes, they said, 'you finish your degree and then we'll understand if you want to go climbing, we'll help you,' so it was OK. I then climbed for a year, living at home for about 6 months, and in France for the rest.
Having studied maths you must obviously understand figures reasonably well, why not go and make lots of money instead of climbing?
That's what I'm doing now! I wanted a year to climb, it was something that I had in me. I

don't see myself grinding down the long road to a pension, I see myself working for two years and then going around the world, going to Australia, climbing in different countries which really inspire me.

What do you do now?

I'm a marketing analyst. I build econometric models which are basically an equation; one side of the equation is market share, and the other side are things like price distribution, advertising; you build models to simulate the behaviour of the market. Big companies can make decisions on how they price relative to their competitors, or how much they advertise, and what effect that will have on their share. You can get very involved, it's almost like a new route project, except the big difference is that you get quite well paid.

What has given you the inspiration to climb?

I think it's two things, one is being out in the country. I love exploring, I'm just as happy tramping around on a winters day in the Lakes, looking for new crags as I am, working on a hard limestone project. Secondly it's also the involvement that you have when you climb. If you imagine 95% of your life when you're doing things, your mind is not totally focused on the thing that you're doing; what you're doing is thinking about other things. Probably the most intense experience that most people have is making love to somebody, and sometimes then it happens. In other areas though, quite often you don't have that sort of complete absolute involvement in what you're doing. When you're on a hard route, or when you're on a bold route; for maybe ten - fifteen

minutes you can be completely and utterly focused on what you're doing. There is not another thought in you head, it's like a drug, it's absolute intensity of thought, complete focus on one single thing.

Does climbing tense you up or release you from stress?

Sometimes I come back from work and I'm really, really stressed out. I'll come back, sit in the flat and have a cup of coffee, I can't switch off, all the time work is going through my brain. I'll just go down the wall and within 5 or 10 minutes of climbing that feeling has gone, it's lifted because I can focus on the climbing. I'm not thinking about whether I'm going to get the shit dropped on me next week, or whether I'm going to get a pay rise. It does relax you.

In that switching off sense, has climbing never become a monotonous, robotic form of activity?

It did to a certain extent, and last year I didn't climb on limestone. I'd had 6 months in France, living in Apt, Provence. Then I was living in a tent in The Verdon for 6 weeks, everything was climbing, you were living with climbers, eating, breathing, talking – climbing two days out of every three. I came back to this country and on the days I wasn't climbing I was bolting. At the end of that summer doing The YORKSHIRE RIPPER was a culmination. I really wanted to do it and was scared to stop going to Malham or Kilnsey in case I got unfit. I was 17 days on that, which is the longest I've been on any route ever. When I did it, I didn't have any interest in doing any other routes, I didn't think I was good enough to do an 8b+.

perhaps because when I did it, nothing wonderful happened to my life, there was no shaft of sunlight, it was like really shitty, cold, wet, rainy day. After that I didn't climb on limestone for a while, I did what I wanted and broke away from what you call the robotic monotony of it. I went to Lancaster and did a Masters in Operational Research, I climbed in the Lakes, climbed on gritstone and that winter did things like BOTTOM LINE and MIND BOMB. I returned to finding lots of new crags and exploring, one of my primary reasons for climbing – being out in the countryside, never knowing what you were going to find around the corner.

Do you feel one can achieve the top grades and explore new bold routes?

Yes, BUT; you can only do one thing, or the other. You can't do both at the same time. I don't know anybody that does both things together, really well. You step off an 8b at Malham and you're heads not ready to do a bold route, then most of the time you spend slogging around the Lakes, hanging on an abseil rope, getting belays and things like that. If you go to Malham you're so unfit that you can't do anything harder than 7b+, 7c.

Do competitions appeal to you?

The only reason they appeal to me is that I see it as a way that you could make a living out of climbing i.e. you could support yourself and go out climbing full time. But the actually physical process of climbing on a competition wall, doesn't really turn me on. The only thing that turns me on is the money if you're good enough.

Does not the on-sight idea appeal?

Yes, but not on something that is artificial, you on-sight, so what? In two weeks time it's back into scaffolding and on the back of a lorry. It's not like if you on-sight something at Malham, Kilnsey or Pen Trwyn; you've on-sighted it and it's been there for the last 20 million years, and will be there for the next 20 million years. I on-sighted the combination of artificial nobs that were put up in Munich, it doesn't really excite me.

What made you attempt the line left of THE CUMBRIAN, THE FIRST AND LAST AND ALWAYS?

It's just exploration really. I had a day off college and didn't have anybody to climb with. That year 1990 I drove up to the Lakes a lot, walked up to a big mountain crag with a guide book and looked for a line that hadn't been done, something really, really outrageous. There's so many routes it doesn't mean anything to fillers in. The point is to look for the most outrageous line that you can conceivably do. 19 times out of 20 you abseil down and think 'that's really outrageous' and won't go. But one time out of 20 you do abseil down something outrageous and you find that it is covered in holds, you've got something that is really special, and if you abseil down a lot of things you find routes like that.

Did you go back and do it?
Yes. Basically because I top roped it in a one'er and said 'that was a really good top rope', it's really really dangerous, it's really unjustifiable. If I do it nobody else will ever do it ever again, what's the point in doing it? I went back to Lancaster, had a couple of weeks wandering around and I just couldn't leave it, because I'd top roped it in a one'er, it was nagging away at me and I couldn't go to another crag and start working another route. It's a bit of a problem really, once I start on a route I have to do it.

Malcolm Taylor

Malcolm is one of the very quiet climbers of our time who has been living very much in the away from the scene, and done his own thing by going to France well away from the main bunch of British climbers. His 6ft 1in frame gives him a great reach advantage, especially when it only has to carry 10 stone along. He climbed very well in 1989 repeating many hard routes in the Peak and added his own route at Ravens Tor, RATTLE AND HUMP 8a. He then moved to France and in the last year has climbed 25 routes of 8a and above, including the classic LES MAINS SALES 8b. Still getting better, Malcolm at 25 years old is looking for that run of good fortune after injury to get established in the 8b grades.

Interview 20.1.91 Hunters Bar, Sheffield.

When did you first start climbing?
At school, I'd have been about 12 or 13. I bumbled along for years really climbing HVS, in the Peak and occasionally North Wales. I had friends at college in North Wales so I used to go over there.

What did your parents think of your attraction to climbing?
It used to frighten my mother to death. I remember the first time I went to High Tor, where there was this big very impressive face that my mother had seen a lot. I went home after I'd been climbing, and my mother hadn't cooked me any tea because she was convinced I was going to kill myself. She did worry about it then obviously, but I think now she's accepted that it is fairly safe really. I think there was more opposition to the fact that I was climbing rather than working.

Did you think that sometimes you might not come home in the evening? Did danger ever worry you?
No. I was definitely scared, I was fifteen at the time and there was two of us. We started out with a tarpaulin rope and that frightened me less than it did when we had all the gear, but it is frightening, if it wasn't we'd have given up years ago.

Where were you living in the Peak?
I was living in Ambergate, South of Matlock. I left school and everybody was unemployed nationally, not just climbers. I did my A levels then left school, '85 or '86 and started climbing full time.

Did you at the time want to go to university?
I applied to do an outdoor education course at Bangor in North Wales and they accepted me for the course. Then they closed the course down with the government cuts and offered me a place on a P.E. course. I wasn't interested in P.E. because they said you had to be at

county level in a ball game, which I'm not. So I jacked that in and applied to Liverpool to do the same outdoor education course at IM Marsh, but they turned me down because I was late in having applied to Bangor, and unfortunately they had filled the course. I didn't really think about it after that.

Was there any resentment that to do the P.E. course you had to be good at ball games?
Not at the time because it didn't interest me. But I learnt climbing at school and certainly it's made me what I am. I don't know if that's a good thing or bad, but I think it should play a greater part in the school curriculum In that respect, if it was then part of P.E. the course could reflect that.

Did you have interest in other sports like football?
I used to play cricket, I like watching cricket

and still I really enjoy it. Sometimes I wish that.... well it's a damn sight easier to make a living in cricket than it is climbing, but that's life.

Then you started doing new routes?
It seemed odd because you used to read the magazines about people like Jerry Moffatt doing ROOSTER BOOSTER. They were new routes and it wasn't what ordinary people did, OR average climbers did. It seemed odd but we had a really brilliant time, they were mostly awful routes, but we did some good ones as well.

Were you looking for the adventure or was it just lack of new climbs to do?
It was adventure definitely, they were definite routes, they were lines and there were big gaps on the crag that we were filling. There was a lot of adventure. There are some routes

Malcolm on the notorious CRACK 8b at Froggatt, one of the last hard routes to be climbed. Moves only of 6c, but very often impossible since invariably poor conditions prevail with the trees so near.

that I lead then, some E3's and E4's perhaps that were serious, but which were probably quite easy in reality.

When did you try the big routes on High Tor like BASTILLE E5?

I tried TALES OF YANKEE POWER E5 a couple of times with my brother but I always got a bit psyched out by it. Those routes at that time, seemed to have a reputation, you never saw anybody doing them. In the guide E1 was Extreme, E2's were hard extreme; E3 and above were cloud cuckoo land, so things like BASTILLE, TALES and CASTELLAN were forbidden fruit, they belonged to other people, the same as I said about new routes, Normal people don't do them which is silly, because sometimes when people see that you're doing a hard route, they look at you as if you're a freak and you're not, you're just some guys going climbing. Sometimes it gets annoying, people just stand and stare at you like you're some kind of weirdo, just because you managed to do something that they consider impossible, well it's not impossible, you just have to try. Climbing in this country is at a very low standard I think, as it is in France also, I lived there for all last year.

What made you go to France?

I had a lot of problems with my tendon for the past 18 months and it was basically climbing in the cold, but it was different and a change, I was a bit fed up as well. I'd do a new route and have people writing letters slagging me off, and people criticizing me in magazines about routes I'd done, and they'd write calling me names which doesn't bother me, but it's a bit pathetic and it grates on you after a while. People who should have known better, wrote to me saying that I was obviously a good climber, why don't you come clean and start climbing without bolts? Why do you bastardize yourself like this? It's like hate mail almost, but if you get five or six letters like that.... well that reason I wanted to get away. Also I'd done most routes in the Peak District.

Why did you choose France?

It was circumstances really, I went over there on holiday climbing, as well my wife and I were looking at property to buy and it was so cheap. It wasn't a conscious decision, let's go to France, it was circumstantial.

Did you go with the intention to remain in France.

We weren't even sure I guess, it was a bit like moving house anyway, it can be a bit bewildering. You don't know how the system works, we didn't know where anything was, and nobody could speak our language. We couldn't speak theirs more to the point!!

Did you buy a place?

Yes, just near Apt in Provence. We were doing bed and breakfast with the passing trade. The village we lived in was just off the main road, so we set ourselves up doing that which in the summer, we made a living at, but in the winter it was difficult because there was very few people around. I was amazed at how little respect people had for other peoples property, they would stay for a night and managed to break so many things, and it gets a bit annoying – I think that's a reflection on society.

Did you learn much about the French people?

Yes, I think French climbers are just like any other climbers. I was constantly reminded of something Ken Wilson once said to me that people at Buoux lurch from bolt to bolt. After a while that sticks out in your head because that's what's happening. They're not really rock climbing, it's very very different, and you certainly get a different sort of person climbing in France, than you do in England. This might sound a bit pompous since I put bolts in myself but you can't get away from it, a bolt is essential, there is no question about that, climbing wouldn't be as advanced as it is now without bolts. I don't know if it's a good thing or a bad thing, because it opens it out to more people. The problem is that you get a lot of environmental damage, you get a lot of litter problems and you get a lot of overcrowding problems.

What was the general character of the people that were climbing in France?

At a higher level of difficulty the French climbers seemed very similar to the English climbers, but I think that's because English climbers are becoming more like French climbers rather than the same sort of people. On a lower level of climbing you definitely get a different sort of person that goes climbing in France. I started because I really enjoyed climbing, I loved climbing mountains and things. That sounds really corny I suppose but it is true. In France you get the impression that people start for the same reason they play football, because their mates do it or because their dad does it. There's no commitment involved, you don't have to commit yourself to learning, you just need to protect your life I suppose – it's very very safe and all the time you get the impression that what Ken was saying is true. People do lurch from bolt to bolt, obviously they're not brilliant climbers.

There are world class climbers like Didier Raboutou, Jean Baptist Tribout and François Legrand; but there are a lot of shoddy climbers in France. I also think that it's how they want it to be, otherwise they wouldn't have developed it the way they have. They have the Alps, and the people who are into mountaineering and mountains and dangerous climbing go there. I think they still see it as training for mountaineering, except for the very few elite people. The majority of people see it as we would see swimming, or they see it as training for mountains so it doesn't matter if they desecrate this crag and that crag. That is their attitude and I don't think they really have a choice because there are very few routes at Buoux that you could satisfactorily protect without bolts, it's a massive equation that you have to balance.

Living in France did you climb with the French people at all, or did you remain distant?

You don't remain distant, but you don't climb with anybody particularly. You get to know people just like you do if you go to Ravens Tor everyday for two weeks. It was the same there, you get to recognise voices and names.

Were the routes that you did in France ever chipped?

We're talking routes, whole complete routes. When some guy did TABOU ZI ZI, 8b it's called TABOU, because it's chipped and it's a series of drilled pockets. Everybody slagged it off and that is not on. ROSE AND THE VAMPIRE 8b, is chipped, and all these famous famous French routes are chipped and I found it difficult to get my head around that, you're doing a route and you're enjoying it, but you know it's got great big chiseled holds in it; but you just have to say in France that is how they do it. I did a new route in Spain quite by accident. Some guy was stood at the bottom blowing kisses and saying "It's beautiful, you must redpoint this route". There was a resting level 3/4 of the way up, and I realised it hadn't got any bolts in the top. He appeared, then abseiled and screwed the bolt hangers in as the top wall had never been done. Thirty foot where he'd just put the bolts in looked totally blank, it was just a series of big chipped holds, and that felt really weird doing the first ascent of a route that was just created, it was definitely climbable with a bit of effort, and without chipped holds.

Does it matter to you that if a rock isn't climbed?

Not at all, it's quite irrational really, there aren't many possibilities left. We haven't got a divine right to climb them, we haven't got any sort of right to climb them, if we're not good enough then leave them be.

What made you leave France in the end?

I came back for treatment on my fingers because they weren't getting any better. It's unavailable in France on the national health. Also because we were broke!

Did you think of getting a permanent job in France?

On reflection, the area we moved to was a good choice for climbing, but employment down there is only 50% of the work force. The other 25% pick grapes for peanuts and it's not that easy to go and get a job with the language problem.

What do you see in the future for your climbing?

I'm having treatment for my fingers at the moment, which is a series of steroid injections and seems to be working. I'd like to do some new routes, that I know about, I have some projects that I'd like to do. I've got some harder routes that I would like to do, I'd like to climb in competitions more. I don't know how realistic it is, but I'm writing a book at the moment, a novel which is something I've always wanted to do, so that would fit in nicely with climbing.

What's the novel?

You'll have to wait till it's published.

Have you alway needed inspiration to go climbing?

The first few years I climbed no, because I was just happy climbing, but once you start to get better you suddenly realise that these people you read about aren't super human. They're just guys going out climbing a lot. You want to get better and I was inspired then to repeat things like THE PROW E7. I did the first pitch and belayed at the top of that and Darren Hawkins came up and we were just psyched out of our brains, because we both just couldn't believe that we'd done this pitch. "The hardest route in the world" quote, and yet there we were and it didn't feel very hard, and it makes you feel odd. We coined a phrase at the time "Prowed out". It was like being psyched out, but it was the aura of the route we were on, rather than the difficulty of the climbing. After a bit you overcome that and think, 'Christ I can do those routes', so you do them, and now THE PROW is pretty easy. It was a brilliant route at the time it was done, dead impressive. I've got a list in my head of projects and new routes I'd like to do, which inspire me.

Do you think competitions will attract more competitive people to the sport?

No. What I think it will do, is inspire people of the new generation. Instead of doing new routes because there aren't any, and to prove their point in climbing, to make their mark, they'll have to do competitions. There is very little left for them to do on the rock.

*Malham Cove in the distance almost hidden by an ageless farmhouse,
a spider with it's web of dry stone walls.*

The Elite

The Elite as ever is a small select group, never ostentatious or grubby. They can be at times a bit snotty, but never in climbing for it is accomplishment that make them the Elite, not society or peer group structure. They climb with care, distinct actions, calculated movement, and make mistakes rarely. They can be future masters in the making, and they are respected as such. They can be past masters in retirement and are honoured equally. Their body's are quite different to other climbers, in the shape of a well cut, clean climbing machine. They have a spark, that of knowing the top game inside out, they're never hustled, they don't grope around in shoot out's. The Elite are above, their skill is wonderful to watch, power immense, and judgement uncanny.

John Dunne

To most climbers the very mention of John Dunne immediately brings Malham Cove to mind. This is only natural since in the years '87,'88 and '89 John put up most of the major routes, which stand today as the modern test pieces for any top climber. They are today's classics such as: BREACH OF THE PEACE 8a, THE GROOVE 8a+, AUSTRIAN OAK 8a+, MAGNETIC FIELDS 8b and PREDATOR 8b. Very impressive for a young lad only 20 years old who had become a full time professional climber. His gritstone achievements also left people wondering who this superkid was: NEW STATESMAN 8b at Ilkley and PARTHEON SHOT 8a at Burbage. Unfortunately John then suffered from a painful shoulder injury, and has recently had 18 months off climbing. After very serious and complicatd operations on both shoulders, he has begun climbing again, and is now building up strength again.

Interview 1.6.91 Ilkley, Yorkshire.

Why did you leave school at 15½?
Climbing basically, I was on for doing 10 'O' levels, but didn't turn up for 6 of them and the two I got, were my good subjects. I did no studying at all and had a complete skive for two years. I was climbing a good solid E5, proper one's like SARDINE in the peak, now given French 7b. I flashed AUTOBAHN E5 6b, things like WHITE HEAT, PUBLIC ENEMY in Pembroke, AXLE ATTACK in Wales. Then just before my 16th birthday I did things like INDESCENT EXPOSURE 7b+ and LITTLE PLUM 7c+.

How hard did they feel?
You might not believe me but LITTLE PLUM felt easier than the rest because it was suited to my power, I did it in a day, dogged the hell out of it, then redpointed it.

That was in 1985, had you thought of doing REVELATIONS 8a+ then?
I'd obviously thought about it, but to me that was THE route of the day, and there was no way I was in that sort of League. I knew I was getting good by doing a lot of these routes, but SARDINE 7b took me 4-5 days with Ben Masterson. I could flash other E5's in the Peak, but this was proper, pumpy E5 climbing. After doing that I realised that REVELATIONS was a long way off, I was still heavy then, about 12 stone, I was definitely fat.

When came the big break through?
After my 17th birthday in Jan. 1986, I did STRAWBERRIES 7c with four falls, which had the aura 'Well he's going to be quite good, better watch him', and all that caper. Then 3 months of doing all the hard routes in the Peak, Wales and Pembroke, I came to Malham and it became a race for the first ascents

between Mark Leach, Martin Atkinson and myself. Dave Kenyon did RAIN DOGS 8a at Malham, about a month later I did it and it felt like my first really hard route. As soon as I did it, that was it, I could look at Basher and see that I was a lot more powerful than him.

Did Malham then suit you?
Yes, it was great. But also it was a shame really, because I climbed there for two solid years, I could burn anyone off there. Then when I went somewhere else, I found things desperate because my field of climbing just wasn't there, only in my last year of climbing did I realise about going elsewhere. It's understandable though, just look at Malham, impressive or what!

Around then in 1988 you put up PREDATOR, one of the country's first 8b's?
Yes, it got to the stage where I'd done everything in Yorkshire that year, and I think it was a case of running out of worthwhile rock. There was this nice line bolted to the right of ZOOLOOK, so I thought 'I'll have a sniff of this'. I tried the moves and couldn't do them, but thought it would be a good route to do. At the time I was jumped up and didn't give a damm about anybody, well if I rob someones route, that's there problem for not getting up it quick enough – it's fair game. Mainly because I knew that there wasn't anyone about who could rob my routes; Ben and Jerry weren't in Yorkshire so I felt quite safe. I did the route

which caused offence, but I still have this attitude that if a piece of rock can be climbed by someone in '89 or '90 it should be, and not in two years, what's a couple of quid for a few bolts. I'm sure Jerry and Ben think that way, Ben does obviously, AGINCOURT and MAGINOT weren't his, he's done them now, they're state of the art. I think if you've waited 2 years for someone to do them, you've missed out.

Is that why you attacked the great unclimbed lines on gritstone?
Well, I wasn't prepared to say, 'no leave it, that's impossible.' You never really know till you've gone on something, what it's going to be like. Routes build up a big reputation and people tend to stay clear, it just needs one person to go in and test the water, and the routes are a lot easier than you think.

Was the route NEW STATESMAN 8b, niggling away at you, did you feel that you had to climb it?
The NEW STATESMAN was a route that stood out as the last great problem in my mind, from when I very first started climbing at Ilkley. Quite honestly the reason why I did it was for publicity, it wasn't for me. It was for glossy photo's everywhere. Maybe now if that hadn't been done, I would have been happy to top rope it and leave it at that.

John completing the last moves on the 'Reps' 8a traverse, Cow and Calf, Ilkley, Yorkshire. The chalk dust from the dyno stil hanging in the air.

Have you always enjoyed the fear aspect of climbing?

Yes, without doubt. The thing is with me, I love fear, it can be anything, it can be climbing, it can be 7 blokes coming towards me on the street, I love it, it doesn't bother me at all. Ever since I was a kid I loved being frightened. I got that on gritstone but never on limestone, it's a different type of buzz. I think I've got a touch of madness in me but I can control it. I've never really been out of control on a grit route, I've slipped and managed to do the business, but I've never gone on routes where I wouldn't be able to keep it together upstairs. When I was younger I didn't quite realise what I was actually doing and I got away with it so many times that you tend to build up a feeling 'I'll get away with it again, I always do.' But you know that's going to come to a nasty end at some stage.

Now I look at it more realistically. Fear and risk are different though because everything I've done has always been a controlled risk, not a kamikaze job, and I think it applies to anybody climbing the hardest bold routes on a regular basis. Take Johnny Dawes climbs, they're bold, but it's all controlled, there are no idiots climbing routes of E8 and E9. People can gauge what their capable of and that's what a lot of people don't realise, you don't go climbing an arete that's 50 ft high and start slapping you're way up it, it's all controlled, you know exactly what to do.

Has on-sighting bold climbs ever appealed then?

Well the style that I'm now adopting, is to climb in a style where I can reverse what I'm climbing. It's something I didn't look into in the past, but just lately I've solo'd to the last move on some routes and solo'd back down again. Believe it or not, in the past that's something I never even thought of. When I went to Froggatt for the first time and solo'd DOWNHILL RACER E4 6a, there was no thought of going back down, you were going up or you were coming off. I still say that a lot of the HARD E8 grit routes that I've done, were so well rehearsed there was no way I was going to fall off them.

You've done routes in the past like PARTH-EON SHOT 8a+, that have been questioned, does it worry you?

It did then, it still hurts a bit obviously, but it doesn't bother me now. To be honest, I'm not bothered what people think me now. If I go to a crag and fall off a VS, I make a fool of myself, so what. I'm out now to prove things to myself. Before I never felt that I reached what I was capable of, now without the pressure I can see what I can do. I was up in the Lakes the other day and did a hard line which was good, it may have even been a project, so what, I was

climbing it for myself, not any guidebook or big media kick. That side of climbing doesn't interest me anymore. One chap even wrote me a letter asking to actually prove to him that I'd done PARTHEON SHOT, send him photos, all that caper. I don't see it's any of his business. I did the route for myself and if I hadn't, I'd still be trying it. I'm not, so I think he's got his answer.

When did you get injured?

Around March 1989. I had twinges earlier but a couple of days before the Leeds competition, my shoulders became really swollen. I took some time off, then went up to Dunbarton and the pain became like an intense hyperdermic needle. I realised that it was very serious and I went to all sorts of specialists. Then as soon as I went back climbing it got really bad and painful again, I thought I'd only ripped some muscle. I then had MRI scans, the whole lot – they didn't want to cut the shoulders open, I mean there's a lot of muscle in my shoulders and it's a bit of a big job.

Did they say eventually what caused it?

Yes, 'too much too young.' I'm not exactly the lightest climber in the world and it was chronic tendonitis in both shoulders. It resulted in an operation costing nearly 6000 pounds. The tendons of the shoulder run along the top of it then go through a hole in the bone. They had become so inflamed and were getting trapped inside the hole. Cortisone injections and rest may have done the trick but the injury had gone on far too long, so the only way to relieve pressure was to make the hole bigger by taking some of the bone off. The tendons had been swollen in the joint and had rubbed away some of the muscle tissue, also spliting one of the muscles as well. That had to be stiched back again and it resulted in a two week stay in hospital. It was done at Park Hospital, Nottingham, and I'm really thankful to them for it. There were no guarantees but it had to be worth it.

Because of the injury you've come out of mainstream climbing, have you benefited from that?

Yes, I have a lot. I've done some controversial stuff in climbing that I've never really recovered from. I got so much stick in the climbing press, the contract with my manager went wrong, I was getting sick of full time climbing and lack of money. Maybe I would have carried on without the injury, but from before leaving school I had the opportunity to go into my fathers building business, and saw it as the best time to accept the offer. The injury has been a bit of a blessing in a way, it's opened my eyes to life. At some stage you have to buy a house, get a bit of money and settle down. You

look at some of the Peak climbers, they're 30 odd, no money to their name, they're going to be knackered when they pack climbing in and look for a job, that's one of the problems. Climbing is one of those things that bites you, and if it does, you know it's always going to be there, so you have to be sensible about it.

Are you climbing as well as before?

I climb a lot better now because I take a more sensible view to training and climbing. I've got less time than before but I tend to use it very sensibly, I've seen that there's no need to climb 7 days a week.

Are we going forward in climbing?

I think we've got to be going forward in terms of things like HUBBLE 8c+, but I think standards have got a long way to go if the rock is there to do it on. I've done several problems on bolders and on routes in the last few months and I've been injured for the past two years. I'm unfit, and can do the moves already on these hard routes, it must signify something.

Are climbers bouldering far harder than actual routes then?

Some climbers are yes, but only some, not very many, there's not that many really hard problems about. Technical standards will rise, like HUBBLE isn't a technical route, it's just pure brute power. Whereas certain grit problems are a lot more technical, and it has to be said, that there is still a lot of grit unclimbed, there really is. I'd written off the wall to the left of the NEW STATESMAN as being ludicrous. I've top roped the arête to the right of WELLINGTON CRACK, so that's on but it's going to be very bold. I'd like to lead it, it's obviously worth leading for getting a nice glossy picture in the magazine but that's not what I want.

You did though when you were young?

Yes. Before when I was doing a lot of the hard routes on grit I was only 17 or 18, and I wouldn't dream of going up to a crag and pulling a really necky lead off unless there were hundreds of people watching. I did a big route on Curbar a few weeks ago, and did it in my own time, not for anyone else, no photos, that's the difference now.

What is there in climbing for you now?

It sounds stupid coming from me but FREE-DOM; because I've done a few naughty things in my time, and I have enjoyed the publicity and the hype of it all. But for me now it's the reflection on really what it originally was all about; it's got to be, going out and doing your own thing. OK there has to be some rules in climbing, but as a general rule there are no rules, you can go and do your own thing whenever you want, and that's what I want now.

John in complete control whilst soloing WELLINGTON CRACK E4 5c, Ilkley Quarry.

Martin Atkinson

Known to most of the climbing world as 'Basher.' Born 20.2.62 at Barnoldswick near Skipton in Yorkshire. He started climbing at 14 on the gritstone outcrops of Brimham and Ilkley in Yorkshire, and developed into one of the countries leading climbers in the Eighties. His contribution was mostly second ascents, and keeping the whole of the climbing scene motivated. His likeable character and enthusiasm, even with limbs in plaster kept standards rising in Britain, when in 1988 he added MECCA at Ravens Tor, Britain's first 8b+. He is undoubtedly one of the best climbing writers today and retains a balanced philosophical view of climbing and its future progression. He is now married and has a very respectable job as Export Manager for Mammut, based in Switzerland.

John Dunne shaking out at the top of WELLINGTON CRACK, ice cool man, ice cool!

Interview 12.11.90 Harrogate, Yorkshire.

When did you first discover redpointing?
In about 1976, I took about 6 months to do WELLINGTON CRACK E4, I did it with about 10 points of aid, then 9 points of aid, and eventually got down to no points of aid. Then 10 rests, 9 and so on, it was the first redpoint ascent!

Did that lead straight to E5's?
Not completely, I attended Skipton Grammar School in North Yorkshire, which was extremely advantageous for my climbing but not for my education. At the beginning of the lower 6th I asked myself; what am I doing A levels for? I left school and headed for the Lakes. I got a job as the cellar manager at the New Dungeon Ghyll pub. With the combination of beer and chip butties I soon got up to a very fat 14 stones, and a 17 year old useless climber. I returned to my parents at Barnoldswick, got a job working for a 'Bricky' and went

on a diet! I then started ticking the E5's around '79 and '80 with classics like TALES OF YANKEE POWER at High Tor in Derbyshire. *That was a respected route then, did you enjoy nut protection?*
Yes totally, we didn't know any better at the time.
Do you think it should be bolted now?
No. I don't think that nut routes should be retro bolted, they should be there so if people want to do them, then they can. Bolt routes are fantastic, but it's great if we can have both styles and types of climbing in Britain. I'm not saying one is better than the other though.
Do you think it will change?
I am not sure if specific routes like TALES will get bolted or not, but I don't think that British climbing will become totally dependent upon bolts because there is a variety of rock types, which is why you can easily define different rules. It's also logical to me that one should have bolts in limestone but not in gritstone;

having said that some of the best routes with best memories are the scary ones like VERBAL ABUSE E7, or having epics like ripping wires out of EYE OF THE TIGER E6, and so on.

Did you ever get seriously injured from falling off?

Yes, I pulled a peg out of WHITE BAIT E6,6c and broke quite a few bones and had my arm in pot for 14 months.

DANGEROUS BROTHERS 8a, next door, what made you bolt that?

To me it was obvious, there's absolutely no value in the route what so ever, except pulling on little holds and getting the next one. You can enjoy the technical aspect if your safe. SUPERCOOL 8a+, again I put the bolts in where it was hard, kept them a reasonable distance apart so people could work it, enjoy it, and then when its easier give it some character with run out near the top. That route happened to work perfectly in that style.

A lot of HVS climbers call for routes to be retro bolted.

Yes they probably do, but that's not a logical progression in any manner. If somebody can climb without bolts then it has to be said that it's better, there's less aid. If you can climb a route in the nude without a rope then it's better. I'm not advocating that you should do it but its obvious that you should always try to do the best effort you can. If somebody makes a statement by doing the route without bolts then that's how it should stay.

When did you start climbing 8a?

My climbing style changed in '85 when I went to France with Chris Gore, before that we were going around and doing things like PROW E7 etc. My motivation at that time was to follow Ron around, do what he was doing, Pen Trwyn and hard routes in the Peak. Then I went to Buoux and saw what was going on over there.

Who was climbing there?

People like Marc Le Menestrel, we learnt what was going on and I started climbing French style.

Did you do any hard routes in '85?

No, we mainly did on-sights, a couple of 7c+ but we were climbing English style, go up, fall off and come back to the ground. Its laughable now, but it was good fun and interesting. We soon learn't, that wasn't the way to go out there, it was pointless.

You then started climbing harder routes in Britain?

Yes, because we realised that if you used different methods to train things, you could climb harder routes, which for me was personally satisfying. Whether it was because I wanted to climb hard routes and tell everyone I'd done them, or because I was reaching my

own higher potential I don't know. I did TEQUILA MOCKINGBIRD E6,6b over 4 days and ten falls, not dogging one move, that's crazy. I could have done it in a day if I'd practiced it on a top rope. To take 4 days is interesting, but it's such hard work for the brain. Whereas after I came back from France, I would have tried to do it on-sight, see how far I could have got. Once I have fallen off I would have climbed the route resting on the bolts, with the aim of practicing the route as quickly as possible and doing it at the first red point attempt. If I couldn't do that, I would

practice every move and red point the route in as short a time as possible. With French technique there's such a logical progression, it's not just a question of top roping a route first. What you do is first try on sight, it might be an 8b+ and if you fail after 20ft and you've flashed a 7c that's interesting. Then you go bolt to bolt, its a logical progression. The problem was that when we were in France in the first place the French were only top roping. They wouldn't try anything on sight and they were ruining all the routes that were anything easier than their hardest grades.

John Welford moving quickly up the crux section of Martin's route, DANGEROUS BROTHERS 8a at Rubicon Wall.

Simon Nadin zooming along the POWERBAND 8b traverse. This was used by Basher all the time whilst training for doing MECCA. Now it has become very popular and is considered to be a route in it's own right at 8b.

Has climbing like that changed in France now?

Yes, because of what people like Jerry Moffatt were doing and maybe to a small extent us as well, but especially Jerry. They couldn't believe he could on-sight their hard routes and now because of competitions, its as important to do an on-sight as a hard route.

Was MECCA the hardest route you'd ever done?

Yes, it is a hard 8b+, it felt like a very big jump from the routes that I had done until that point, I'd done a couple of 8b's but easy ones. If you are working on a route in your own area it is much easier to stay in shape and keep your body in peak condition. If you go abroad you usually go to get fit, you stay for three to four weeks and then have to come home again. You don't have the time to accomplish any major routes. That was my problem on TO BOLT OR NOT TO BE, 8b+ at Smith Rocks in the USA. If I'd have lived there, then I would have had the time to work it and do it, as I did MECCA.

After getting to the top grade you changed direction?

Yes, Switzerland and a job! I was 26, happy and the thought of full time climbing for the next five years or so seemed most appealing. With the climbing contracts that I had at the time I could survive and have a reasonable life: buy a house, run a car, take a holiday and most importantly climb. A fantastic lifestyle in terms of doing what I wanted to do, but what of the future? A serious accident or injury would have left me without an income or possible career. I was offered a full time job with Mammut, and it was an offer too good to turn down.

None of your four A levels are languages. You speak fluent German and French how come?

German went with the job and it was a case of learn it, and learn it quick! I learnt French from Jean Baptiste Tribout. I went to France and met Antoine le Menestrel and Jebé. We drove down to Buoux and dossed on the plateau for two months. There were thirteen French people and I, the English went on for about 6 hours and that was it. They were really good times, it was then that I started climbing 8a's. At the time there was a list in a French magazine of how many 8a's the top climbers had done, Marc, Antoine and Jebé had done 13, the next guy down had done nine. I had done 11 which was crazy, more than most of the French guys, and I didn't get a mention! Still it was a fantastic time, I learnt so much from Antoine, Marc, Laurent Jacob, Fabrice Guillot etc. Those boys were where it was, in France at the time.

Chris Plant having finished the hard 6c part of MECCA 8b+ and pulling round into the never ending groove where the stamina is tested beyond reason. Mark Leach on the absolute limit, the very final move of MECCA, leaving the groove after 60ft of overhanging 6b/c awe inspiring climbing.

Was it inspiring climbing with them?
Yes of course it was, at that time they were consolidating 8a, doing them very quickly, like in a day. They were putting up new routes like La NUIT DE LéZARDS 8a+ which I worked on with Jebé. One day Marc said he had a new line to show me, he led me around to beneath what is now CHOUCAS, nobody had ever been there. We looked at Choucas in amazement; absolute amazement, When I returned two months later and Wow! Marc had it bolted and was hard at work on it. Just the way he was doing it was definitely 8b, it was outrageous. That summer they did LA FLUID ENCHANTé'8b, CHOUCAS 8b, and LES MAIN SALES 8b.

Jean Baptiste Tribout, Jebé to everyone. A regular visitor to Britian having ticked CRY FREEDOM 8b+ in five days and YORKSHIRE RIPPER 8b in two. His world travels are very impressive with new routes everywhere including SPECTRE 8b+ at Buoux and TO BOLT OR NOT TO BE 8b+ at Smith Rock, USA.

Did you feel Marc was the most prominent climber at the time?
Yes, but the most talented was Antoine, and the most determined was Jebé. Marc now has other interests, like his studies. as does Antoine but can still do the odd 8b+ when he feels the urge! Jebé is battling in there doing the business.
Did you feel that Marc was in a different league?
No, I felt that Marc was better then myself, because he was stronger and more motivated, Antoine was better than I, but more importantly was that he was in a different league to everybody. Jebé and I were in same league as me at the time, but he pushed himself much harder and kept on pushing. It did't worry me at the time that Marc and Antoine were better than myself, as was Jerry and also Ben, but it did worry Jebé. He found it hard to accept, not because he was bitter and twisted, but there was this obvious rivalry between three guys that had started climbing together, and at the time they were living, eating and still climbing together.
You left out the other top climber Edlinger?
He wasn't part of the group, let's say he wasn't exactly popular with the Parisiens! *Was that justifiable or understandable?*
It was understandable in that Edlinger was a mythical person to the French public. He was earning a fortune, he was climbing routes that perhaps weren't as hard as some of the Parisiens were doing, and he was a southerner, most climbers were Parisiens which is a big difference. They never got in contact with each other which leads to problems, as it does with Sheffield climbers and Welsh climbers, whether its right or wrong, and, they were jealous. Justifiable, no because you should never hate anybody because there either a better climber or a better bullshitter, it's just not worth it.
When Antoine solo'd REVELATIONS 8a+, what effect did that have on you?
It had a very big effect on me and also on a lot of other climbers. They were staying with us and because I spoke French we spent a lot of time together, one night we had a very interesting conversation and I could tell that Antoine was seriously thinking of something. Of what I wasn't sure, but it was something big. He knew what he wanted to do and the next day went out and did it: he solo'd REVELA-TIONS. I knew that he was a brilliant climber but to actually watch him do that was incredible. I couldn't even work the route at the time, and to watch someone come along and solo it really knocked me out. He really kicked ass, he certainly kicked Jerry's ass. It was an outrageous thing, the hardest route in the country got soloed. Everybody had to ask themselves 'are we men or are we mice'.

What other things could you compare with the soloing of REVELATIONS?
Nothing that would directly compare with that but things that also impressed me were: Jebé doing an 8a on-sight at Smith Rock, that was the first time I saw an 8a done on-sight. The most impressive series of ascents was Stefan Glowacz who did two 8a's and an 8a+ on-sight in two days, whilst preparing for the Arco competition.

Does somebody like Ghersen impress you?
Yes, of course I'm impressed by Alain Ghersen. He is the strongest man in the world, one of the best boulder's in the world, and yet he is out there soloing the AMERICAN DIRECT on the Dru, outrageous! That is probably one of the most impressive thing that one could ever imagine in climbing really, to be doing a hard boulder problem at Fontainebleau today and a hard route in the Alps tomorrow.
Had you ever thought of doing anything like that?
Yes, I'd love to but I don't want to kill myself and I haven't got the time or application. I couldn't just go out and learn all that without giving up other things.
Have you always enjoyed climbing in France?
Yes.
How about Spain?
No, I don't like it, Spain is a toilet. Italy I like, which is similar to France in '86, there is so much discovering going on.

Now you're in Switzerland, have you met their top climber Philippe Steulet?
Yes, that's who I climb with most of the time.
Is he a nice climber?
He's a nice guy, Philippe is classic, what I would say 'an English type climber.' A complete stamina merchant, hanging in forever and just bumbling his way through the moves, keeps going, he's a real star. He's not what you would call a power boy, but he's a good climber.

Do you like the Swiss way of life?
No, not particularly, it is a bit of a social disaster and very different to England.
Do you think the English way of life helps climbing?
Yes, the English crags help climbing, they are so varied. You can do big routes, small routes, boulder, climb in any weather, there are always people to climb with because of the social set up and system, it's perfect.
Do you miss climbing in England?
I miss bouldering with the lads.
Any plans for the future?
Yes, not to stagnate. I think I'll always be part of the working team, but six months off to go climbing would be the best bonus I could get!

Ed Morgan

I call Ed the mathematician purely from his climbing style which is incredebly calculated. On a probem he will study the holds quite closely, then seemingly zoom up the problem with a dazzling display of fingertip strength.

Weight is not one of Ed's problems since he is just under 10 stone and 6ft. 1in. tall. He represents the epitomy of the modern rock gymnast, slim, very powerful shoulders, and a complete application of bouldering into red-pointing. He has climbed less than 10 grade 8 routes, yet most are the hardest routes in the country. His best effort so far is MECCA 8b+ at Ravens Tor in the Peak, but his efforts on repeating Jerry Moffatt's route LIQUID AMBER 8c, have been very impressive.

Interview 17.1.91 Longsight, Manchester.

Coming from Cambridge in the flat lands, how did you develop an interest in climbing?
My brother started about 2 years before I did, in the venture scouts. I criticised him in a big way for actually starting, I thought it was crazy. I had the usual public image of it being really dangerous, but nevertheless he kept on at me to give it a go. There was a good climbing wall built about that time in Cambridge, so I had a few goes there, then he took me up the Peak, had a weekend there and it took off. His input was quite important and I wouldn't imagine I'd have started if he hadn't, he gave me the opportunity to go climbing.

Did you do any sport prior to that?
At school I played cricket, then I played golf for about 4 or 5 years; I got quite good at that but then in the 6th form I started climbing, that took over from everything.

Was that the first time you got into any exciting sport?
Yes it probably was.

That didn't worry you that it was this dangerous sport?
I soon realised that it was as dangerous as you want to make it: so I made it very safe. Obviously every so often you get gripped, but I didn't think it was as dangerous as I had thought.

Glebe Farm with summer hay making in full progress, sits on the promontry above Millers Dale, to give fantastic views over the Wye Valley and Ravens Tor in the distance.

You did brilliantly at school with three grade A's at 'A' levels in maths, physics and chemistry. Was there any temptation to stay in Cambridge?

Not really; Cambridge, obviously had the attraction of being a very prestigious university, but I did want to get away and also start climbing. I didn't consider Oxford since a lot of consideration was choosing a good course for what I wanted to do – Oxford's not particularly good in that respect. Cambridge didn't do computer science and Manchester seemed to be the best option to combine my academic interests alongside climbing.

Do you think that you were lucky discovering climbing other than that would you have become a complete academic?

No, I don't think so. I could still become a complete academic, as well as being a climber. I always think perhaps one is compromising the other and I go through phases of thinking about this, at the moment I have no work deadlines, so I can fit the climbing in as well as I would if I had no academic work.

Do you think if you had met Ben and Jerry you might have been persuaded to give up studying completely and become a climber?

I don't think I would at that stage, because I didn't have any expectation of climbing at that sort of level. I was just beginning, I really enjoyed it, it was just a pastime like I played golf as a pastime; so in that respect I think I would have gone to university whatever.

When did you begin climbing better than you brother, and did it affect him?

I don't think it really affected him, he has always encouraged me in a very supportive way, there was never really any competition.

Was there a significant time that you started climbing a lot better?

Yes absolutely, just going into my third year at university. Mike Collins just started his first year, he was a mature student and he was very keen climbing E6/E7, so I started climbing with him. We'd go down to Rubicon and go bouldering there, I think that was the incidence where I started climbing on limestone I hadn't really before that other than going to

France a couple of times: Monaco, Verdon and briefly Buoux. Before that I just didn't know what was available on the limestone. There's a crag down in South Wales called Dinas Rock – there's an E2 that goes up the big face and there's a peg and a wire 40 foot up. You do a tricky crux about 5c and then just run it out on easy ground. I'd was doing fine till a hand hold broke and I ended up with a 40 foot plummet head first, that really shook me up a lot. I got the impression that all limestone was like that, holds breaking all the time.

So climbing with Mike changed that?

Yes, he just opened my eyes to what was available in this country with sports climbing. Limestone seemed to suit my climbing abilities quite well, and I enjoyed going out bouldering as well.

Without sports climbing would you have continued to sustain an interest?

Yes, obviously it would have been in a different direction, but I think from day one when I started climbing I felt there was something that really motivated me.

Have you flashed many routes?
No, not really, it's not something I've concentrated on. My enjoyment comes from bouldering and redpointing, sequencing moves together. The routes that I've flashed have been very enjoyable, but in a different sort of way.

Can you see yourself doing more flashing in the future?
Perhaps I will change my emphasis a bit, a lot of it comes from just finding the time to do all these things. Working routes is very time consuming, you're doing very hard moves which for me, leaves me tired for a day or more afterwards. There is no way of working a route, and then going off and trying to flash stuff afterwards, I give everything on the working of a route or trying to redpoint a route. It's tiring to fit in work as well. I'm left with just one or the other, and I just chose the one I enjoy. Conceivably if I have a bit more time I'd like to obviously concentrate on both.

When did you climb MECCA?
In November 1989. It was after I started my Post Graduate course.
Had you done may 8a's before that?
Very few, I'd done CAVIAR 8a+, and one other.
What then gave you the confidence to go onto MECCA 8b+?
Again it was a lot of influence from Mike. He was not afraid to get on these routes and work them, it was a case of getting on and seeing how we went. We didn't know any of the moves that were on it, it was just a matter of working them out ourselves and it took us a couple of days before we even worked out what all the moves were. It was getting towards the end of the year and a case of, 'choose a route and redpoint it before the end of the year', I chose MECCA. It doesn't seem to make any sense does it! But the moves felt O.K. and I felt... I don't know if I was ever confident that I could redpoint it, that year. But it was that I just had to try, there weren't really any other routes.

Was redpointing MECCA mentally strenuous?
Yes, horribly. It was standing at the bottom not knowing what to think before getting on it. Friends tell me before I got on the route I was just too psyched, wide-eyed and really tense.
Did you enjoy that?
No, because I always fell off. When I got nearer to doing it, I became more confident so I could relax, but it was also that the conditions were getting bad. It was cold and there was a lot of mist about, I was conscious of the fact that it was going to get wet soon, so each day I had on it I'd get nearer and nearer the top on redpoint but not quite make it, and then I'd

just think I'd blown it because it would get wet by next time. So there was that added pressure of wanting to get it out of the way obviously, before next year.
Do you get psycologically tense when you go climbing or is it something that relaxes you?
I think it does relax me. I just think it's really good to get away from your work and just go out climbing that's one of the things that attracts me – it does get me out of Manchester.
How long did it take you to do MECCA?
It took me eleven days.
Did you think, Oh sod it....?
Yes, I gave up on it for a month when I started my PhD, I didn't really get out very much. Then I went about it the wrong way, but I learnt a lot about how to redpoint routes. Before MECCA I'd work the moves and then start from the bottom trying to redpoint it, instead of trying to link big sections to the top

and not starting at the bottom, a lot of days were spent getting links from the bottom and then not being to get the clips further up. But after the break I came back and got a big link through the crux and then I realised that perhaps I could do it.
Were you fairly happy when you did it?
Oh yes, absolutely. It didn't really sink in for a week or two perhaps that I'd done it, it just seemed so unfeasible.
Is the concept of linking sections as opposed to starting from the bottom, important do you feel?
It's because on the top section there are the bits you get to when you're tired, you've got to be most familiar with them; so by linking from half way up to the top you get more familiar with the top section. Perhaps it's not, so important but it's just something that happened to me on MECCA, something that I

Sights typical of the scene at Llandudno in the heat of summer: Ed Morgan working away on LIQUID AMBER 8c, the pensioners enjoying a stroll along the pier, and young climbers leaving the shade of the parks and Parasella's cafe.

spent a lot of time trying to link. I'd have three or four attempts in the day, just to try and redpoint it. Then you get half way up, and just dog to bolt out to the top, to get the gear out. Finally I linked it throughout to half way up, clipped the bolt and just didn't know what to do for the next bit, I was lost; but if I'd worked it properly, that wouldn't have been a problem.

What is important, where is the most power in extreme climbing?

I think it probably does lie in the fingers, certain moves you obviously have to be strong, whatever muscle groups they are; but at the end of the day, you are always hanging on with your fingers.

What made you go on ZEKE 8b, after you'd done MECCA?

It had just been one of my goals to do ZEKE and MECCA – as simple as that. In the Peak District there weren't really any other routes to do in the E8 bracket. Last year it was a route that I wanted to do.

Does HUBBLE interest you?

Absolutely, it's just another route to get on and see if I can do, something to train for but perhaps LIQUID AMBER motivates me more, it's more sustained.

What about Zippy's project?

Absolutely excellent!!

do you feel like going and stealing that?

No, No, I don't. Some would say it might serve him right because he's done that to a few people...No that's just not done, there's a certain amount of etiquette involved.

Do you enjoy that etiquette with other climbers?

Yes I think so, because a lot of people respect that you've put a lot of effort into doing a route, and it's a new route. I'd hope that if someone was getting nowhere with a route they would let someone else do it, rather than persevering, but I think that if someone's made the effort to clean a route, bolt it up, then it should be left to them to try and redpoint.

Does climbing on grit interest you?

No, although I haven't really given it a chance, all I've done is some of the easier slab routes which all seem to have the same sort of move on, so I get bored with it.

How about soloing?

Not really, no.

Don't you feel like being the first person to solo MECCA?

No!! absolutely not. It doesn't really attract me. A few things at Rubicon might be solo'able but it's too hard to justify doing it really.

Are you keen to go and do AGINCOURT?

Yes, but again it's finding the time. I think there are 8c routes in this country that I'd like to do more, but it will be up there on the list of priorities.

Tony Mitchell

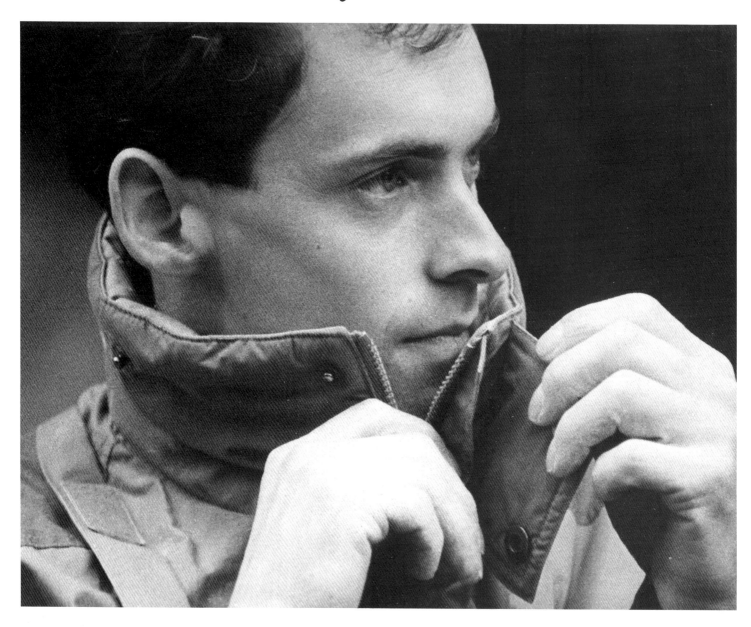

In 1990 Tony somewhat shocked the climbing world by redpointing CRY FREEDOM 8b+ at Malham Cove. His climbing skills were well known but his life differs so much from any other climber in the top standard, ie. 8b+ grade; he has a full time job and only climbs on odd days of the week. His life as a full time G.P. and father of 2 children, leaves him little enough time to climb, yet in managing CRY FREEDOM he has set future standards for other working climbers. Along the way he has added new routes such as TECHNICIAN 8a, at Kilnsey and PRIME EVIL 8a, at Chapel Head Scar. He has repeated a lot of the hard 8 routes in Yorkshire including those such as PREDATOR 8b, YORKSHIRE RIPPER 8b, MAGNETIC FIELDS 8b and BAT ROUTE 8b+.

Interview 2.2.91 Accrington, Lancs.

What made you decide to take a career in Medicine?
At school I was quite interested in biological sciences and the teachers suggested that I could be a potential candidate for medical school. I looked seriously at it, and it seemed an attractive career because it gives you lots of options, whether you want to specialize in hospital branches of medicine, or General Practice. I picked Leeds University which fitted in nicely with the climbing, I did know that when you are doing a medical course, there's a lot of very hard work, not a great deal of spare time, so therefore it's important to be near the crags.

Didn't it seem a rather safe career to get into?
Yes. There are lots of advantages and disadvantages doing medicine. It is bloody hard work, and there's a lot of book work and learning to do; but it is a very interesting subject. It covers vast areas and deals with people, which is what I quite like doing; everyday is different, there are always new things to learn and it's quite challenging.

When you were studying did you want to put more time into climbing?
Yes all the time! It's a constant battle to maintain fitness, to get out on routes that you want to do, particularly when you start. The first two years are normal study work, but by the time you get to the third year you are starting to work in hospitals. You're working a lot of nights and a lot of weekends, so you really have to plan your time well or miss things. It certainly wasn't easy, but being at Leeds in the early eighties, we had the best

climbing walls around and a lot of accessible bouldering crags to go to. As long as I passed my exams I would get my degree at the end of it, which is what I wanted. There were times when I wanted to jack it in and climb full time, especially when you were seeing other lads getting out and doing things when you were tied in at hospital.

How far did you want to go in Medicine?
Well, I didn't want to be a hospital physician or a surgeon, I had decided that quite early on. I wanted to do General Practice which gives you more time, and you are also well paid from early on. I think if I had decided to become a surgeon etc. then the the climbing would have just gone completely. I knew several G.P.'s and was climbing with John Hart at the time, he was a General Practitioner and had a very good

standard of living, plenty of holiday and spare time. I know doctors who just work as Locums and they take 6 months off in the year, go around the world and travel. They do locum work for a short period of time, but eventually one has to settle down and it becomes more difficult to do that. You make sacrifices early on, and at the end of the day it works out better.

You're one of the top ten climbers in the country, if you could earn the same salary climbing as your medical practice, would you have taken climbing up full time?
If I was climbing all the time I think it would lose something, it would become a job and to me climbing is leisure, even though I do take it very seriously. It's a release from the stresses of bringing a family up and the stresses of

working as a doctor. The climbing I do is quite stressful as well, so maybe I'm just a person that thrives on stress! I'll probably have a coronary at the age of 40. If I was only climbing then that would become very stressful, having to meet the demands of sponsors, having to do well in competitions or having to climb certain routes. Knowing some of the lads who do make a living out of climbing, it is very stressful and it puts great pressures on you, I wouldn't want that from climbing, it's a separate thing.

Have you ever been at a point in climbing where you have been too psychologically stressed, and have had to stand back from it?
It got a bit that way with CRY FREEDOM. I got annoyed because I couldn't get out when the conditions were just right. Obviously one has

Tony going for the ultimate training pump out on the CRAIG Y LONGRIDGE 8b traverse. No moves ever need be harder than 6b on this 30° overhanging traverse, but at 400ft. long it takes no prisoners.

Tony caught in the ultimate grimace on the crux power move of MAGNETIC FIELDS 8b, Malham Cove.

to go on the route when you have the free time, but often it would be a bit wet or too hot, the conditions wouldn't be right or you're feeling tired. If I was climbing full time I could pick and choose the days, pace myself better and maybe do the route quicker. It gets even harder the more difficult the route you get on. If you're trying to fit a full time job around climbing and maybe you're trying to take your family out for the day, you're trying to squeeze your climbing into certain times, so you really have to discipline yourself. I do a lot of mental exercises to try and get my psychology right for doing a hard route. Of the routes I've done, the longest I've spent on a route is 5 days before CRY FREEDOM, it was a big psychological barrier to do that route. I'll probably go back this year and try something equally hard, but for the addictive reasons you always want to do something that is harder. Sooner or later you're going to have to say 'this is just silly' because you're just getting totally obsessed, and it's not possible unless you're climbing full time. You always get a bit fitter over the winter and think 'can I do something a bit harder?' that's the nature of the game.

Is climbing addictive then?

I think sports climbing is, without a doubt, you get obsessed about difficulty, and you do get a great sensation once you've worked a route. You get a similar sensation when you're soloing, moving freely, you are not faffing about trying to place a wire, and the moves are so good and so hard that it's just sheer pleasure in the movement. Then one gets obsessed with difficulty, wanting to push the physical difficulty all the time. The feedback you get when you've done a really hard route is tremendous, so it's addictive, you juš̃come obsessed, and it's a bit illogical really. It took me 28 days to get up CRY FREEDOM; you think 'what am I going back for but you've just got to complete the route. I think climbing in general is addictive, you get some sort of feedback, some sort of adrenaline, some hormone which makes your body feel good; but of all the aspects of climbing, I think sports climbing is the most extremely addictive style. Saying that, Messner has climbed all 14 peaks over 8000 metres so I guess to some people mountaineering has that addiction also.

How can you combine fitness with a full time job?

Most days I get in about 6.30 in the evening after quite a stressful days work, then you have to think about training. A lot of the time you just don't feel like it, but you have to make yourself do it if you want to keep on top of the fitness. If you relax and let it slip, it's much harder to get back to that level, you haven't got the time. Effectiveness is the key to training; I

do a lot of work on the finger boards, because it's not a lot of use going down to local climbing walls, they are too busy and you can't really train, so it's a wasted evening really. Walls become a social occasion, so I tend to go on personal facilities and get much more effective training out of that.

Can that training do a lot of damage to the body?

I'm sure it does, I'm sure the fingers take a lot of hammering, particularly on the finger boards, one doesn't tend to warm up as much as you should particularly on a cold night. I've had finger strain and tendon problems, but if you keep the fitness levels up, and the strength in the tendons and the muscles, and you do try and warm up a bit, then you're less likely to injure yourself. There is always the risk in a hard training session, that you could injure yourself unfortunately.

Are top climbers today going to be more injury-prone than they would have been 10 years ago?

Without a doubt. We've seen in several top climbers over-use injuries due to inappropriate or over-training and incorrect training, I'm sure we'll see a lot more of it unless they are very careful to train properly, especially young climbers coming along now wanting to climb really hard and not really building it up over a number of years. They are wanting to climb 8b, 8b+ within two years and they are sat working on finger boards and doing power pulls and ladders. There is no doubt that there are going to be injuries because they haven't built it up gradually. I've built it up over 10 years; people like Jerry, Ben, Mark and Chris Gore, their strength has been built up over years and even they get injuries.

By not climbing full time, do you regret not putting up lots of new routes?

No because I've never been particularly motivated to doing new routes, I've never had the pioneering instinct, I just love to climb and it's much easier to go along and do a route that someone else has done already. Occasionally I'll do the odd new route but I'm not vigorously motivated to be a pioneer. One could say, that you could have put up routes, and as hard as other people at the time in theory; but I think some people are more motivated to do that. It does take time to clean new routes and suss them out. Some people just want to climb new routes all the time and I suppose some people get a buzz out of seeing their name in guide books and magazines – there is that aspect. My main motivation is to climb because I love climbing, I like to do hard things but I'm not that motivated to do new routes, over the years I've probably done about 20, but that has not been the main thrust of my climbing.

Were you ever enticed to be an expedition doctor?

No, not really, you always think about the possibility, because you get lots of offers to go on expeditions. Originally, before I started climbing, I was quite into the hills and mountains, did a few routes in Scotland and the Alps. The prospect of just going on an expedition and not being involved in the main part of getting to the top of the mountain is not me. I wouldn't be content sitting in a tent treating people with frost bite and cerebral oedema, I'd want to be up there doing things. On the practical side, if I got involved in Himalayan mountains I would be quite ambitious, so that would be dangerous and I don't want to get addicted to that.

What takes the biggest side to competition,

the piece of rock or the other climbers?

A bit of both really. I can be out on my own just bouldering and become obsessed with a problem. Then if I go to the wall there may be a bunch of lads there, and I want to be the best, I want to get up problems that they can't do and I want to do harder routes than they can do. I think all climbers are competitive even at climbing club level, if they are out with their mates everyone wants to do something that the others can't do. There is a lot of competition in climbers which is why climbing competitions came along. There is also the climbing for yourself and trying to justify your own capabilities.

Do you give in easily?

No never, if I'm bouldering I have to do the problem, I'm very competitive, I always have been. It annoys me when I can't do something, I always think 'why can't I do that?' So I go back to get stronger or fitter to do it. You have to draw the line somewhere as routes get so hard, and I just haven't got the time in life to put into them; but still you set yourself goals.

Does climbing harder and harder routes need an aggressive attitude?

It's a controlled aggression, it's a way of venting your frustrations. There's a lot of energy there which can be channelled into doing that, you've got to be aggressive to do a hard route, you can't be a namby pamby, you've got to get stuck in and give it some oomph.

From a professional point of view, there are a couple of girls that have done well, are they exceptions or can women climb 8a etc.?

I'm sure women can, and I'm sure given the right approach they can climb 8b+, 8c. On the very, very powerful routes, I'm sure it becomes much more difficult as a woman just can't

develop the muscle structure to do the very, powerful moves. It's mostly in the right approach and training.

How much of their femininity do they have to lose to climb 8a?

I don't know, Isabelle is quite feminine, again it's the controlled aggression, you get a lot of mild mannered blokes that can climb 8b and above, it's channelling that energy which is probably a better word than aggression. A lot of women are quite good as far as technique and style goes, and that accounts for a lot, even on a very powerful route. Technique counts for a lot, and now all top women climbers are good technicians, Lynn Hill is an excellent technician with perfect technique, as well as being really strong and light.

Does balance count much or is it just pure strength?

Obviously strength is the most important thing, but there are moves where a subtle use of balance of body language helps, even on very steep routes you have to be aware of you position and balance, although a lot of times it is just pure power. Technique is important also, I've always concentrated a lot on technique and I like to climb things in good style.

Are you tempted to move to a practice in Derbyshire or Wales?

No, it's not that easy to keep moving practices. Once you get established in a practice you generally stay there, it's a long term commitment and you just grow with the practice. I've moved around enough in the last ten years; Merseyside to Leeds to Lancaster and back down to East Lancashire. To keep up-rooting and moving, especially when you have children starting schools, gets a bit wearisome. Also the fact is that I prefer it in Yorkshire than Derbyshire anyway, I certainly wouldn't move to Llanberis! – I can't think of anything worse, but don't quote me on that one Dave.

Jason Myers

Jason is the least known top climber in Britain by a very long way partly due to his continual climbing abroad in the South of France. His exploits at Buoux have been very impressive with excellent repeats of routes like SPECTRE 8b+, LE MISSION 8b, and the second ascent of Didier Raboutou's route TOTAL TRANS-FERT 8b. He has never been the lightest of climbers and in consequence has suffered from elbow injuries which in turn have made him retire at the early age of 22.

Interview 7.1.91 Hathersage, Peak District.

When you were a child did you feel that you might end up being an engineer in the wool industry like your father?
I didn't have any clue to what I wanted to do, I just plugged along doing my own thing and seeing what would happen. That's pretty much the way I am today, I've never been a great one for forcing destiny.

Did your friends at school go off to firm careers?
Oh yes, Everyone I went to school with went either into Banks or university. A great tragedy, none of my friends went travelling or did anything like that, they were all normal.

Do you know what attracted you to study physics at Sheffield in 1986?
Friends I had here that were already at university and poly. climbing, it's a nice place, reasonably close to home, and close to the climbing obviously. In 1984 it became established as the centre with Jerry, Basher, Andy Pollitt, Tim Freeman etc.

When you started at Sheffield, what standard were you climbing at?
I think when I got to Sheffield I had done some E6's at Malham, things like OBSESSION 7b+ and MAIN OVERHANG 7c.

What did you do in your summer off after A levels?
That was it, I spent it at Malham! I Just worked my way through the routes, made a couple of trips to Pembroke – holidays from Malham! That's what we used to call them.

How did you view the climbing styles in Pembroke? (Placing gear etc.)
It was good and I was into it then, I was into everything. I did some bold routes, soloing on gritstone but nothing spectacular. I enjoyed my time at Malham as much as I did in Pembroke but Malham was so much more

convenient. You'd hitch up in the morning, climb all day, hitch back at night and do the same the next day or sleep there, no problem.

Pembroke was more of a jovial holiday trip?
Yes. We enjoyed it, we tried quite hard on routes but difficulty wasn't the main thing.

There was no psychological draw for the more bolder routes?
No, not really. I quite enjoyed putting in gear and doing fairly safe stuff, but I made no effort to seek death situations, definitely not into that.

At the time were you intense on improving your standard or was climbing just a form of relaxation?
I think I was fairly intent on improving, I think that started with finishing A levels two years before. I finished my 'O 'levels, had a long summer and started getting into it, bouldering and trying quite hard; then working through the 'A 'levels I used to work at my bouldering – coming along slowly but surely, then Malham, spending loads of time there and definitely pushing it.

Your standard had obviously shot up over two years, to E6, is there any single thing you could point to that has helped that?
Having a couple of really good boulder crags on my door step. When I lived in Baildon I had Baildon bank, which despite it's reputation is a really good base. I developed the bouldering there and did most of the routes, spending lots of time there. There are some really good problems, good traverses to work out, all that sort of thing, it was great fun. The same with Shipley Glen which was dead close, importantly going climbing was never an effort, it's always been incredibly convenient, it's always been on by doorstep.

Did you develop any other interests at the same time?
Not really. I became interested in photography and took a fair number of pictures when I had the chance, but all my energy went into climbing.

Then you went to Sheffield and you studied physics, then what happened?
I did the first term and was dead keen and worked very hard, was conscientious and did well. Then I started getting more and more into climbing, did more and more climbing and training and hanging out on the scene, and less and less physics, so by the end of the second term it was one or the other. I knew I wanted to do one or the other very well, but there was no way I was going to be able to do both, so physics was put on the shelf for the time being.

Did you leave Sheffield?
No, I stayed in Sheffield but quit the course and signed on.

Have you had any regrets since in doing that?
No. I'd do the same thing again. I think I've been quite lucky, it's worked out very well for me. Going to university then was really nice, it was good because it got me away from home. If I'd gone straight into a job I think it would be a lot harder to get out of, you'd be a lot more committed. It gave me the option of seeing what I wanted to do, then enjoy climbing and still have the option of going back and doing physics eventually. If I'd stayed home there is no way I would have got into it and I'd probably got really bored. I've had my climbing days as it were and now because of the elbow injury, the climbing was put to one side. I've gone on to do other things and landed quite a nice number here in Hathersage working in the climbing shop.

Where was the first crag you visited in France?
Buoux.

Did it ever enter your mind that you should go somewhere else?
Yes, but the first time I went it liked it. I can always remember driving down the valley the first time, there were these little crags which were small compared to the main thing. You'd think, bloody hell these look really good, and then you'd come round the corner and see all the overhanging bits and the Bout de Monde which makes you speechless, I'll always remember it. I just thought this is it, this is for me, I want to climb here and it worked out really well because the style of the climbing suits me very well. Climbing on pockets, long lock-offs, reaches, nothing too technical, basically thuggy which as you know suits me, I haven't got much in the way of brains and virtually no footwork, which made it just right. I love the area, it was spot on.

Did you fair well on your first visit?
I did OK, I did REVE DE PAPPILLION 8a. I think I did a lot better than most people on the first visit, I was lucky the style of climbing suited me, pulling on pockets is a lot different to crimping edges in Britain. I had the right sort of strength to pull on pockets, good arms so the overhangs suited me.

Have you ever been to areas of climbing where you've just instantly felt at ease and immediately want to go away?
The slabby bits of Buoux, some of the areas round the west face are just Ooooooo.

Do you look at that as climbing perhaps which doesn't suit you, or perhaps that you're not willing to take up that sort of challenge?
Both, it didn't suit me therefore I didn't want to push it anymore. I'll just stick to what I'm

good at and I enjoy myself which is a bit of a cop out, because you should be working on your weaknesses to benefit you all round as a climber.

Did you try REV on-sight hoping to get up it?
No! No chance, you wouldn't stand a chance on it, because it's hard to move on, you'd pull on a hold and you're off straight away because you've pulled on the wrong one, there's too many to chose from, it's far too hard, there is no messing around it was straight hanging on the bolt feeling all the holds, no messing around.

Was there any great sense of elation doing an 8a?
Yes there was, I was chuffed with myself, it was a break through, it's a magic number.

Are the celebrations afterwards an important part or is it more personal, is it something you think about a couple of months after and have that glowing feeling?
It is very much at the time, the longer you spend on something the less of an elation it is at the time, but the more it is afterwards. A climb which isn't too hard but you do quickly say, at the time you feel really good, but the next day, you've forgotten about it. CHOUCAS 8a+, I had an epic on, it just took me forever, at the time I just thought, no big deal, but I look back on it and think great, that probably lives on with me more than Rev.

How did you get over to France on that trip?
Went in Ben Masterson's car, which was an epic, there were storms in the channel, it kept breaking down, we got done for speeding.

How did Ben take that?
Remarkably well, especially when he locked his keys in the car, he said "Oh well I suppose we'll just have to break the window then". I was stunned. We were speeding down the Route Nationels, went through towns and shot through a couple of red lights, crossed the white lines, and eventually got pulled up by gendarmes and guns. They said right, £100 fine now or you go nowhere, even then he took it quite well. Obviously he wasn't pleased but we had a whip round and had just about enough money to get down there.

Did an incident like that fray tempers between the climbers?
No I don't think so, it was all part of the adventure. I don't think I've been in any situation where there has been particularly frayed tempers. You get a bit pissed off with somebody every now and then but it doesn't last long, ten minutes later it's forgotten.

Has going to Buoux always held that enjoyment?
I love going down there and meeting all the foreigners, it was very cosmopolitan and you make lots of really good friends.

Jason's early adventure playground Malham Cove.

What do you remember about doing CHOUCAS?

It was such a big tick, it was world famous, pictures had been all over, there was loads of Americans, French, Germans, Italians they all wanted to do it. I think most of them were without a hope really to be quite honest, probably a bit like me the previous Autumn. This time round, in Spring, I thought I was capable of it but in the end I got bored with it, so I left it. Actually I officially gave up on it, pulled my rope and walked away from it, I had had enough. I knew I could do it but I was just so pissed off with it, falling off the same move

all the time, and not getting any more out of it. ***You didn't feel it was too hard for you?***
No, I did other things that were as hard and harder, so it was just a feeling that that was enough.

Why did you keep falling off?
At first it was just too hard, then I just didn't try hard enough, you don't want it bad enough whatever, I don't know; you don't concentrate. The thing that was stopping me was this business of the jump, I could get the height every time. You are jumping into a pocket, which is like the top of a pint glass, and you

catch it, when you get it there is no problem, I was going for it and just missing all the time, or I'd get two fingers in or one finger either side, I was just never quite getting it right, but I'd had enough. Then one night I was sitting around the campsite with these Americans getting mellowed out and this guy Darius was talking about a route in America where he had to do a figure four. We realised it at the same time, looked at each other and it was like having light bulbs on our heads YES! First thing next morning it worked perfectly first time, easy. Darius was the first guy to do the move, and get pass it on lead. It was a really busy day down at Bout de Monde, because the shade comes on in the evening, and everybody goes there to try the routes or watch people try the routes. All the French were sitting there saying 'Bloody hell,' big queue of foreigners wanting to try CHOUCAS, Darius tied on and sauntered up the first bit. They thought here's just another guy going to fall off any minute. He went for the figure of four, and everybody just had eyes out on stalks, they couldn't believe it. They hadn't seen anything like it and they all came running forward gasping. The best bit was that Mark le Menestrel was there, who first did the route quite a while before thought, it was absolutely brilliant. You can understand him being quite upset that it had been made easier, and he was well into it, saying 'what did he do, he's brilliant!' It was so funny, they were absolutely gob-smacked. I think some of them were a bit pissed off, the French pride and joy had been reduced to a static move. I'll never forget it.

You had done TABOU ZI ZI 8b, along with CHOUCAS, how did you view 8b+ climbs?
Well that's a different league. I've always considered myself second division, always B Team, I don't think I was ever one of the best. So I thought I could do it but not that year, maybe the next.

Which was the first 8b+ that you started on.
Probably The RAGE DE VIVRE, I always wanted to do that. I never really got onto the top bit, I just went up there once to have a look at it, but I always had a hard time with the start of THE ROSE, the very first move, I seemed to be too tall to do it the normal way. I had a real problem getting all my legs into this undercut position, I just couldn't get my centre of gravity close in like everyone else yet I still wasn't tall enough to do it the tall man's way, so it was really frustrating, I'm sure if I'd been stronger I'd have been able to do it, you can always do anything if you are stronger. It always seemed to me to be a bit unfair that first move, the rest of it I could do O.K. no problem, but that meant I couldn't do the rest of it unfortunately. I suppose I could have done Rage de Vivre instead of THE RAGE DE VIVRE.

Are conditions important at Buoux?
Yes, even though everyone seems to think it's just pulling on pockets all the time, which it is. But the crux's are always when the pockets aren't pockets or edges aren't edges, they are dimples, in which case friction is of the essence and conditions have got to be just so.

What was your first 8b+?
First and only, the SPECTRE which was the following spring in 1988. I'd seen Didier on TOTAL TRANSFERT the previous Autumn and I really wanted to do it. I did that after a while

and SPECTRE is next door to it. I did TOTAL TRANSFERT the first try of the day, and it felt easy, so I felt because it's an effort to get up there, I might as well take a quick look at it. I think I did all the moves straight off, they all seemed reasonable, even the top bit which was supposed to be terrible but never seemed that bad to me. I didn't think I'd do it, It appeared way too hard, loads of people were trying it and falling off time after time on the top bit. So I went back the next day, I'd only dogged it out once the day previous, and somehow managed to get myself up to the crux, the jump. I caught it the first time and fell off in shock, I hung there thinking I've done it, better give it a go. I was off then and that was a surprise, I thought oh well, I suppose I can do this, better stick at it. It wasn't what I went out there to do. I wanted to do the Rage.

How long did SPECTRE take you?
I think it was 5 or 6 days. First day I dogged it out once, next day I caught the hold from the ground, which is like a big sticking point. The next day I had a bad day, I couldn't get anywhere near it, I was climbing really badly. Then the next day I caught the jump twice, I went for the next one where you jump across yourself, caught the last hold, swung off it, came off. I really lost my cool because it was a big tick. When I did it I was really made up. Before that this was the thing that almost had me in tears, another day of jumping for the hold, catching it, and falling off.

After doing it didn't you get an injury?
Yes. We stayed in France another month and went climbing in the Verdon, then came back and it was up at Malham climbing that I had a little twinge. I didn't think it was anything untoward, rested and it was fine. I went out to the crag again, worked out, no problem. I got up the next day, it felt a bit sore, I usually try to listen to my body and if I have any twinge, I'll leave it to rest. But every time I went out climbing, I'd get up the next day and it was sore, it just didn't go away. That was it.
You felt the injury was bad so you gave up climbing?
Yes more or less straight away, I had a couple of times when I rested it for a couple of weeks, then went out, and it was obvious it wasn't up to it, so I just spent the summer in Sheffield, wandering around on the Moors, doing a bit of bouldering, and soloed happily at E1, I think I did it a lot of good just to keep it exercised, any bad injury like that, if you stop, as far as I can gather you want to keep it moving, so I think that was a good thing to do?
Did that satisfy you, just going out bouldering?
Not really, I wanted to be doing hard things, progressing and improving.

What appeals to you cycling?
The exercise, the fresh air, just a totally enjoyable thing. It was something I was into before I got into rock climbing, going back to square one again really.

What do you see yourself doing over the next ten years?
Just sort of take it as it comes, go back to university and finish what I started there, apart from that, who knows.
Do the alpine routes appeal to you?
Yes totally, that is where my commanding direction is now, Scotland and the Alps, maybe bigger.

Do you look up to figures like Christophe Profit, Tomo Cesen?
Totally, they are in, not a higher class, but a different class to the rock climbers. I think people like Tomo Cesen, are in a different class all together to everyone else. It is unreal what he did. When I was a climber I had no comprehension of what these people were doing, but now I've broadened my horizons a bit and know a bit about how fit people can be from cycling that is really impressive, the sort of things they do are outrageous, the big link ups they do in the Alps are so good, to be that fit, to keep going. Getting back to that shows how far climbing has got to go. As far as I can see they are still playing at it. Not through any fault of their own, people are still finding out. I think sport climbing is barely one generation old now. If you look at cycling for example, it's probably 6 generations old, and how scientifically they approach it, climbing is going to go a long way.

Is it alpine Solo Climbing or part alpine with climbing?
I'd like to do solo's and things but it's not worth the risk, I don't think there are too many things that can go wrong that are out of your control really. You can be walking along quite happily and then can just plop down a crevase, you won't even see it or anything, whereas if your roped up with a mate, there is no problem.
The Himalayas, they hold a fascination?
Absolutely yes, I've got quite a desire to travel, and climbing and travelling is a good way of doing it. I know a lot of people who have just travelled, have been all over the world, seen great places, but the way to do it is to go somewhere, and do something there, you get more out of it.

Is that because climbing memories hold a strong part for you?
Yes, I like to feel I've achieved something as well, and pushed myself a bit. That is very important to me.

Sean looking mean and incredibly powerful on POWERBAND.

Sean Myles is one of the new breed of climbers in Britain keeping in the shadow of the stars and avoiding magazine publicity quite subtly by not climbing the hardest new routes or taking part in climbing competitions. Sean has abundant talent in not only climbing, but as a great humourist about the crags and bouldering areas. This also reflects his character of an easy going climber with a thirst for new areas to visit and climbs to succeed on. He has climbed across Britain putting up a complete cross section of routes: MONUMENTAL ARMBLASTER 8b, Cheedale limestone; BUNGLES ARETE 8b, Llanberis slate; RODNEY MULLEN E7 6c (8b), Yorkshire gritstone and CAPTAIN INVINCIBLE 8b in Burbage Quarry. He repeated Scott Franklins SCARFACE 8b+ very easily in the USA, and has done a worthy selection of French 8b climbs at Buoux and Volx.

Interview 31.10.90 Llanrwst, Wales.

You went to St. Edmund Hall, Oxford University, did you have a particular career in mind?
You mean a career! as in working! God no. I knew that wasn't going to happen for sure. At the time it was expected of me and it's something very concrete to do, if I'd known of the social scene in climbing then I wouldn't have gone. I came very close to leaving on several occasions but you say no. It's kind of intimidating thinking I'll go to Sheffield and go climbing. You might go to Sheffield and find that nobody wants to climb with you and so in consequence blow out on both accounts.
You got three grade A's at 'A 'levels and then only a '2.1' at university..
You bastard!! – only a '2.1' the cheek!
Didn't you consider that a failure?
No! not at all why? It's a different standard isn't it. It's like flashing a 7a and then thinking you've done badly falling off an 8a.
Were you studying as hard as you were at school?
I studied harder at university. At school I didn't

really study, because at 'A 'level standard if you're good at science you could do Maths, Physics and Chemistry without any real effort, and provided you have an aptitude there is no studying required really, and little knowledge requirement. At university level, physics seemed to me that it actually took a lot of thought and actual study time. I worked hard for my final year.
So it came as no surprise to you to get a '2.1.'
I thought I was capable of it, I was told at the beginning of my final year that I was going to fail so I thought I'd better do some work now, I knew I was capable of doing reasonably well and really happy to get a '2.1.'
Did climbing and studying clash?
Yes, mainly until the final year. I was too interested in climbing, even when I started university, I started in geology and kept thinking should I give it up and just go climbing. I did and took up physics then thought, should I give up physics and just go climbing, it kept niggling at me and after a couple of years I thought well, now I've made this commitment I might as well finish it off and actually get something out of it.

Sean on the second ascent of George Smith's SWIFT
UNDERCUT 8a. The route takes the hard way up the
underside of Joe Brown's 60's classic testpiece, the
ochre slab on VECTOR E2 5c. A short route but
completely upside down and very airy.

Sean working BUNGLES ARETE 8b prior to his first
ascent. The climb takes the rib at the top ot the
Rainbow slab commanding the quarry. Incredibly tiny
and awkward holds enable the overhanging arête to
be succumb.

With other sports, did they also conflict?

I have tried a lot of sports and felt fairly natural at most of them. Most of them seem to have drawbacks and you get bored with them. Climbing seems to be the most addictive one and it's the most individual sport I've tried. You can't keep on trying things but have to stick with something. It's nice and easy to judge how well your climbing, whereas something like table tennis or squash it's 50 per cent on how the other person is playing.

Have you stayed in climbing because you're successful at it?

No. I don't think I'd have taken a career whatever had happened, it just doesn't interest me in the slightest, as far as I can see the only reason for taking up or doing any job is to get money, and it's very rare to find satisfaction in a job other than just getting money out of it.

Do you get any money from climbing?

No, not really, it's not part of it. There's no way you should climb to get money, it's pointless.

Can you see yourself staying climbing over the next 10 years?

Yes, but not in the same way, not tied down in Britain doing the same old thing, I can see myself travelling in climbing for quite a while. If I had a serious injury such as tendonitis I'd go back to college to do some kind of research. I'd certainly not earn money to buy a house or anything like that.

You wouldn't get married?

Where's a bucket! It hasn't even crossed my mind.

Do you like climbing on your own?

Sometimes, it's really mood dependant, you can go bouldering on your own but its really hard to get the enthusiasm because you need someone to motivate you, that's unless you happen to be in a really good mood. It's nice to go soloing with someone else and do a load of routes you've done before.

Who do you boulder with mainly?

I guess Zippy and Ben Moon, Jerry Moffatt when he's around, Johnny Dawes when he's not too fat.

Is Johnny Dawes in the same league as Ben and Jerry?

Yes, and on his own thing he's even better, way better. He could do a route that they couldn't do, which does bear out the point that you should find out what your good at. You shouldn't try to compete with people on their ground, unfortunately I can't seem to find any particular ground that I'm better than everyone else.

Which climber impresses you the most?

I think Jerry really just because of his tenacity and the fact that he's nearly always motivated, and he always puts 100 per cent in. Ben is so naturally strong but he's quite different to Jerry. Johnny because he climbs on pure talent, and totally individually.

Do you see any similarity between the English and the French climbing scenes?

Not even vaguely. They're in general posy, it's perhaps becoming more posy in England but it's different somehow, you'd never get a group of Frenchmen at Stoney Mid. in the mud, freezing cold, polished rock; that's England, it's got no pose value.

When you were in France you climbed the Rose 8b, failed on the the RAGE 8b+ are you tempted to go back and try and do it?

No, but mainly because that if it were in the Peak I would try, but I couldn't stand being in France anymore. I'm fed up with it.

Have you any plans for climbing in Britain?

Yes, I'm going to move to Llanberis, but after being here for the past two days in the rain I think I've changed my mind again. I'd like to move away from Sheffield and do something different like slate which is dead interesting.

On your visit to America what was your impression?

The depth of good standard climbing is very shallow, there are the exceptions of people like Scott Franklyn, Jim Karn and Ron Kauk who are strong climbers but the whole scene is very different. The most noticeable part is the lack of history in their climbing. A lot of the people I climbed with didn't appreciate climbing and its history of evolution. The other difference is the lack of bouldering, which is also the same with France, yes they have Fontainebleau but that's it, whereas in Britain there's steep bouldering in every area so you can always get out, even it its raining. Bouldering is just perfect when you just want to go climbing without ropes or hassle.

Does bouldering effect the local climbers temperament at all?

Yes, it must make a difference but I've not ever thought of why or been bothered to think why. When you go bouldering with a few people it's much more intimate than on a rope where your always separated by 30 or 50 feet, one person is doing something and the others are bored stiff, whereas bouldering is far more active between climbers, you have to spot, work out moves together.

Has bouldering improved your climbing a lot?

Yes you just get stronger. You also use your imagination a lot more as well, when you go bouldering you realise that its much more fun and so you end up doing not so much route climbing because your not so satisfied with it somehow.

A bouldering area like Fontainebleau, is it mainly strength or technique?

It's mainly conditions to be honest because you don't do problems on sight, they're technically awkward, and so after that it's just down to the friction on the day.

Do you feel that someone like Ben has more strength than you?

Oh yes, definitely.

Do you feel that you could be as strong as him?

Well if he didn't climb for the next five years maybe. He's just naturally stronger, if someone's genetically stronger than you then that's it. Also we have a completely different background. I didn't start climbing full time until I had left university and by that time he'd been at it full time for 6 years. It's a huge difference and you just can't make it up. Also I've had injuries which are related to late starting in climbing, your arm and stomach muscles are built up and strong but your individual climbing muscles aren't. The tendons and ligaments haven't developed equally and consequently you put too much stress on them in the early stages. If you start climbing early on in your teens your finger and shoulder muscles grow at a good proportionate rate.

Do you feel experience is invaluable?

Yes totally. You get stronger year by year, but in other ways you go up and down. You get more solid at things, before you might do a move easily but occasionally fall off. Now you do them every time even if you have an off day.

Do you ever find a climb new to you boring because you've done all similar moves bouldering?

No, if the moves are interesting even less so, the moves just aren't the same, there's always something different about them, except that a route say in Cheedale might feel just like blocks on a wall, or the strings of pockets in France, but you never get bored because it's similar to the one before. It's like eating some particular food that you've eaten it before; you like it and know it, but it is different, and then it's down to the variety, which is why Britain is so good a place to climb, it's interesting.

What makes you climb in Britain at the moment?

Not the weather that's for sure. I think it's the routes basically, they are far more interesting than those on the continent. That's it really, I've climbed all over the world and at the moment the only place to go is the South of France, and the only thing that makes it worth going is the weather. The routes are good but there all the same in general, lines of pockets, some chipped and some not.

Would you ever move to France?

No definitely not, the French are really boring, there's no social scene there at all, my French isn't that good but I would say that's partly down to the fact that the people aren't very friendly.

Does danger appeal to you?

No not really. You get a thrill out of doing bold routes, and you do things that are sort of dangerous occasionally but not very often. You just have to be in the mood for it. Sometimes you're in a mood for doing things which are dangerous but then when you do them your so worked up, you're fit, co-ordinated and you climb in control which in turn makes it not dangerous. Theoretically it is, but danger provocation such as going into a ludicrous climbing situation without preparation does not appeal to me.

Chris Plant glues back a tiny flake off THE MEDIUM 8a+. Sean Myles did the second ascent a few minuites later, without the glued hold, at a grade a lot harder than Johnny Dawes on the first ascent. The crux involves stepping up on the left foot, and using wafer thin flakes to the best effect, slab desperado!

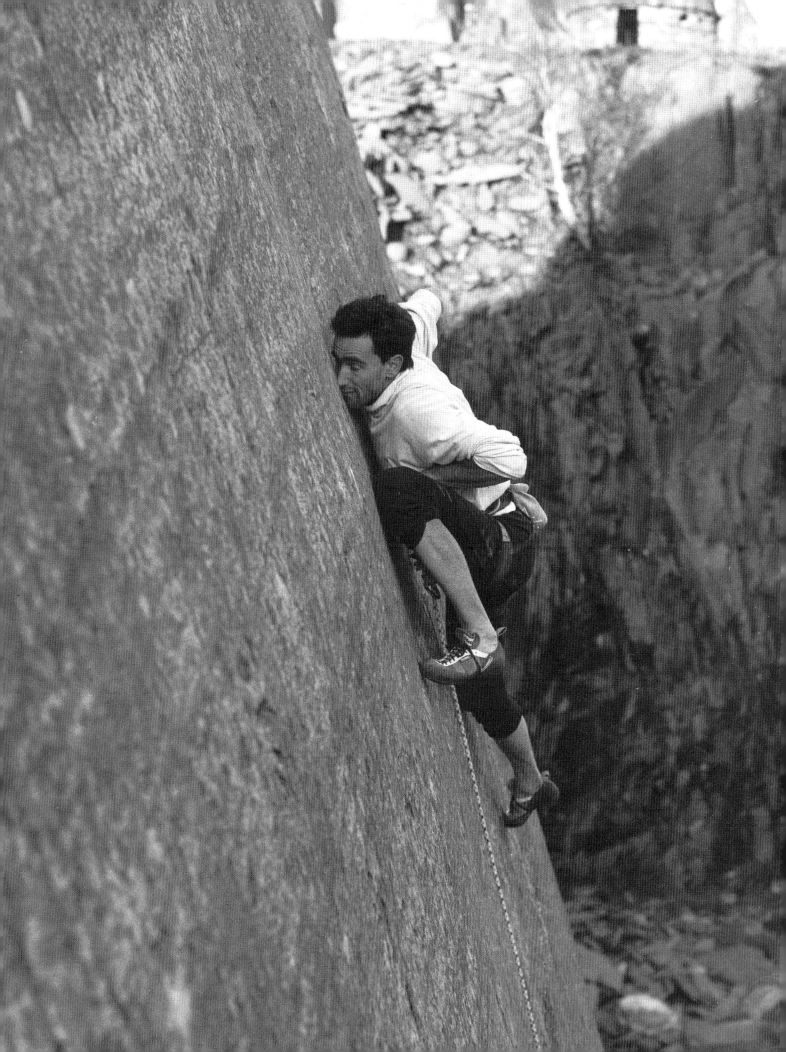

Mark Leach

Mark is the real powerhouse of British climbing today, and has the muscles to prove it. Anyone who can do 7 one arm pull ups on either arm must be quite strong. His place at the top of British climbers has been established since he repeated routes like MASTERS EDGE, and REVELATIONS back in 1985. From then he was a major developer in Yorkshire climbing with many new routes at Malham Cove and Kilnsey. His early climbing in the Lancashire quarries put him in good stead for future projects. In 1988 he took the major prize at Malham Cove by free climbing the old aid route of Controversy to give CRY FREEDOM 8b+. Later on that year he free climbed the great central roof at Kilnsey free top give MANDELA 8b. His other good additions to British climbing are too numerous to name but his latest project at Malham nicknamed TROUBLE is one of the great unclimbed lines left in England.

Interview 24.1.91 Nether Edge, Sheffield.

How much do you train for climbing?
It depends on the time of year, but it's got to be at least three times a week, even when I'm not doing that much, and then at the most it could be five times. Each day when I train hard is like a three tiered day; I start by going bouldering or climbing, then I come back and work out on the finger boards or the weights, and then go for a long run – that's a complete full day.

Is the training linked to doing actual routes?
Yes, because I have a goal, something to aim for, and then once I've done that climb, that's one stage complete. I then look to the next stage, the next grade, look for something even more outrageous.

Has training ever become more important to you than climbing?
It's good fun! Sometimes I get right into the

finger boards, I find that just as good fun as the crag, because it's less hassle and it's like bouldering indoors.

Could you do a one arm pull up when you were a child?
No I did the first one in Germany in '84 just by chance. I climbed solidly for three months in Europe, then the first one I really tried I did. Maybe I could have done one before that but I was never that strong when I was a child.

Is strength that useful to climb hard routes?
It depends on the route, it's not going to matter so much on a slab other than maybe finger holds, but all the hard limestone routes, are the hardest routes in the world at the moment. A lot of it's power; if you haven't got the power, then you're not going to be able to

Mark on 'cruise control,' at Malham Cove – the classic RAIN DOGS 8a.

do the moves no matter how much stamina you've got. Things like HUBBLE at the moment are pure power, but in five years time you might have routes which are four times as long as that, which are going to require power stamina.

How do you quantify power, what is it?
For climbing in it's purest form, I guess it's just getting a hold and cranking on it, that's pure force, pure strength. If you can't pull on a hold then you can't do the move.

You did a lot of climbing in '85 in Lancashire with Paul Pritchard, were you surprised that Paul went into more mind games with climbing?
No, because of the routes we were doing at the time. We used to have competitions on doing new routes, like we'd have five goes each and I was always stronger than Paul, but he had a massive reach and really thin fingers, so he used to get away with a lot of things on thin cracks and really thin holds. He was much better on bold routes, even though we both did bold things in Lancashire, he just liked it better than me.

Has bold climbing ever appealed to you?
Yes, I did quite a few bold things on grit in '85, MASTERS EDGE E7, BEAU GESTE E7 at Froggatt, and I did a lot of soloing on grit. I didn't want to injure myself so I'd do one every now and again because it is exciting. I do believe though that if you do it too often, then it's going to catch up with you, you're going to injure yourself or kill yourself!

Do any other routes of that time stand out in your mind?
In '85, ZOOLOOK 8a, REVELATIONS 8a+, MASTERS EDGE 7C+, those are the three, I did so many early repeats, but those are the three that really stand out.

Were you at college then?
Yes, I did two HND's in Mechanical engineering, at Bolton. I finished those in about '87 and then I had the winter and although I was working at the time I could train and boulder and just got stronger and fitter.

Why two HND's?
The course I did meant that I came out with two, it was just horrendous the hours you had to do to pass them.

Did that not make you want to take up a career in Engineering?
I always wanted something to back me up for when I didn't want to climb again. I'd been studying engineering for three years before that, trying to get an apprenticeship because it's more interesting making things. I couldn't get one so I thought I'd carry on with the academic side, I still tried to get a job when I'd finished but I was getting more and more interested in climbing.

Around that time you started to climb with John Dunne, was there any competition between you?
I'll say there was, we were good friends but we both had projects at Malham, we knew what we wanted to do, the trouble was that we both had the same ideas. It was the case of, you do that, I'll do this. We always used to do second ascents of each others routes every time. I'd do one and John would repeat it a few days later, John would do one and then I'd repeat it. It was friendly competition but it was good, it meant that we both got fitter and stronger and we were both thinking along the same lines of what we wanted to do.

Was that important for your improvement?
Yes, for both our improvements. You do need competition, without it you're not going to try your hardest and you're not going to put 100% into it. Certainly you do need it over a long period of time. That was one of the reasons I moved to Sheffield because there is competition and it's a way to improve.

Mark doing the modern hard equivalent of aid climbing to gear up MECCA, one arm pull ups on every bolt, placing quickdraws on lead, 14 in total.

The 6c start to MECCA 8b+, involving an above average physique!

Mark's latest project and a real candidate for 9a, TROUBLE between CRY FREEDOM and BAT ROUTE at Malham Cove. RAIN DOGS below is cruised up and then it starts to turn very nasty, steep 7b moves across ever overhanging roofs.

You got better and eventually climbed CRY FREEDOM 8b+, how long did it take you?
I spent 46 days trying the route which must be a record on any climb. I was getting up to the crux, which is 100ft up near the top after 2 or 3 days. Then I was trying this 7a/b boulder problem which took me 5 days to do. Then I couldn't link the boulder problem from the ground and because I was using the route to get fit on, the time taken was really in getting the stamina fitness. It is better to gain the fitness on other routes, cellars, bouldering etc., rather than on the route.

Did you think that you might never be able to do it?
I alway knew that I could do it because I had the psyche, and I wanted to do something really, really hard, and I wanted to do the next grade up. I never felt it wasn't worth trying because I wasn't going to do it.

Did it ever worry you that John Dunne might come in and do it?
Yes we were both like that on each others routes; very paranoid about each others movements. I don't think we'd steal routes off each other, but he's known to pinch routes off other people which I don't think is on really, if someone is trying the route. I don't mind people trying my projects, but sometimes you may have brittle holds on it and they pull them off. Most people are normally pretty good about it. The classic instance is in '86/87 when I did THE CRACK at Froggatt. I was dossing at Basher's house in Sheffield, and I was Trying THE CRACK every other day, and on the days I was resting, Basher was trying it. But he didn't let me know and I only found out the year after, he kept it completely quiet. I think you

can be a little bit annoyed at the time because obviously he wanted to do the first ascent or maybe he was just interested in the way I was thinking at the time and what I wanted from climbing. Maybe he was interested in the grade and the way things were progressing. I think as long as people only use projects as interest, but I think it's a bit bad to steal. If the person says right 'I don't want to do that route anymore and I'm not interested in climbing it', then it's as an open project.

What would you do if someone chipped a route like CRY FREEDOM?
I'd find out who it was and ask them why they did it, and kick their head in. Honestly nobody likes any route being chipped I'd just go and fill them in and try and make a good job of it.

I'd sprinkle limestone dust over the seam so hopefully you couldn't tell that it had been chipped, I'd try and put it back to it's natural form.

Are you glad that European climbers have come and repeated your routes?

Yes, it's good because a lot of the people in Britain are climbing the same grade and it's good to see other peoples attitudes towards your own creations. All the British have been going to Europe for a long time repeating their creations, so it's good to have some of them come over and see what they think.

Did you meet Jean Baptiste when he came over?

Yes, he's a good friend, I stay with him when I go to France. It's good just to talk to him about these routes, he thinks they are good routes, creative crags. He was really pleased that he did CRY FREEDOM, it was one of the things that he wanted to do.

Did it surprise you how quickly he did it, in 5 days?

No, not really it always takes much longer to do a first ascent even though you're convinced that the route will go. You are always trying new sequences and then once a few people get on the route, you're getting more ideas to doing the moves on the route. With CRY FREEDOM I just saw one set of moves on the crux, and then Jebe came along, looked around, had different ideas and thought of another sequence. The more people you get on a route makes it easier, you do find an easier sequence. It happens on all the top routes, Jean Baptiste saw his routes downgraded because other people had found easier sequences, it always happens.

Will CRY FREEDOM ever get soloed?

I doubt it because you could spend a lot of time wiring it, and even if you get a dead positive sequence, that one mistake and then your dead. It's like you're going to die from that height, 150ft straight down the cove.

Could soloing it be classified as a step forward for climbing?

Yes it would, because it would be fantastic commitment, you would have a sustained route leading up to a definite crux. There is no way people could chuck you a rope off because the thing is so overhanging, it's committing and frightening even to think about.

Has soloing any of the Malham routes ever appealed to you?

Yes, I used to solo quite a lot of things but thought, yes it is good fun but I'd rather do things that I could take a long fall off. I don't mind taking long falls, it's the same kind of adrenalin rush, the same commitment but you don't really die but you may get injured. Whereas if you're soloing you still have the same feelings, but you're going to die if you don't make it. I'd rather do something which is bold but safe.

Is doing a new route more important than repeating someone else's hard route?

I alway find repeating routes easier because you know the route has been climbed. You know that someone has done a route, and you know that you have the same ability, so you try their route. You want to do other people's routes because then you see the way they are thinking and what they are trying to get out of the climbing. It is important to repeat the climb as soon as possible. It's nice doing new routes because they are your own, but it's equally as good in repeating others.

Is doing a route like INDIAN FACE important to you?

It used to be because I've always wanted to do it, and then a few years ago I changed my mind, just because it really means death, and I don't want to die. For Johnny, it's great to do the first ascent, the same with a lot of the bold routes that Paul Pritchard and Johnny did. You go for the first ascent and commit yourself totally, the creation of a brilliant route. I think the major part in putting your life on the line is in creating that route, proving to everyone that it can be done, that's the point of a new route. But what are you going to get as a second ascent; it's not the same is it, you're not creating. Your putting everything into it, you have to still put in the same commitment, all you have to do is slip once and you are dead! On HUBBLE one slip and you start again from the bottom, even though you have to commit yourself to bold routes and the bolt routes as well, you can have another go on the bolt routes, with bold routes you may never have another go, you always have to get something out of climbing.

What do you see yourself doing after you can't climb 8c any longer?

I've always said that when I can't improve any longer then I would stop and do something else, so I'm just hanging on in the sport. I think I will still always have attachments to climbing, I'd just boulder. You can go out for a few hours and get really good enjoyment, rather than training really hard and trying to do horrendous routes. I can see myself climbing a a lot harder grade wise, perhaps in my thirties, but then I'll stop doing routes and just go into bouldering because then it gives me more time for a 'proper job.' I think I'd still train to a certain extent just to keep fit, but I'd branch out and look at other things to do but I think I'd always go bouldering.

*Ravens Tor, a few hundred yards from Millers Dale, a bastion of rock
with a striking appearance to both climbers and walkers.*

The Masters

The Masters needs little explanation, can there be more than one even – only in the case of climbing where there are separate disciplines: there is the natural climber who is both a boulderer perfectionist and willing to display that skill in the face of certain death, E10 if you like. There is the on-sight specialist and competition climber with machine like fluidity; and there is the technician, power over steep rock on small holds, the ultimate in difficulty. All are Masters, the best in the world at a time in history. The three in this chapter receive the highest accolade and join the ranks of the other modern Masters: John Gill USA, Pete Livesey GB, John Bachar USA, Ron Fawcett GB, Ron Kauk USA, Patrick Edlinger F, Tony Yaniro USA, Jim Collins USA, Jerry Moffatt GB, Antoine Le Menestrel F, Marc le Menestrel F, Johnny Dawes GB, Stephan Glowacz GER, Wolfgang Güllich GER, Simon Nadin GB, Ben Moon GB, and François Legrand F. Standards go up and more is demanded from the current Masters, yet history allows one to always marvel at achievements gained in the past. The respect is fantastic and is never lost.

Johnny Dawes

Most climbers top climbers fit into the 5ft 11ins, 9½ stone bracket. Johnny is the exception at 5ft 5ins and size 3½ climbing shoes. His climbing style has developed to cope with the lack of reach by the perfection of the dyno to leap through the air where others simply climb. He first really came to prominence in 1984 with an on-sight solo of ULYSEES 7b+ at Stanage, a very brave undertaking. Over the following years he climbed various 8a routes on slate such as WINDOWS OF PERCEPTION, and THE QUARRYMAN 8a+. He put the history books straight with the first true ascent of the major direct line on Cloggy's Great Wall with INDIAN FACE E9. A climb with no significant protection and a French top rope grade of 7c. Over the years '88 and '89 he proved to the climbing world that he was an all rounder by climbing a lot of Buoux routes in quick style such as CHOUCAS 8a+, TABOU ZI ZI 8b, and MAUVAIS SANG 8b. Then in 1990 he climbed the first 8c on Welsh slate THE VERY BIG AND THE VERY SMALL. More of a sustained technical problem than a complete power stamina route it's remained unrepeated for over a year with attempts from all the top boys.

Interview 3.4.91 Llanberis, Wales

When were your best, most exciting times in climbing?

The early times back in 1983 when I was doing things like THE CAD E5, LORD E6, and TEENAGE MENOPAUSE E7 and things like that. It was really fun we used to come up here to Llanberis and get pissed every night, you'd climb very hard and still get pissed then, the high cost to pay for modern climbing! TEENAGE MENOPAUSE on Idwal Walls was probably the first route that scared me. Nick Dixon couldn't afford the RP for it which is the only runner on it and if you don't have that you hit the ground. Nick Dixon's life at that stage was worth £3.00, he had a really old hex that didn't fit in the placement. I went on the route and managed to get up it but it shocked me that Nick could be so strange as to not buy a runner, so that scared me for his sake. I got committed on that route like I had never been before.

You remember those times with affection?

Yes. You just think back to all the silly things that you do. There was one time, you'd be with a girl down by the lake or something and your mate would be dossed and next to you in the

morning he'd tell you everything that you'd said to her, you didn't know he was there and stuff like that. We used to have time trials down the Pass, all that sort of stuff. There was one time when Bob Drury and I jumped on the back of Dick Griffith's van, we just thought he was going to collect his rope from his house. In fact he was going to Pen Trwyn with Paul and I ended up on the Bangor by-pass hanging on the side of this van, traversing across to get into the window all at 90mph – brilliant!

You're now 27 and have gone back to university to study, can you see yourself becoming a pure academic?

No. It's too introspective, you can think with your senses and you can live by your skills, but I think the best things happen when you use both. The intellectual side of me was neglected with climbing and I'm now just balancing things up really.

Do you have any thought about where this degree will take you?

I'd like to make films really. I think the more people you meet, in order to change the situation in the Third world I think you've got to change peoples attitudes here, I don't think that you can divorce the fact that we have cheap coffee with the fact that these countries are poor, that's just a simple example; we use all the energy, all the fossil fuel so I'd like to make a film bringing out things like that because I think you can do more good by changing things here than you could by actually going over there and changing things on a small scale. I think you have to do it from both ends obviously. I think people need to see the damage that they have done, awareness of people in the west isn't very high really.

Is something like that study becoming the same as climbing?
No, it's much much quieter but a lot calmer feeling, it simmers away.

Have you become calmer do you think in the past five years?
Much calmer, but that has a cost because you don't get as excited. It's bound to be like that because there are so many things that have been exciting so far. If you do a lot of exciting things you're bound to find it hard to find other ones.

Are you prepared to accept that?
I've got no choice really.

What is the single most important part of your life?
Now it's meeting different people. It's more important to me than climbing, but I think that if I'm unhappy and I don't get rid of my aggressive energies on something, then they will always blister up somewhere else. I've been down at college for two terms now and I've found myself getting really down for 2 to 3 days; I'm not racing karts, or I haven't got a girlfriend, something like that. Without those things I can get unhappy, then I meet some people and get the biggest buzz.

Has being so heavily involved in climbing inhibited those other interests to a detrimental effect?
I think for a long time the people side of it wasn't that important to me, friends were important, but that was because we used to go climbing together. In the pub you'd talk about climbing a lot and that would be great.

What side of people interest you?
The person you meet, and different people mean different things. Some people are funny, some people are interesting and some people are a challenge. Recently people have been really quiet and over the period of a whole term I've got to know them. Often they've got a really dry wit that you didn't even notice at first, before they would have said something but you missed it. It seemed to me that learning to listen and relax with people is one of the biggest challenges; nicest and most rewarding challenges you can have.

Why do you think that climbing has become less important?
I just feel that rock is not as interesting as people.

It's taken you 27 years to find this out?
Yes, I always knew it, I just didn't think I liked people before.

What then made climbing on slate interesting?
When we climbed on slate we were really just trying to work with it, to work out what new methods you could use to climb something. I wasn't so much trying to climb harder routes just for that, but was trying to find new ways to climb; really that's the main thread that's gone through my climbing career and the interesting part.

Can doing a climb for a second time then ever interest you?
If I've not climbed it well the first time maybe yes, but not really. When you talking about hard climbs of the type we were climbing then things like WINDOWS OF PERCEPTION 8a, QUARRYMAN 8a+, or the more technical masterpieces, those which had to be done perfectly. You couldn't shake your way up them, which is what appealed to me compared to the limestone routes, you could do them without climbing well if you wanted.

What were your most memorable slate routes?
Probably the QUARRY MAN, to have spent so much time. The nicest time I've had on slate really is walking up to the quarries and bolting it, looking at new lines, every time I looked at the crag it surprised me because it kept giving unusual moves. Virtually every crux on the routes up there is a unique move that I've never found anywhere else, it's really good movement.

Has that derivation of control always been important?
I started climbing up trees and buildings a lot and I learnt a lot about edges and posture in that form of climbing. Then when I started to climb on rock the holds were too far away for me, then I started jumping to develope those sort of skills. I always used to do gymnastics and I would play at all sorts of tricks, I'd try to run up walls and do mantleshelves, more than climbing, it's sort of imaging movement in my head that I like.

Does dance interest you in that respect?
Yes things like, there's a Japanese gymnastic troop that works with different forms, they have different poles that they jump from one to another horizontally and spin in the air, so the dynamics of the movement is the part also in climbing which I like.

Do you need the will to improve on technique, or is is simply satisfying in doing it?
Yes because the routes become more interesting in that way. To launch into an analogy, you can go round a corner in a car in lots of different ways, you can go round without

squealing the tyres at all, then you can understeer and squeal the front tyres or put the power on too early and oversteer so the back comes round; so that would be like your first and second generation cornering. A classic four wheel drift which was in the sixties, but then as the power of the cars got higher, you could actually change the attitude of the car by using the power of the brakes to lock the front wheels momentarily, to lift the rear so that the braking would do the turning for you, so that you brake with a slight amount of turn on, then the car would change angle by the steering, the brakes and the throttle. Then you get fourth generation where you actually set the car up into the slide, but you control the slide at the same time as you are putting it into it, by applying opposite lock and incepting the car; by that method you can get faster out of the cornering and get more pull.

In that you are predicting the future and you also rely upon the past in a more definite way, the whole thing is more natural some how. In the way that if you look at waves coming in to a seashore, the big waves may be coming in but there might be a small wave rippling back, in order to image those sort of things you obviously can't think from A to Z to do them, you have to just allow your intuition to do that for you, that is 'fourth generation' and I think climbing moved into that sort of spectrum around 1985. There are probably boulder problems around that were fourth generation, but not dynamic fourth generation, they were form-fitting to a trick type of skill, now you've got imaging skills where you might have to look at all the holds, or you might have to make something into a hold by pressing into it, using your momentum, and that momentum continues into the next move, you get these backwards and forwards, past and future plays. Do you understand what I mean?

Oh exactly, Yes Johnny, Whew! How do you relate that sort of working out style of climbing to on sight bold climbing?
Do you think that's working out? I don't think that's working out. You don't work it out with your head, you just play with it, it's like skate boarding, you can't think how you're going to do it very much. You can get somebody to give you an idea but it's natural.

Do you look at on sight climbing in same respect or do you climb very much in control?
I think because on sight climbing is so dangerous you have to be pretty much in control, but I think if you let go, if you have a fatalistic attitude to it, if you have accepted the fact that you could die on something, I think you are in the safest position, that's a paradox, but it's true I think, because then you're not worried about hurting yourself, you can focus

Johnny explaining the crux of BOBBY'S GROOVE 8a+ across breakfast to sleepy onlookers. Nick Harms just passing the crux and entering the final slippery groove to a slithery finish perhaps.

so in that way, both of them involve you and letting go of thinking, trying not to put too many rules around it.

Can you think of any routes that you think are particularly dangerous?

I think the first one's were on grit really, ULYSEES was probably the first route where, I climbed and let go but you'd probably just sprain your ankle if you fell off that. There have been all sorts of other routes mainly in Wales I suppose, like COMES TO MOTHER is incredibly serious, I very nearly died on that, more recently PROFESSOR WHITTAKER on the LLeyn Peninsula, they were both on sight climbs.

What made you do something like PROFESSOR WHITTAKER?

It didn't look as hard as it was, I found myself committed on it and I couldn't down-climb, and I was really unfit so I had to keep climbing, the same with COME TO MOTHER. We tried a route to the back of The Zawn and that had proved too hard so we ended up climbing this route to the left which went up the arete, and made it about 80 foot out with no gear that would hold me. There was about 8 holds on this roof, and of the eight that were there, I pulled off three, and Paul then pulled off two, those were the two that I used when I pulled over the roof, that is a really serious situation! When I got over the bulge there was a friend crack, but I had the wrong size friends, nothing would fit in, so I had to hand traverse the lip of this roof 80 foot up, just a big fin of rock and I was jamming at the back of it with my arms stiff, so that I could actually leave my forearm flat, but have my body underneath the overhang without actually leaning on the fin of rock with my forearm, if I hadn't done that it might have broken anywhere in front of my hand and I would have died.

In your understanding when you started climbing the route, did you know that it was going to be incredibly serious?

It seemed to have cracks on it, which when I got on the route seemed to be really awful. It looked like normal Red Wall rock, in fact for some reason it was really talcy and all the quartz crystals were incredibly loose.

What do you think made you carry on climbing and getting to the situation where you couldn't down-climb?

A notion that climbing serious routes was important. Also the fact that the climbing I'd already done on the route was really brilliant. I thought it was a superb form of rock with fins of quartz and really nice patterns and things up this arete. I did want to do the route, that was with Paul Pritchard, his pitch was also very dangerous.

Does the safety level really worry you when you attempt hard routes?

Yes it does but if you go on a route and you are really scared of it then you are going to be in danger I think, it's a double think, like Orwell's double think, you have to think that something is wrong but then you have to tell yourself it's right. For some reason that was quite a natural way of thinking for me anyway.

Is succeeding on a climb important?

It depends what mood you're in really, at times when you need a boost, then it's nice to think of the routes that you have done, but if you're well balanced then I don't think it does matter much. The MELT DOWN means more to me now because I haven't done it, It takes up more of my time, it inspires me more than if I've done it – it's another one of these catch 22's. The moment when you do the route, all the effort up till then hits you, and you get glimpses of the future, from the fact that you've just done this route and it brings you up a level

in standard, and you think from this place, where can I go, develop further from here. I think that it's not necessarily doing the route that's important, it's the opening of new possibilities. But in order to sort of dump that new possibility with a sword; it means you need to have the routes done.

Did you think that the VERY BIG AND THE VERY SMALL 8c, was going to be one of the hardest routes in Britain?

It was Nick Harms project and Nick pulled one of the holds off it and couldn't do one of the moves on it, I was training to do a route in the top quarry, The MELT DOWN and that seemed like a really good place to start.

Does it feel like being one of the hardest routes in the country?

It probably is because it took me longer to work that, than it took me to work HUBBLE 8c+ on Ravens Tor, although the actual crux on that is a slap for a hold and I was almost getting it. A little bit more strength and timing, I would be able to work that. But the difference between working and doing, is actually a lot bigger on HUBBLE.

Why does gritstone have it's own characteristics that appeal to you?

It's on a human scale gritstone, it's about six times your height, it's not a massive monolith, you can look from the bottom the crag and see the route that you are going to climb, and get a feel for it; it's not closed in or as secretive as other rock. It's open rock, you climb on arete's and on open slabs, it's just shaped, it's a really beautiful rock to look at and to climb.

Don't you find the moves very awkward and intricate?

Not really, I think it leads you on a lot more than other rocks, the moves come to you in a really strange way.

When you try a route and don't do it on sight do you think you should leave it alone?
I'd liked to have had the time to try INDIAN FACE E9 6c, on-sight, but I think people would have done the same thing as me basically, I was forced into top roping it a lot by really wanting to do the climb.

Is INDIAN FACE dangerous?
Yes Dave, it is!! it's frightening!!! no protection really, 6c moves 100ft up, that's fairly dangerous I think!!!

What made you do INDIAN FACE?
I watched Jerry Moffatt do MASTERS WALL E7 6b, on Cloggy and always wondered why he traversed off it. It was the obvious challenge up that piece of rock.

Do you ever feel a sense of guilt that you have stolen from the future so many good new routes?
Not really because I don't think I've bashed them into submission, OK maybe one or two but the rest were ready to be done.

Does not doing one great route then leaving the rest for future generations have an appeal?
It would be a good idea but I've certainly never thought about it, I like nicking other peoples routes off them as well anyway. It's good fun doing a route and knowing that someone else has failed on it. I think there's a false kindness about climbing now, that peo-

Johnny forever out playing, trying a new sequence on his own route THE UNTOUCHABLE 8a, Llanberis Slate. This short overhanging arête packing a lot in over the space of 30 feet.

ple leave routes for other people once there bolted, half the fun of climbing is that it's cut throat. It has changed essentially though from the past because people are now into producing products, it's gone from being natural to someone abseiling down it, preparing it, serving it by doing the first ascent, and then the punters come along to consume it.

Simon Nadin

Simon's reputation in the climbing world goes back to the early 80's when rumours spread across the Peak to Sheffield about the fantastic Buxton stickmen, insect like creatures. These 16 years old kids, who could out perform any of the climbers on the Buxton Wall, yet were never seen on the crags. Then came an onslaught of E5 and E6 new routes, on the Staffordshire gritstone a couple of years later and the climbing world woke up to the best of the stickmen, Simon Nadin. Living 10 mins. from Cheedale gave him the perfect opportunity to develop in climbing and in 1985 pioneered many bold Grit routes, PARALOGISM E7, on the Roaches being one of many. On limestone he put up GONADS 8a+ in Cheedale and repeated routes like CHOUCAS 8a+ in France. Simon followed the footsteps of Jerry Moffatt in flashing 7c+ routes abroad, demonstrating his tremendous ability and immense cool headedness. His physique developed very well indeed and even after a motorbike injury, and awkward recovery he came 3rd at the international competition in Leeds in 1989. A year later he really showed the world by winning the first ever climbing World Cup. It was a very great achievement considering the intense level of competition by brilliant climbers from France, Germany and the USA. He is one of the best mannered climbers in the world, which in turn is reflected in his quiet yet friendly attitude about the crags. His appetite for routes is similar to a beginner who has just started climbing, yet his success puts him at the complete opposite end of the scale.

Interview, 14.1.91 Buxton, Derbyshire.

When did you first go to France?
In 1985, the first place I went to was the Verdon. A group of friends who were cavers dropped us off at the Verdon. I was climbing with Mark Pretty and a few of the lads from Sheffield. I think at the time I flashed a 7c+ and that was definitely '85. I'd always been into putting as much effort as possible on a route and getting up something first try, it's something I've always enjoyed.

Where did you learn that?
You don't learn it anywhere really, it's probably a lot to do with a traditional upbringing on traditional routes where you don't fall off hopefully. There are so many dangerous routes with poor gear, you just hang on for grim death! Hang on as much as you can.

Did you have any nasty moments early on?
I've always managed to come through without hurting myself. I've had a few scary moments but I've never actually hurt myself climbing, only over use injuries like skin and tendon problems. My injuries have always been from stupid things like motorbikes and rodeo rides.

Does it make sense for you to climb the bolt routes in the same purist style as the nut protected routes?
Yes, but obviously it depends on the routes. Some routes you can't expect to flash but in a way that's one reason why I've never done any of the very hard routes. I've always preferred to do things quickly, I don't like to spend a lot of time on something. I'm fairly confident that I could get up a lot of the hard routes if I spent the time on them, it's just a case of building up that specific power, for those specific moves; which doesn't really mean you're improving your climbing, you're only improving strength for those few moves. My idea of climbing is that you need to be all round, you need to be able to do everything, all the different types of climbing that are involved, and do them quickly. It's a lot slower process; building up your skill, power and stamina; all at the same time. You don't end up doing the hardest

routes, but you do quite hard routes quickly. The hardest limestone routes are very narrow minded as far as I'm concerned, I prefer a lot more variety which is also why I've never really stuck at them. I also feel sorry for the poor second, stood there for hours on end belaying. I do enjoy some of the harder routes, they're absolutely brilliant, but it's not what I get out of climbing.

Is flashing routes always exciting?
It varies, sometimes it's great to have a really hard struggle on a route and just manage to scrape through, slapping for the holds, just catching them, your power's going and your stamina but you just manage to hang on and get to the top; it's a great sense of achievement. Bolt routes don't always give me a big buzz after having completed them, often I think, fine I've done that one, now I'll go and do the next, mainly because I enjoy the physical side of these routes, the satisfaction of the total pump. I get more lasting memories from routes that have got a bit of excitement in them. That's why I've always liked grit routes or nut protected limestone, EYE OF THE TIGER E7 6c in Dovedale must be one of the most satisfying climbs I've done on limestone.

Where have your favourite places been on grit?
I like a lot of the quieter places, Skyline at The Roaches is one of my favourite areas. Unfortunately there's not a lot there to do but I've always liked Staffordshire gritstone.

Is that soloing or a leading sense?
From the age of 15-16 I've always had the habit of soloing for some strange reason, I hardly ever used ropes. I was soloing so much that I was really confident, I just knew what I could do, soloing E4 6a on-sight all the time. I couldn't do the same thing anymore because I've lost the confidence. I'm stronger, I can probably do harder routes but I'm not climbing as well. That's mainly because it's harder to get the new experiences all the time since I've climbed for so long, and done all the routes before.

Are the odds against you in soloing?
Yes. It got to a point where I thought that if I continued soloing I would sooner or later hurt myself, that's why I don't do much now. I still solo but not to anywhere near the same standard as I used to. It's something I keep thinking I'd like to get back into, but only thinking! I'm too old to continue frightening myself.

Did you get that same feeling when you were 17-18?
Then I didn't seem to be worried, I'd see a new line that I wanted to do, it might have no protection, but that didn't matter, it might even

be at the limit of my abilities. Obviously I'd top rope them first, 4 or 5 times and I still might fall off a couple of times out of those tries; but you end up going for it one day and well, I don't know whether it was the looking for glory or fame in the magazines or not, I'm not sure. It's pretty stupid looking back on it, but a worth while experience.

Do you feel that French climbers miss out on that gritstone experience?
Yes. I think in France they miss out on a lot of what are the most important things in climbing for me really. They haven't got the same variety. They have got the adventurous routes but most people tend to stick to the safe ones, it's a different upbringing, no real sense of tradition.

Have you come across any European climbers who are similar to yourself?
No, the climbers I've met are totally into steep, overhanging limestone, which I'm not into really. The only person I can think of really is Wolfgang Güllich, he seems as though he's a lot more into the adventurous side as well as the powerful side. He's one of the few people I can think of who's climbed really hard and also done dangerous routes, he's in Patagonia at the moment which sums it up.

Does Alpine climbing appeal to you?
Yes it's something that's tempting me a lot more now. I'm keen to go to the mountains to try and find an aid route on a big wall that's possible to free climb, and spending quite a while trying to do that. That would be a really good achievement. I really admire Todd Skinner and Paul Pianna for doing SALATHE WALL free, I think that's great. It must be a lot of hard work, but something to look back on and be proud of.

Do you climb purely for yourself?
I've always tried to, which is one of my problems at the moment. Now I'm climbing professionally and making a living out of it I'm starting to question my reasons for climbing. I'm being paid to climb, I have to climb and consequently I'm loosing interest. I feel that I have to stop to try and regain the enthusiasm, and the want to climb again; to realise for myself that I do still need it. But maybe that's because I've climbed so much over the last few years anyway.

What made you climb in your first competition?
It was a case that there was a competition in Leeds, I thought I may as well have a go.

You didn't have any strong feelings against competitions, having enjoyed perhaps the more purist attitude to climbing?
No, I didn't have any feeling against them, people can go into competitions if they want to, it's up to them what they do. I just went along to see what they were about, just for the experience.

Were you surprised how well you did?
Yes, I was gob-smacked, I couldn't believe it. I think it's a case of pressure really, which at the time I could handle because I had the will to climb and win, It's all a mind game really.

So all the climbers were just about as strong as each other?
Well I can think of a lot of climbers who were and still are, a lot physically stronger than me; but I was really enjoying my climbing and perhaps more than them, for me that is strength.

For you the competitions came at the right time?
Yes. Before '89 I hadn't been climbing because I'd crashed my motor bike and damaged my shoulders in August '87. I was still ticking over

Simon going for the redpoint on Sean Myles route,
FOUR DOOR DOSTOYEVSKY 8A+
Cornice, Cheedale.

doing a little bit now and then, but nothing serious. I started working for high rise services, an access abseil company. I was enjoying working and earning reasonable money, it was a good job because I could work for a while, earn good money, and then have a few weeks off and go away wherever I wanted. I wasn't sure if I wanted to compete for a living at first and kept on working after the Leeds competition as I wasn't really sure whether it would spoil my enjoyment of climbing. After the second competition I decided to make a serious go at it.

You won the second competition?

Yes, but it wasn't a real victory. Jerry and I were the only ones to finish the final route, so we then had a climb off and both of us got up it. Then it was decided on time, I won but obviously I didn't, the same again happened in Italy.

How do you view Jerry Moffatt as a climber?

I'm very impressed with Jerry because he has done a lot of different types of climbing and he still seems quite a traditionalist really. I think he likes other things in climbing other than just power climbing, he's done so much. I admire his incredible enthusiasm for climbing.

Do competition routes ever look appealing?

Yes, I've done some that I've really enjoyed, yet others have been absolutely awful. I've always enjoyed the ones in places like La Riba, Spain due to the type of wall used. Other walls can be very limited with the holds that they have. The wall that was used for Madonna in Italy this year was flat panels with bolt on holds; you had a hold for you left hand, hold for your right hand and so on. You just look at it, there's nothing there that makes you want to climb it, it's just a test of you physical strength and nothing else. That doesn't interest me, there's so much more to climbing than strength, that's what makes it so interesting.

Are there any vibes that you know someones going to do well at a competition?

No, normally I won't notice or should I say, think about what anyone else is doing in the warm up area. At certain competitions you know you're going to win, and are very confident and happy about being there. That's the most important thing with competitions. If I feel that I'm only travelling to competitions, just for the competition, then I tend to lose interest, I have to try and make it feel like it's a holiday or that I'm going somewhere new and exciting. Going to America this year was great because I've only been there once before and I'm climbing in a totally new area, it's a country I really don't know a lot about and it's great. You forget why you're there so you relax more and just enjoy yourself.

What is it drives you in the day?

I think it's my idea of what climbing is. Just to on-sight basically, putting as much effort as I can into getting to the top of a route without falling off. That's what I've always enjoyed. I think living in England I've gained a wide variety of experiences, different rock types, different situations, I think that really helps. In France there are a lot of very strong climbers, but I think you get very limited skills from the type of climbing that they do.

Do you think it's important that we keep that variety by not bolt everything up?

Oh yes, totally. It would be terrible if everything got bolted up. I can't see that it every would happen really.

But say with retrobolting routes, like TEQUILA, GOLDEN MILE at Cheedale in the Peak?

Well they don't need to be basically, and it would be a real waste if routes like that were bolted. You just don't get the same experience from bolted routes. You have an exercise but that's not what climbing is about, developing judgement, assessing the situation and taking calculated risks, which is so much more important than ticking numbers. Obviously you need to be climbing a little below your limit, but the grade is not important is it? If you have a route that you've got to put gear in, and it's not 100% that it's going to stay in; you get a different experience every time, it's the excitement side of it.

So people who want those bolted routes should really be prepared to travel to France?

Not necessarily, but there are plenty of bolted routes in the Peak and Yorkshire; there are enough to go around. You can't expect everything to be bolted, if you want to do that you may as well climb indoors on the climbing walls or just top rope climbs, because on most of the bolted routes you may as well be on a top rope.

Is England you're favourite country to climb in then?

It has been, but over recent years many crags have become too familiar to me, making the enjoyment wane a little. Obviously I've done too much climbing over the past few years so it's hard to be objective. I really enjoy going away, America is brilliant because I've had great times there, so many new routes to go at and new things to see. I do have a lot of good memories of the Peak District though, it was in the area which I grew up. Realistically, in England you have so many different rock types it has to be enjoyable. America doesn't have the variety and in France you don't have the bouldering, just a large flashing potential.

How many 8a's have you flashed?

I don't know, about 10 or so, and a couple of 8a+'s.

Is there a big difference between 8a and 8a+?

Both the 8a+ routes I've on-sighted have been stamina routes, there are hard moves on them but there not powerful. You can have a short 8a in the Peak, or even 7c+ that you stand no chance of flashing because the moves are so hard. Whereas for me the big longer routes in Yorkshire are reasonable to on-sight, it's just a matter of stamina really.

Having flashed 8a, does that put pressure on you?

Yes, that has been a problem this year. I've put myself under too much pressure because of the on-sight ethic. I've realised that I need to be on-sighting routes. I will consciously think about this rather than taking things as they come. It's very much a stupid personal pressure, which is hard to get away from.

Can you ever see yourself flashing 8b's?

Yes, definitely. I was hoping to this year but things sort of fell apart. There are some routes like the MISSION at Buoux, SORTELIGES at Cimai, which could be flashed. I was so close to flashing an 8b at Roche de Rame, Briançon; I wasn't really climbing well (not that I'd admit it, if I was), and was doing the moves a lot harder than they should have been done. I then ran out of steam, but if I'd have seen the easier sequence, I could have flashed it, only one more move to go which wasn't that hard. It is one of my major ambitions, to flash as hard as possible. I'm not really into the hardest routes, I would love to do them but it is nice to save routes, then hopefully one day when I am good enough I can have a good chance of flashing it.

Do the hardest routes like MAGINOT LINE 8c and AGINCOURT 8c, hold any other interest for you?

For me it's really important to have a line and interesting features, something interesting to make me want to climb a route. Obviously these routes are hard but they've got nothing that inspires me. I certainly believe the moves to do and link are very hard, but I need more than that to make me want to do a climb. I like features, something that makes you want to climb, not routes that are just a blank bit of wall between two other good routes.

Simon on a 6c boulder problem start to Ron Fawcett's MINT 400 E6 6b. The route takes the direct up the East Wall of Froggatt Pinnacle. See page 53.

The progression in standards of climbing in Britain over 30 years has left a string of names who stand out in particular, Joe Brown, Pete Livesey, Tom Proctor, Ron Fawcett, Jerry Moffatt, Johnny Dawes and now Ben Moon. There have been other great climbers of course but each of these do stand out as complete legends in their own right. Ben was born on the 13th June 1966, at Kingston in South London. After drifting into climbing by going walking with his parents, he made a trip to North Wales, in the summer of 83, halfway through his 'O' levels. It was the end of schooling but the start of a far more beneficial education, that of how to climb. He started at VS and a few months later with the tuition of Messrs. Moffatt, Pollitt, Atkinson and Gore, he left leading E5. He moved into the scene at Sheffield and the following year put up Britain's second 8a climb STATEMENT OF YOUTH, at The Orme, then repeated Jerry Moffatt's REVELATIONS 8a+, in 3 days. The following year he went to France and did the 3rd ascent of CHOUCAS. In 1986 he consolidated the 8b grade with his new route ZEKE THE FREAK in Derbyshire, on the infamous Rubicon Wall; and did THE ROSE AND THE VAMPIRE at Buoux. A broken wrist the following year put him out for quite a bit but then in 1988 he really came hot on Jerry Moffatt's heels in being the second person to complete the Buoux trio of 8b+'s. SPECTRE on the Monday, THE MINIMUM on the Friday, and then THE RAGE DE VIVRE on the Wednesday. Jerry was still the man to beat, and the following year Ben stole the biggest prize of all, AGINCOURT, the world's first confirmed 8c, the French beaten on home ground, and by an Englishman. This was followed by another climb in France MAGINOT LINE, then 8c; the French pride was lower than rock bottom and Ben was the new top climber. 1990 saw Ben rise to new heights with the completion of his route on Ravens Tor, Derbyshire; efforts spanning over two years resulted in the worlds first 8c+, HUBBLE. During the first year of it's creation it has not been repeated, doubtless to say that it most probably will be repeated, but the challenge has been there. If someone does, they will be chasing Ben a year late, when 9a or 9a+ might be on the table.

Ben Moon prior to his first ascent of CULLODEN 8b, Tideswell Dale, Derbyshire; so called because it was Scottish Ben's project.

Interview 24.1.91 Nether Edge, Sheffield.

Where did you get the name HUBBLE from?
My brother suggested it and as you know it's a special telescope, I simply quite liked the word.

It didn't seem as provocative as other route names like AGINCOURT?
They weren't mine either, I don't enjoy route naming. AGINCOURT and MAGINOT LINE were both Sean Myles, he's the one responsible.

Did you think Hubble would be as hard as 8c+ when you started on it?
I'd thought it would be hard and I thought it would take me a lot longer to do than it did, but I seemed to make progress on it a lot quicker than I first envisaged. I went on it 2 years ago and had my doubts whether it was possible, then a year later I did most of the moves bar a couple, and then last year it came together quite quickly.

You did STATEMENT OF YOUTH 8a, in 1984, did you get the same sense of elation as when you did Hubble?
Oh yes! They were both big highs, and so was MAGINOT LINE and AGINCOURT, also things like CHOUCAS, THE ROSE, THE RAGE and the MINIMUM. Things that I really wanted to do at the bottom of my heart.

Are there any routes now that you want to do?
Not really, not hard repeats. I'd like to do LIQUID AMBER, Jerry's 8c but it's not a priority since 8c isn't hard anymore. I'd like to do another new route but I don't know where. If

you're going to do something really hard, it's nice that it's your own creation, rather than repeating someones maybe. It's a lot of time and effort.

Up until 1989, you were just chasing everyone, people like Jerry Moffatt, Didier Raboutou, and Marc le Menestrel. Was it a surprise to be at the top?
I very nearly did RAGE DE VIVRE 8b+ in 1986, which would have been the second ascent, but I wasn't very professional about it. I was doing red point technique and didn't work the top part enough. I fell off it five or six times and shouldn't have. I knew I could do the other ones because I had done Marc's other hard routes like CHOUCAS and THE ROSE. It took longer than I thought, and I also had an accident when I broke my wrist in 1987, falling off a building onto a concrete pavement with Johnny Dawes in Manchester.

Who got you into the position?
It was me being stupid. We had just arrived there and we were going to do some filming for Alan Hughes, it was all green, in the winter and it was horrible. No one was spotting me and I just jumped on this arete, was laybacking up it and I shot off, landing on my wrist.

Then you broke your thumb?
Yes I broke my thumb skiing, I've broken my wrist twice on one and once on the other, my nose and my toe.

But it's not affected your climbing?
No, I've had a lot of lay-offs over the past three or four years and I have always come back really strong, which is really bizarre.

What have you done in those lay-offs?
Nothing really, rode motorbikes, I studied for a little bit one winter when I was out for three or four months, it was quite nice really.
Have you ever thought of giving up climbing?
No, it's funny that you should say that. No I don't want to give up climbing but there are some things that I'm finding it hard to get motivated for, like I find it very hard to go abroad, down to the South of France, for even 2 or 3 weeks now. I can't handle hanging out down there, not having a house, it's all too familiar. If I want to do competitions, I can't really stay in this country now because the weather is so bad, I'm not going to be fit enough, but I can't bring myself to do it.

Then you must enjoy living in England?
Yes I do, the climbing is getting a bit limited though. I couldn't ever move to France, it's seems such a boring country to live in, nobody does anything in the evenings, it's just dead. I mean I don't know what people do, it makes me so Ahhhh! We were at Fontainebleau the other week for five days, we used to go out in the evenings, to cafes and it's just not like England, you don't go out and there's not a lot of totty; people just don't go out, I don't know what on earth they do!
Are you a party raver or do you think of yourself as a serious person?
Yes, I'm serious when I have to be, but I like to go out you know...
Is the social side of climbing important in your life in England?
Yes it is really important. I like going out and getting really boxed with friends; also going out climbing and having a good laugh as well, going out bouldering with a group is really good and important.

In your climbing, have you had to teach yourself, or do you think you've learn't from others?
No, I think I've taught myself really from my own experience, I've picked a lot up from Jerry, but I'm mostly self taught, I have my own ideas about how to approach something.
Where do you get those ideas from?
It has just happened as I've climbed and as you make mistakes, I guess you find what works best for you to get you up a hard boulder problem, or a route, or an on-sight or something like that.
Is the scenery important to you for climbing?
Yes it is, it's really nice to climb in beautiful scenery, but again it depends what you are doing. If you're on something really hard, you're not going to notice the scenery because all your concentration is taken up with the rock; whereas if you go out for an easy day

Ben placing the final bolts into HUBBLE. Looking down on the master as he leaves the dyno 7b undercut to easy 7a ground above at a mere 45° overhanging. From here a dynamic lunge with the right hand to the obvious sidepull is made.

soloing or bouldering in the Peak District, the Burbage Valley or up on Stanage Edge, it's really nice and you do appreciate your surroundings.
When you've been bouldering have you climbed with anyone more powerful than yourself?
No. Both Jerry and I are really strong, and sometimes on some particular holds Jerry is stronger or more tenacious, his determination makes him better on some things than me. Sometimes though I'm better than him on some problems. Apart from that there just isn't anyone.

Would you be surprised to meet someone.....is it possible, stronger than yourself?
Oh no! It would be great to go bouldering with someone who is stronger than me, but it would have to be on an equal footing. There would be no point in someone who is stronger than me say, bouldering at Cressbrook with Jerry and I, because we have the problems wired, and even if he is strong he is still going to find them really difficult; it would be nice to go bouldering together in an area where we hadn't been before. Also I'd love to watch someone do HUBBLE.
You might be kept waiting for a long time!!
Maybe Jerry might do it this year.

Do you like the challenge of hard things in life?
Some things. It's a challenge to make a living isn't it? I'd love to have loads of money, not to worry about work, and be able to direct all my energy into something like climbing or fast cars or driving bikes; I have no shortage of things I'd like to do, so yes I do like challenges.
When you're working a hard route like AGINCOURT...
It isn't a hard route any longer, it might be for some people but it's not for me. I did that two years ago, and a year after when I went back to it, I did it straight away, it's not state of the art.
When you were doing it...
Yes that does sound really contentious, conceited and arrogant but it is true.
When you were trying it, was there much pressure on you to do it?
Not really, no.
Did you not lie awake at night thinking....?
No. For a while you'd lie there just going through the moves in your head like everyone does, you'd wake up in the morning on the day that you were going to redpoint it and you'd be going through the moves.....
Is it nervousness?
No, on routes I don't get nervous no. I don't find that there's any pressure on, whereas there is a hell of a lot at competitions. I get

nervous at them because there is a lot more pressure to do well, I put pressure on myself obviously, and there is pressure from what people think of you, I'm one of the guys who's meant to win the damm thing.

Why haven't you done so well in competitions?

I don't know, fucking hell! I don't know, I just don't know! I haven't got the head for it, I don't like saying that because it seems really negative, but you have to be realistic about these things; I've been in lots of competitions now and I've had a chance to do really well, just at the last moment I've fucked it up. Every competition you do it, you make a mistake and think 'what did I do wrong there' and you find yourself analysing it all the time, which I don't know if it's a good thing. I think my concentra-tion lets me down a lot of the time, maybe.

Is succeeding on a route important, or is it more the thrill of the moves?

With the view that I am going to succeed one day, yes it is. But I also enjoy working things and it's the movement, the climbing move-ment, which is why I like climbing.

Can you describe any of those movements?

No, not really, no. I just like the movement of going from one hold to another, there's something special about it; making three movements and how it flows together, or when you're climbing really well on-sight, or something like that, everything you do is natural and there is no thought involved, you feel really at one with the rock. Then there's when you are doing a hard redpoint like HUBBLE, you have all the movement wired, and it's having the power to link the moves together. That's kind of different in a way, maybe you're getting off a bit, on the power involved doing the movements.

What then makes bouldering so addictive?

For me it's where you do the hardest move that you are physically capable of doing, which is something that I really like. When one is bouldering everything is very much in control until the moment you do the move or fall off. Hold preparation, grease, weather, your mind psychology; everything can be on your side. All your concentration is going into learning about your body and it's relation to the problem. It's also very uncluttered, you don't need anything but a pair of boots, chalk bag, resin cloth and mat; it's really nice to go bouldering with some friends.

Scenes of down t'dale in the dizzy summer. Ben caught creating HUBBLE, looks like 3c+ to me! 'Just making sure the holds don't get any bigger Dave, otherwise the Yorkshire lad's will be on it.'

Sean Myles working his roof project, Zippy belaying and Ben the boy racer with the GTI. Sean placed all the bolts standing on the roof of his car, the first ever drive in climb.

Opposite Ravens Tor the fisherman
couldn't give a monkeys about Ben
creating history with the first ascent of
HUBBLE.
The best use for a quick draw,
cramming feet into undersize boots.

Ben in extremis on the 7b undercut of HUBBLE. Ben joining
REVELATIONS on the first ascent, with 100° concentration.

Are the moves that you do on bouldering problems harder than routes?
Oh yes, way harder.

And the same with HUBBLE?
Yes HUBBLE as well, because it does make a difference having a rope and a harness on, even if it doesn't weigh hardly anything. That's what makes me feel you can do something really really hard with a rope on, because of what we have done on boulder problems.

Do you enjoy routes that are more physical than mind puzzling?
Both really. I don't stay interested in just pulling from one pocket to another pocket, the holds have got to have some interest, and the feet in a particular position have got to be interesting. I think they both come together and there is a lot of technique in powerful moves, similar to very powerful formula one cars, having the power is necessary but you have to use it carefully and to the best effect.

Do you think it's a pity that we can't have harder routes, placing your own gear on lead?
No, not really because you're defeating the whole point of the red point technique. On hard red pointing all the gear is in place, you clip a biner in point one of a second and loose no energy in doing it. If you do, then the bolts in the wrong place, or your a pretty useless climber. The concept of using up strength on clipping gear is old hat, the route's too fuckin easy if you can do that, the red point ethic allows you to finally lead the hardest route possible. The ironic thing is that, there's going to come a time when you will get a really hard route, and you're not going to be able to clip a bolt, you're going to have to top rope it. Then there will be all those people who have been against bolts saying, well you should have top roped them in the first place.

But does top roping a route give you the same satisfaction?
No it doesn't, but it would if top roping was no choice, if you had to top rope it because you couldn't stop to clip a bolt.

Do you think climbing benefits from not having rules?
You couldn't have rules could you. There are ethics of like, no bolts on grit, no bolts on mountain rock, certain ethics but not rules.

Do you always find yourself at home with those?
Yes. My ethics are different to someone like Ken Wilson's aren't they, what I think is acceptable, he doesn't.

Does it worry you that other people think differently?
It doesn't worry me, it just pisses me off some peoples attitudes, but I'm sure they're really pissed off with my attitude.

How do you see the younger generation coping?
There isn't any bloody younger generation, there is no one coming up, no really good young climbers.

What you've brought up there is an interesting point, why aren't there?
I don't know I really don't know! Maybe the scene is just getting a bit stale.
Is it just social changes?
Maybe.

Is it a good lifestyle being a professional climber?
Yes, I guess it's a really good lifestyle. I shouldn't really complain because I do do exactly what I want more or less, and I make enough money. I don't make very much but I make enough to go where I want and have a nice car.

Do you see yourself getting married and having a few children?
Oh yes Dave, I want a massive white wedding at St. Paul's Cathedral, seven children all running around being noisy and messy. Not seriously though, I don't know about getting married, I don't really see the point. Yes, I might have kids one day, I don't know? I don't know what I'll do, I don't really think of it. It's kind of worrying in a way, I'm making money from climbing, but what if I do climbing less seriously? how am I going to make my money? I guess it's much like that for most people really, even someone in a secure job is only secure for a year or so, because in a year, industry changes and he could lose his job, I'm sure I can manage and get by.
To sum it up, what power does climbing have over your life?
The Power of Climbing, it's enormous! It dictates my entire existence.

Roll of Honour

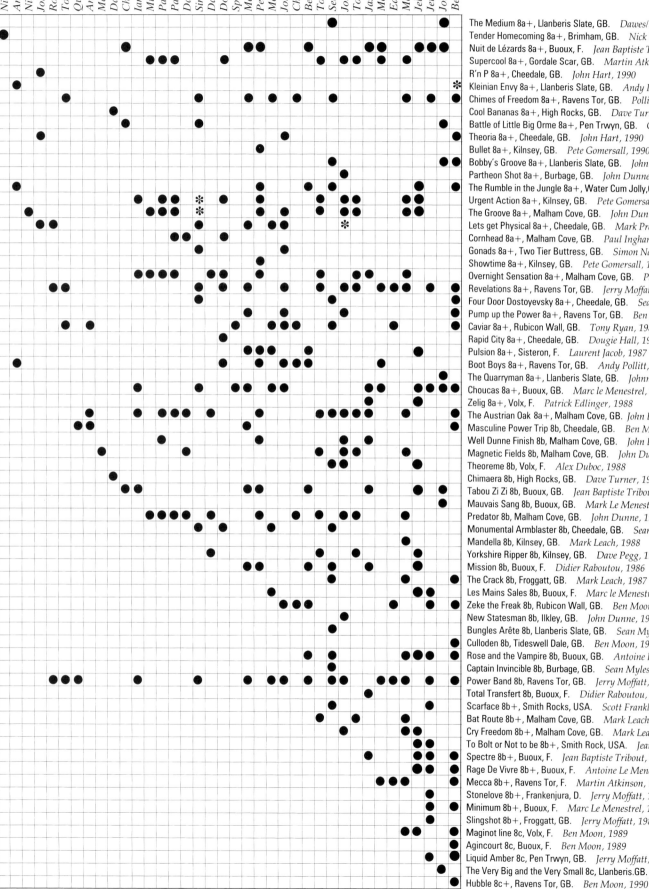

Column headers (left to right): Nick Dixon, Andy Pollitt, Nick Sellars, John Hart, Robin Barker, Tony Ryan, Quentin Fisher, Andy Goring, Malcolm Smith, Dave Turner, Chris Plant, Ian Vincent, Mick Lovatt, Paul Craven, Paul Ingham, Dave Cuthbertson, Simon Nadin, Dave Pegg, Dougie Hall, Spider Mackenzie, Mark Pretty, Pete Gomersall, Malcolm Taylor, John Welford, Chris Gore, Ben Masterson, Tony Mitchell, Sean Myles, John Dunne, Tony Mitchell, Jason Myers, Martin Atkinson, Ed Morgan, Mark Leach, Jebé Tribout, Jerry Moffatt, Johnny Dawes, Ben Moon

- The Medium 8a+, Llanberis Slate, GB.   *Dawes/Sean Myles, 1990*
- Tender Homecoming 8a+, Brimham, GB.   *Nick Dixon, 1990*
- Nuit de Lézards 8a+, Buoux, F.   *Jean Baptiste Tribout, 1985*
- Supercool 8a+, Gordale Scar, GB.   *Martin Atkinson, 1987*
- R'n P 8a+, Cheedale, GB.   *John Hart, 1990*
- Kleinian Envy 8a+, Llanberis Slate, GB.   *Andy Pollitt, 1987*
- Chimes of Freedom 8a+, Ravens Tor, GB.   *Pollitt/Moon, 1986/90*
- Cool Bananas 8a+, High Rocks, GB.   *Dave Turner, 1987*
- Battle of Little Big Orme 8a+, Pen Trwyn, GB.   *Chris Plant, 1989*
- Theoria 8a+, Cheedale, GB.   *John Hart, 1990*
- Bullet 8a+, Kilnsey, GB.   *Pete Gomersall, 1990*
- Bobby's Groove 8a+, Llanberis Slate, GB.   *Johnny Dawes, 1988*
- Partheon Shot 8a+, Burbage, GB.   *John Dunne, 1989*
- The Rumble in the Jungle 8a+, Water Cum Jolly,GB.   *Andy Pollitt, 198?*
- Urgent Action 8a+, Kilnsey, GB.   *Pete Gomersall, 1989*
- The Groove 8a+, Malham Cove, GB.   *John Dunne, 1988*
- Lets get Physical 8a+, Cheedale, GB.   *Mark Pretty, 1988*
- Cornhead 8a+, Malham Cove, GB.   *Paul Ingham, 1989*
- Gonads 8a+, Two Tier Buttress, GB.   *Simon Nadin, 1985*
- Showtime 8a+, Kilnsey, GB.   *Pete Gomersall, 1989*
- Overnight Sensation 8a+, Malham Cove, GB.   *Paul Ingham, 1987*
- Revelations 8a+, Ravens Tor, GB.   *Jerry Moffatt, 1984*
- Four Door Dostoyevsky 8a+, Cheedale, GB.   *Sean Myles, 1989*
- Pump up the Power 8a+, Ravens Tor, GB.   *Ben Moon, 1987*
- Caviar 8a+, Rubicon Wall, GB.   *Tony Ryan, 1987*
- Rapid City 8a+, Cheedale, GB.   *Dougie Hall, 1990*
- Pulsion 8a+, Sisteron, F.   *Laurent Jacob, 1987*
- Boot Boys 8a+, Ravens Tor, GB.   *Andy Pollitt, 1987*
- The Quarryman 8a+, Llanberis Slate, GB.   *Johnny Dawes, 1986*
- Choucas 8a+, Buoux, GB.   *Marc le Menestrel, 1985*
- Zelig 8a+, Volx, F.   *Patrick Edlinger, 1988*
- The Austrian Oak 8a+, Malham Cove, GB.   *John Dunne, 1988*
- Masculine Power Trip 8b, Cheedale, GB.   *Ben Moon, 1989*
- Well Dunne Finish 8b, Malham Cove, GB.   *John Dunne, 1987*
- Magnetic Fields 8b, Malham Cove, GB.   *John Dunne, 1987*
- Theoreme 8b, Volx, F.   *Alex Duboc, 1988*
- Chimaera 8b, High Rocks, GB.   *Dave Turner, 1990*
- Tabou Zi Zi 8b, Buoux, GB.   *Jean Baptiste Tribout, 1986*
- Mauvais Sang 8b, Buoux, GB.   *Mark Le Menestrel, 1986*
- Predator 8b, Malham Cove, GB.   *John Dunne, 1987*
- Monumental Armblaster 8b, Cheedale, GB.   *Sean Myles, 1989*
- Mandella 8b, Kilnsey, GB.   *Mark Leach, 1988*
- Yorkshire Ripper 8b, Kilnsey, GB.   *Dave Pegg, 1989*
- Mission 8b, Buoux, F.   *Didier Raboutou, 1986*
- The Crack 8b, Froggatt, GB.   *Mark Leach, 1987*
- Les Mains Sales 8b, Buoux, F.   *Marc le Menestrel, 1984*
- Zeke the Freak 8b, Rubicon Wall, GB.   *Ben Moon, 1986*
- New Statesman 8b, Ilkley, GB.   *John Dunne, 1989*
- Bungles Arête 8b, Llanberis Slate, GB.   *Sean Myles, 1990*
- Culloden 8b, Tideswell Dale, GB.   *Ben Moon, 1990*
- Rose and the Vampire 8b, Buoux, GB.   *Antoine Le Menestrel, 1985*
- Captain Invincible 8b, Burbage, GB.   *Sean Myles 1991*
- Power Band 8b, Ravens Tor, GB.   *Jerry Moffatt, 1986*
- Total Transfert 8b, Buoux, F.   *Didier Raboutou, 1988*
- Scarface 8b+, Smith Rocks, USA.   *Scott Franklin, 1988*
- Bat Route 8b+, Malham Cove, GB.   *Mark Leach, 1989*
- Cry Freedom 8b+, Malham Cove, GB.   *Mark Leach, 1988*
- To Bolt or Not to be 8b+, Smith Rock, USA.   *Jean Baptiste Tribout, 1987*
- Spectre 8b+, Buoux, F.   *Jean Baptiste Tribout, 1987*
- Rage De Vivre 8b+, Buoux, F.   *Antoine Le Menestrel, 1986*
- Mecca 8b+, Ravens Tor, F.   *Martin Atkinson, 1988*
- Stonelove 8b+, Frankenjura, D.   *Jerry Moffatt, 1988*
- Minimum 8b+, Buoux, F.   *Marc Le Menestrel, 1986*
- Slingshot 8b+, Froggatt, GB.   *Jerry Moffatt, 1987*
- Maginot line 8c, Volx, F.   *Ben Moon, 1989*
- Agincourt 8c, Buoux, F.   *Ben Moon, 1989*
- Liquid Amber 8c, Pen Trwyn, GB.   *Jerry Moffatt, 1990*
- The Very Big and the Very Small 8c, Llanberis.GB.   *Johnny Dawes, 1990*
- Hubble 8c+, Ravens Tor, GB.   *Ben Moon, 1990*

Redpoint: ●   Flash: ✳